# K9 DRUG DETECTION

**Other titles in the *K9 Professional Training Series***
*K9 Behavior Basics, 2nd ed.*
*K9 Decoys and Aggression, 2nd ed.*
*K9 Investigation Errors*
*K9 Personal Protection, 2nd ed.*
*K9 Scent Training*
*K9 Schutzhund Training, 2nd ed.*
*K9 Search and Rescue, 2nd ed.*

**Other K9 titles from Brush Education**
*Aggression Control*
*K9 Complete Care*
*K9 Explosive Detection*
*K9 Officer's Manual*
*K9 Professional Tracking*
*K9 Scent Detection*
*K9 Suspect Discrimination*
*K9 Working Breeds*
*Police Officer's Guide to K9 Searches*

# K9 DRUG DETECTION

## A Manual for Training and Operations

Dr. Resi Gerritsen
Ruud Haak

*K9 Professional Training Series*

An imprint of
Brush Education Inc.

Copyright © 2017 Resi Gerritsen and Ruud Haak

25 26 27 28 29 6 5 4 3 2

Thank you for buying this book and for not copying, scanning, or distributing any part of it without permission. By respecting the spirit as well as the letter of copyright, you support authors and publishers, allowing them to continue to create and distribute the books you value.

Excerpts from this publication may be reproduced under licence from Access Copyright, or with the express written permission of Brush Education Inc., or under licence from a collective management organization in your territory. All rights are otherwise reserved, and no part of this publication may be reproduced, stored in a retrieval system, or transmitted in any form or by any means, electronic, mechanical, photocopying, digital copying, scanning, recording, or otherwise, except as specifically authorized.

Printed in China

Brush Education Inc.
www.brusheducation.ca
contact@brusheducation.ca

Editorial: Meaghan Craven
Cover Design: John Luckhurst; Cover image: Shutterstock—Monika Wisniewska Interior Design: Carol Dragich, Dragich Design
Illustrations: Chao Yu, Vancouver

Photo credits (pages): **Four Winds K9:** 9, 12, 14, 15, 34, 43, 65, 70, 117 (bottom), 143, 146 (bottom). **Four Winds K9 / Chris van Cromvoirt**: 36, 117 (middle), 140 (bottom). **Dog Training Center Oosterhout**: 2, 4, 19, 23, 30, 31, 33, 38, 39, 41, 42, 46, 52, 53, 56, 58, 59, 62, 63, 72, 90, 91, 98 (top), 105, 109, 111 (bottom), 115, 121, 128, 131, 133, 136, 137. **Drug Enforcement Administration (DEA):** 97, 98 (bottom), 103, 107, 111 (top), 117 (top), 119, 122, 123, 134, 140 (top), 146 (top), 151–241, 254 (top), 255. ***Onze Hond* archive**: 246, 250, 251, 252, 254 (bottom). **Ruud Haak**: 49.

**Library and Archives Canada Cataloguing in Publication**
Gerritsen, Resi, author
K9 drug detection : a manual for training and operations / Dr. Resi Gerritsen, Ruud Haak.

(K9 professional training series)

Includes bibliographical references and index.
Issued in print and electronic formats.
ISBN 978-1-55059-681-6 (paperback).—ISBN 978-1-55059-684-7 (epub).—
ISBN 978-1-55059-682-3 (pdf).—ISBN 978-1-55059-683-0 (mobi)

1. Police dogs—Training—Handbooks, manuals, etc. 2. Drug traffic—Investigation—Handbooks, manuals, etc. 3. Drug control—Handbooks, manuals, etc. 4. Drugs of abuse—Handbooks, manuals, etc. I. Haak, Ruud, author II. Title. III. Series: K9 professional training series

HV8025.G45 2017         363.2′32         C2016-906044-6
                                          C2016-906045-4

## Contents

*Introduction* ..................................................................................... vii
1 Selecting the Drug-Detector Dog and Handler ........................... 1
2 Basics of Drug-Detection Training ............................................ 16
3 Accidental Drug Uptake: First Aid for Your Dog ....................... 45
4 Reading Your Dog ...................................................................... 55
5 Influence of Air Currents in Search Work ................................. 73
6 Planning a Search Action ........................................................ 100
7 General Information on Drugs, Drug Laws,
  and Penalties .......................................................................... 125
8 The Different Drugs ................................................................ 148
  Conclusion ............................................................................... 257

  *Appendix A: Canada's Controlled Drugs and
  Substances Act: Drug Schedules I–IV and VIII* ......................... 259

  *Appendix B: Canada's Controlled Drugs and
  Substances Act: Punishments* ................................................. 270

  *Appendix C: United States Controlled Substances Act:
  Drug Schedules I–V* ................................................................. 274

*Appendix D: United States Federal Trafficking Penalties for Drugs Included in Schedules I–V* ............................................. 277

*Notes* ............................................................................. 281

*Bibliography* ................................................................. 283

*About the Authors* ...................................................... 285

*Index* ............................................................................. 289

## Introduction

In 1930, R. and R. Menzel, a husband and wife team of doctors, wrote: "The world of odors and search work is a closed book for us people. Here, we are in the unpleasant situation where the dog has to teach us something, instead of the other way around!" Still, even as we rely on our dogs' noses as we conduct search work, we should also be aware of scents and other distractions that can influence our dogs. In this book, we impart the most current information about how K9 drug-detector handlers should train their dogs, as well as essential knowledge about various influences on dogs' search work.

In the fight against drugs, K9s have been proven to be of great value, so people the world over train dogs to detect drugs. A dog's reliability and ability when performing this task depends on how suitable the dog is for the work and how well the handler can train and assist the dog in operational situations. We hope this book will provide an aid to those on the ground.

Be warned. Your well-trained drug-detector dog is a valuable tool for those wishing to flush out a particular aspect of the drug trade; because of this, your dog is a real hindrance to those operating in said trade. Criminals will not hesitate to try to poison or kill your dog. Always be careful with strangers who want to approach your dog or offer a food reward. And always make sure your dog is lodged in a safe place.

We wish to thank the U.S. Drug Enforcement Administration (www.dea.gov) and Four Winds K9 (www.fourwindsk9.com) for permission to use their photos in this book, as well as Claudia and André Boomaars of Dog Training Center Oosterhout (www.hondencentrum-claudia.nl) for the photos of our training methods and the information they contributed to this book. We also want to thank the Port Security Rotterdam (HBD) and the Rotterdam Police, especially Jan de Bruin, head of the dog training center of the Rotterdam police force, and Nico Ram, who sadly died too young, training instructor for police dogs of the regional police Rotterdam-Rijnmond, for all their advice on training our drug-detector dogs and for transferring their vast knowledge to us.

—Dr. Resi Gerritsen and Ruud Haak

## Disclaimer

While the contents of this book are based on substantial experience and expertise, working with dogs involves inherent risks, especially in dangerous settings and situations. Anyone using approaches described in this book does so entirely at their own risk, and both the authors and publisher disclaim any liability for any injuries or other damage that may be sustained.

# 1

# Selecting the Drug-Detector Dog and Handler

Only mentally and physically healthy dogs should be trained for drug-detection work, which requires a variety of skills in many different situations. Dog breeds with problems like hip and elbow dysplasia, which prevent normal movement, may or may not have problems with drug-detection work, but dogs with other hereditary physical defects like epilepsy and eye disorders are definitely unsuitable for the job. Training will only lead to success if the raw material is sound, so you must carefully examine the characteristics of the dog you want to train. It is equally important to look at the characteristics of the handler who is going to teach the dog and to look at what kind of team the dog and handler might become. Scent training is mentally challenging. It requires a stable, mature mentality in both the dog and the handler.

## Physical Characteristics

Drug detection work is physically strenuous for dogs, so it makes sense to train healthy animals. Many kinds of illnesses and medications affect the dog's nose. Training a dog while his sense of smell is not optimal will lead to all kinds of unnecessary, stressful situations that are detrimental to the training. The physical

If you want your dog's training to be successful, you and your dog must love one another.

characteristics important for a dog undergoing scent training include the following:
- Overall good health
- Normal movement skills
- A strong and muscled body
- A good sense of smell
- A healthy mouth (Missing teeth are not a problem, but we have found bad breath as a result of plaque can be detrimental.)
- Optimal fitness and stamina
- Strong legs, and paws with strong pads
- Adaptability to weather and climate
- A coat suitable for the work

## Mental Characteristics

Scent-detection work also requires intensive mental work on the dog's part. It requires much more from a dog than, say, tracking activities do in terms of cognitive ability. Instead of just following a given human scent, the dog must "memorize" a number of target odors and be able to detect them everywhere. Usually, dogs are trained to detect the following different substances: cocaine, GHB, hashish, heroin, LSD, marijuana, and MDMA. Depending on the context, drug-detector dogs may also learn to recognize other substances like khat, morphine, and poppers. As well, time and again, the dog must be able to detect odors that are slightly different from those memorized. A stable, mature mentality is a must for both the dog and his handler. The characteristics of a potentially good scent-detection dog follow:

- A placid outlook: self-confidence, stability of character, not nervous or afraid
- A lively and interested temperament
- A willingness to work and to continue working even if there is no immediate reward
- Intelligence. We distinguish between *instinctive*, *practical*, and *adaptive* intelligence:
  - By *instinctive intelligence* we mean all hereditary skills and behavior. For instance, the hunting drive: every pup runs after a moving object.
  - By *practical intelligence* we mean the speed with which, and the degree to which, the dog conforms to the desires of the handler. Roughly said, practical intelligence is measured by how quickly and how correctly the dog learns the different exercises.
  - *Adaptive intelligence* can be divided into two abilities: learning proficiency (how quickly the dog develops adequate behavior in a new situation) and problem-solving ability (the dog's ability to choose the behavior needed to solve a problem).
- A good searching drive: the natural ability to use the nose to find objects
- A moderate prey drive: if the dog defends his reward too fiercely, he will become focused on his reward too much, and this will prevent him from searching well

- A high bring drive: the dog should be highly motivated to bring his reward to his handler. He shares it with the handler, which is good for the team.
- An ability to cope with mistakes: if corrected (a verbal correction should be sufficient), the dog should remain composed, willing to work, and not lose his drive to search and retrieve. Dogs that cannot cope with correction are difficult to work with.

These mental characteristics are only found in mature dogs. You can start your dog on scent-detection training before he reaches puberty, but in our experience, early training will not significantly shorten his training time or have a positive impact on his final performance level. Instead, prepare your young dog for detection work by socializing him, teaching him general obedience, and stimulating his search and bring drives by playing games. During this pre-training phase, make sure your dog learns to search with his nose because he will need to do so during scent-detection training and beyond. As well, don't allow him to become too possessive of his reward toys; this can lead to problems with sharing retrieved objects with you, the handler, in later training.

Of course, some the mental characteristics listed above will develop during training and may not be discernable when your

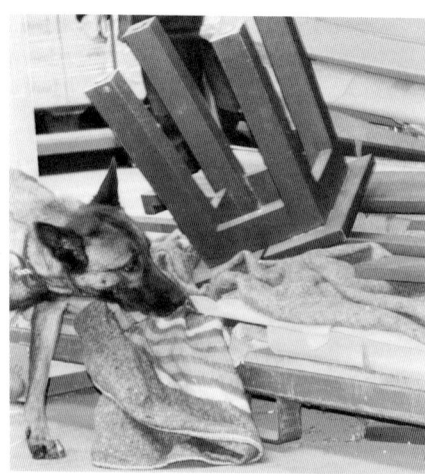

Follow your dog as she performs her search work, and carefully observe her behavior.

dog is young. One can try to test a young dog's will to work, for example, but in the end, the true test of this comes when the dog must maintain a certain level of industry as he performs detection work in a variety of places and under many different kinds of conditions. A dog that seems willing to work in pre-training, or even during training, may buckle in the face of "real" work. Your dog's ability to cope with mistakes also cannot be tested before training.

## Selecting the Dog

Dogs that are suitable for drug-detector training must possess and demonstrate certain desired characteristics and qualities and should be able to perform at a high level and stay at that high level in real-life working conditions. When you select a dog for training, be aware of the following different characteristics: drive, instinct, perseverance, sensitivity, boldness, social behavior, noise shyness, ability to retrieve, and breed and variety.

### DRIVE

We distinguish between two types of drives: *psychological* (pack drive, for example, or territorial behavior [also called guard drive]), and *physical* (the drive to procreate, for example, and the drive to monitor, pursue, kill, and retrieve prey). These drives are important for wild dogs, of course. For example, if a dog does not breed, the pack will become too small to be sustainable. If a wild dog does not chase and kill prey, he will starve. He will also starve if he does not guard his prey, because other dogs or species will take it from him. For our purposes, working dogs must demonstrate they have healthy drives, one of which relates to searching. If the drug-detector dog does not search for his "prey" (drugs) and bring it back to his "pack" (his handler), the "pack" will "starve" (not get their job done).

Every dog possesses extraordinary olfactory ability—but the drug-detector dog must have the urge to use this sense of smell. This is one of the most important things to take into account when selecting a dog for scent training.

## INSTINCT

Many people confuse the word "drive" with "instinct." Both drive and instinct determine a dog's behavior. A drive is the impetus to a certain behavior, while instinct is a complete act or an inherited behavior that is always performed in the same manner.

To be called an instinct, a behavior must meet four requirements:

1. It must result in a certain efficiency (save or enhance the life of an individual).
2. When performed, it must always be done in the same way (stereotyped behavior).
3. It must have been caused by a particular stimulus.
4. It must be innate, present in all animals of the same species.

Examples of instinctive behavior in dogs include burying a bone and marking out territory. The prospective drug-detection dog should have pronounced instinctive behaviors—the dog should also be keen to use his nose intensively. A dog training to smell for drugs should be excited to explore his environment and be able to move easily over different types of terrain, such as slippery floors, stairs, rooms full of objects over which the dog must climb, and so on.

## PERSEVERANCE

When selecting a dog for drug-detection training, you can test a dog's level of persistence in a few different ways. Consider throwing a ball for a prospective dog to retrieve several times. When the dog starts to show signs of fatigue, throw the ball some more, but now keep the dog at heel and only let him go to retrieve the ball a minute after the ball has been thrown. Despite his fatigue, a persistent dog will continue searching for the ball and will want to retrieve it. If the dog proves he is persistent, he also proves he is willing to work hard for his reward.

An alternative test would be to throw the ball for the dog a few times, and then, when the dog shows fatigue, put the ball up in such a way that the dog can see it but cannot reach it (e.g., by placing it in the branches of a tree). To prove he has perseverance, the dog should do everything he can to get the ball.

### SENSITIVITY

A dog with a gentle nature can definitely be trained to be a drug detector. Remember that sensitivity should not be confused with fear. A dog that is easily impressed but has the ability to recover quickly (during selection and training) can serve as an operational detector dog. Dogs that have "firm" characters, however, can handle a variety of situations with greater ease than "soft" dogs. Firm dogs are not cowed by difficult or intimidating circumstances and can cope with a high level of stress, such as a noisy and unpredictable search environment. For this reason, firm dogs may be easier to train for drug detection than soft ones. However, some handlers have insight into properly training and working with sensitive dogs. In fact, some handlers may prefer working with sensitive dogs; never discount personal preference when selecting a dog to train.

No matter the training, however, a dog that is too sensitive, or is hyper-aware of physical contact, may be readily distracted and will not be able to focus on search work. Note that a sensitive dog with a strong bring drive can be a good search dog; his desire to fetch acts like a set of blinders, focusing him on his search work and blocking out all other distractions in his environment.

As well, it should not necessarily be a problem if a dog is very sensitive to his handler's voice. You, the handler, can control your voice level and use a quiet voice to influence your dog if he is sensitive.

### BOLDNESS

When a working drug-detector dog is confronted with everyday influences such as noise, large crowds, or other human activities, he must keep focused on the task at hand. When selecting dogs for training, a minor response to such things is acceptable, provided that the response merely reflects a lack of education. Focused training may correct this behavior. If, during the imprinting phase of his life, a young dog has not been exposed to many varied situations, he may have difficulty coping with variety later in life. Prospective drug-detection dogs should be exposed to different types of terrain during imprinting, too—slippery floors, stairs, obstacles to climb—and to places full of different kinds of people so he will not be afraid of odd terrain and crowds later in his life, especially during search actions. The main imprinting phase occurs during the third to the 12th week of a puppy's life. Socialization and the dog's attitude toward his environment are determined during this period.

### SOCIAL BEHAVIOR

Drug-detector dogs must demonstrate positive social behavior toward humans and other animals. During a search action, after all, the dog will encounter people and other animals. If the dog responds to others with antisocial behavior, he will lose concentration on his search work.

### NOISE SHYNESS

A dog that is afraid of loud noises must be considered unsuitable for work. The startle response and accompanying anxious behavior will distract him from his task. However, do not assume a dog has noise-related anxiety if he seems surprised at the sound of a sudden loud noise, especially if he undertakes immediate recovery after that startle reaction.

### ABILITY TO RETRIEVE

One of the key features a prospective drug-detector dog must possess is the bring drive. When a dog is not driven to fetch, he will make no effort to use his nose to find his reward. A dog with a developed bring drive, however, will eventually be able to retrieve many different objects during training, which will help facilitate the training for search work.

## BREED AND VARIETY

An enormous variety of breeds are qualified for search-dog training; each breed has its own particular temperament and physical qualities, and each dog has his own particularities, regardless of his breed. For example, an individual Labrador retriever may seem slow compared to a Malinois, but he may be very quick compared to other Labs. In essence, when selecting dogs for training, you must assess each one individually within the parameters of his breed and not compare one breed with another.

Within the group of sheepdogs, the shorthaired Belgian shepherd, called Malinois, and the shorthaired Dutch shepherd, also called by its Dutch name Hollandse herder, differ in character with the German shepherd. The German shepherd has an exceptionally

Generally speaking, the crossbreeds known as X-Malinois and X-Dutch shepherd are perseverant, resilient, and determined.

good nose but, on average, a softer character than a Malinois or a Dutch shepherd. The latter two breeds, just like the crossbreeds X-Malinois and X-Dutch shepherd, are best known for their perseverance, resilience, and determination.

Within the group of hounds, we mostly select Labrador retrievers, golden retrievers, and spaniels. The Labrador is known for his friendliness, interest in food rewards, and perseverance, especially the males, which sometimes results in problems during training. For example, his perseverance may cause problems during obedience training—sometimes Labs do not want to learn certain exercises and will persistently refuse. As well, the Lab's focus on food might be so intense that the presence of food will always distract him from his duties. The golden retriever is also a friendly dog with a very gentle nature, and again, the males of the breed tend to persevere. The spaniel—especially the English cocker spaniel, and English and Welsh springer spaniels—has a difficult character; he is both sensitive and busy. However, spaniels generally are driven to work, so when teamed up with the right handler, a spaniel can become an excellent detector dog.

More information about the characteristics, physical defects, and specialties in training of different breeds can be found in our book *K9 Working Breeds: Characteristics and Capabilities* (Brush Education, 2007).

## The Dog Handler

Handlers who work with drug-detector dogs need to be in top physical condition because they must be able to handle often-excessive physical strain. Handlers must walk and stand for long periods, and they must also frequently bend down, squat, and kneel, as well as climb over and up different objects.

Drug-detector dog handlers must also have stable characters and not be easily agitated by their dogs' behavior. They must have learned to interpret the behavior of different dogs and be able to read their signals quickly. They must have patience, be willing to review their own training critically, and be prepared to regularly take a step back in training.

Handlers must be aware of the possible pitfalls they may come across in this work. They especially need to understand how important it is that the dog *not* pay much attention to the handler when working, which is a situation quite the reverse of normal obedience work. The dog must work independently and not respond to inadvertent cues from the handler or others in the area. Everyone who has ever tried to teach a dog something knows that dogs respond very well to handler cues. Most of these people also realize that dogs pick up on cues that were not specifically taught to them. For example, if you put on your walking shoes, the dog will stick to you like glue because he expects to go for a walk. Dogs may also pick up on cues so subtle that you yourself are completely unaware of them.

We call problems resulting from such cues "Clever Hans" problems, so named for the horse, Hans, which lived in Germany at the turn of the 20th century. Hans's owner worked with his horse to develop what the owner thought were mathematical abilities. For example, the owner would ask the stallion, "How much is five plus two?" and Hans would start tapping his hoof, stopping after tapping it seven times. At first, people were stumped. How was Hans able to do sums? However, in 1911, a psychologist watched both the owner and Hans, as well as other people asking questions of Hans, and he deduced that the stallion responded to people's unconscious slight leaning forward as a cue to stop tapping his hoof when he had reached the correct answer. Hans's impetus to tap out the "right" number included food rewards like bread. This kind of cue learning has inspired certain 21st-century studies done in Hungary, where it was found that dogs easily learned and responded to experimenter-given cues such as pointing, bowing, nodding, head turning, and glancing. The Hungarian experiments illustrate how well dogs can learn to "read" us.[1]

During search work, you must always be wary of influencing your dog.

With Clever Hans in mind during training, we want dogs to respond only to consciously given, relevant cues. For example, when a dog is searching for an odor, the only cue available to him must be the odor. However, when we observe handlers training their dogs, sometimes they provide obvious cues, consciously and unconsciously. We have seen some dogs performing searches while carefully watching their handlers or the instructor. A glance at or minimal movement toward the place the dog must find is often enough of a cue for a searching dog.

If dogs are able to learn and pick up on such minimal cues, how can handlers and instructors stop themselves from "helping" dogs to search? The answer is obvious: work blind. You, the handler, like your dog, should not know the position of the hidden odor during training exercises, and preferably no one around you should know it either, since this person could also unconsciously cue the dog.

Dog handlers must thoroughly understand that the search dog is the only one who can smell well enough to solve a real-life problem. So handlers must never try to force their dogs into a "discovery," but rather, they must ensure that training includes exercises that allow dogs to understand what is expected of them. Handlers must therefore be intelligent and sensitive trainers who stay one step ahead of their dogs at all times, even as they allow their dogs to do the work they are trained to do. If you want to be a handler, take a good look at yourself and make sure you can do the job correctly.

An inadequate handler can ruin a potentially good dog. A good handler can go quite a long way with a not-so-good dog, but even that dog will not be able to achieve the high standard necessary for operational work. With that in mind, when choosing handlers, or even if you are a handler yourself, take a look at the handler's work critically. When it comes to dogs, if things do not go well in training, stop. Bear in mind that handlers must like the dogs they work with; there should be no tension between them during training or outside of training. Dog and handler should be constantly deepening their relationship on the training field and off it. A stressful relationship between dog and handler will show itself in scent training and play an important, negative role.

## Selecting the Dog Handler

When handlers work with search and detection dogs, they provide limited supervision and guidance. The dog must, of course, always obey the handler, but he must also be allowed to work independently as much as possible. So search dogs must be independent in their work but also respond appropriately to basic obedience commands.

Experienced dog handlers who begin their work in obedience, or other areas, and then switch to working with search or detector dogs often have some difficulty to adapting their process to the new task—more difficulty, certainly, than that experienced by a new handler starting out in the profession directly as a search- or detector-dog handler. Dog handlers who have focused on other areas of handler expertise before coming to detection work are used to having dogs performing only according to handler commands. Of course, search dogs require a certain amount of supervision, but only in rare cases do search dogs require strict supervision. So in order for handlers to work well in the search milieu, they must have the abilities to adjust, use the voice, and control their actions.

The detector dog is the only one in the search area who can smell well enough to solve the problem at hand.

### ADJUSTING

A detector-dog handler must be able to adapt to the dog and must also be able to assess each situation individually. Because handlers are dependent on their detector dogs to complete a search, as much if not more than they are dependent on their own initiative and knowledge, timing and appropriate actions are very important. In addition, handlers must be understanding of and empathic toward their dogs in order for the team to achieve good results.

### USING THE VOICE

During training, handlers must be able to use their voices to help their dogs achieve results. Handlers should be able to employ a variety of tones, levels of sound, and different emphases on words. Handlers may, for example, need to increase the volume when the team is working in a large area where distance is a factor, or when they need to issue commands as punishment or rejection. In general, a loud voice has no tonal differences, and to dogs, which have

# SELECTING THE DRUG-DETECTOR DOG AND HANDLER

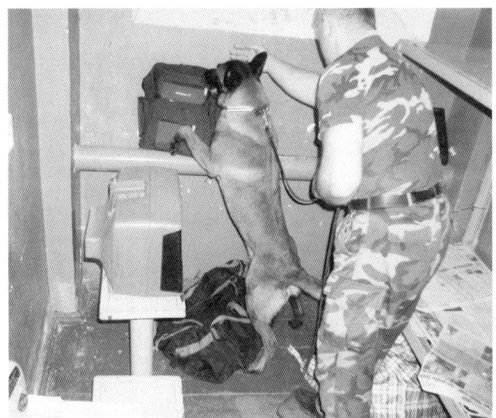

The dog and his handler: two colleagues, each with a specialty.

sensitive and acute hearing, loud voices signal commands as punishment or rejection. Dog handlers must also be able to use their voices in a conversational way, adapting their tone to the individual dog's character.

**CONTROLLING ACTIONS**

Handlers employ actions as a form of nonverbal communication to influence their dogs. Bit by bit during training, handler body movements and actions become more and more important in guiding prospective detector dogs. In most search actions, handlers do not use voice commands so as not to disturb their dogs. As a result, handlers' body movements and actions help guide search dogs' behaviors. Through their actions, handlers should be able to stimulate their dogs' curiosity and interest in such a way as to encourage the dogs to thoroughly and systematically search an object or building.

In the end, the difference between success and failure for a detector handler–dog team depends on the relationship between handler and dog. In addition, the handler's knowledge, understanding, and empathy determines the successful training and operational deployment of a drug-detector dog.

# 2

# Basics of Drug-Detection Training

A dog will only become as good as her handler permits. In other words, the handler-dog combination must be right in order for the team to get positive results. First of all, you, the handler, must rely on the quality of your dog and know everything about the principles of dog training. You must also know how to influence your own dog, know how to read her body language, and you must know about the substances your dog is being trained to detect. Most important, you must be able to work with your dog, together as a team.

## Training without Pressure

We believe detector dogs should be trained without compulsion or pressure. Of course, this manner of training demands certain requirements. First, the dog must have a strong bring drive and you must give the dog enough freedom to learn how to work independently. You and your dog should work together in such a way that you are not always in the dog's face; the danger of "helicopter" dog handling is that the dog will pay too much attention to you, depend too much on your cues, and lose concentration on the search work.

Also important to training without pressure are your conscious and unconscious movements, all of which influence your dog's behaviors. Your body language is important for giving nonverbal commands. For example, you can use body language to draw your dog's attention to a particular place or object. And of course, your voice—all the sounds you use to arouse your dog's curiosity, or to motivate or correct her—is also inseparable from the non-compulsion training method.

## Training with Pressure

We prefer non-coercive training; however, that method is not always possible. Sometimes, dogs that work too independently can wander and encounter dangerous terrain or people. This means that sometimes you need to use pressure when training, and some dogs need a strong approach to corrections outside of search work.

## Principles of Training

Make sure you adhere to the following five rules to create a strong foundation from which to train a detector dog:

1. Do not employ strict discipline or harsh commands when training your dog, unless the dog's nature requires it (for example, a dog that does not easily accept instructions from her handler).
2. Do not use sticks, rocks, or other such objects for fetching, unless you are using them as training tools.
3. Always end the training session with an experience that is pleasurable for your dog—for example, asking her to fetch her favorite toy.
4. Throughout training, do not force your dog to relinquish her toy by giving harsh commands. Instead, to encourage her to give up her "prey," offer her treats such as cheese or sausages, or a dog biscuit.

5. Searching, finding, and temporarily retaining an object forms the basis of search-dog training—these activities should always be pleasant for your dog.

## Equipment

The following equipment is essential to train a detector dog.

### COLLAR

We use light plastic or leather collars in training, which our dogs also wear when we take them for walks. Our dogs wear their collars when we ask them to do a search exercise on leash (long or short), as well. Always make sure your dog's collar fits well—if it's too loose, the collar may come off; if it's too tight, your dog may have trouble breathing, which of course negatively affects search work.

### SHORT LEASH

Use a short leash when you want to keep your dog close to you. A short leash allows you to be able to correct your dog almost immediately and so it makes sense that it is mostly used at the beginning of a dog's training. When your dog can adequately perform the training exercises, you can transition to a long leash. At this point, use the short leash only when you want your dog to follow you on leash, or in situations where your dog needs to be kept close in order that she stays out of danger.

### LONG LEASH

The length of the long leash is mostly a matter of personal preference, but for search work it is usually about 9.8 to 16.4 feet (3–5 m). Because leather long leashes are hard and heavy, we often use a plastic one, which allows for greater maneuverability. When she is on a long leash, your dog is always liable to get tangled up in something. As well, the leash may drag through or touch artifacts in the search area. So make sure you take account of obstacles when conducting searches using this tool.

# BASICS OF DRUG-DETECTION TRAINING

The long leash allows your dog to work more independently than when she is on a short leash, even as it allows you a level of control over your dog. It allows handlers to slowly build distance between them and their dogs during search training. As well, you may wish to use a long leash later on, in search situations where you feel it is necessary to keep your dog under some degree of control.

## TRAINING TOOLS

During training, you should always carry a retrievable reward/motivational item that your dog enjoys working with. You should be able to easily handle this training device, and it should be safe

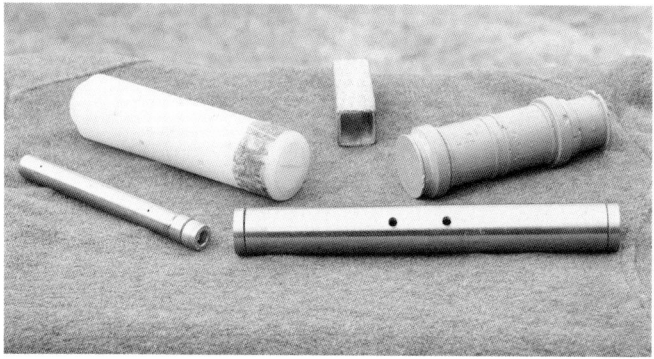

Training tools: a Teflon pipe and metal tubes.

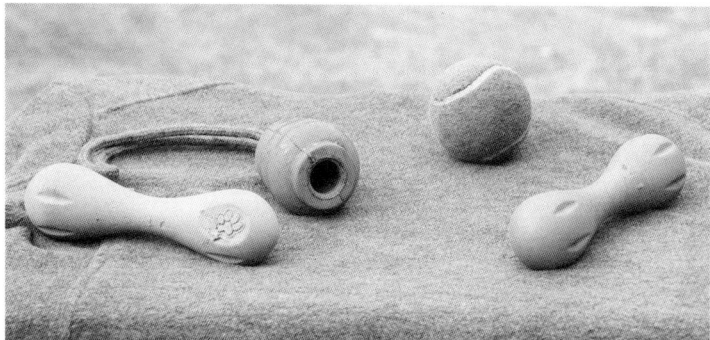

Reward tools: on each side, the Westpaw Hurley, and in the center, the Kong and a tennis ball. All of these items can be satisfying fetch rewards for your dog.

for your dog: no sharp edges. After all, you want your dog to have a good experience when retrieving this item. When choosing the item, make sure it is of a size that your dog cannot swallow. Some examples of retrievable objects include Teflon pipes, rubber balls or tennis balls, Kongs, or Westpaw Hurleys. We prefer the Hurley because it doesn't roll away.

Narcotics can be very dangerous, so, during training, use the retrievable object as a guard against your dog coming into contact with toxic substances. When training your dog to find the odor of a particular drug, for example, place your Hurley near the odor in such a way that your dog can never be in direct contact with the drug but will be able to fetch the Hurley. If you are using a Teflon pipe, ensure that no unpackaged drugs can find their way into the hollow of the pipe. Only very well-packaged drugs should be placed inside the pipe, and they must always be well-protected against destruction, damage, or loss.

## Detector-Dog Training Principles

The principles of detector-dog training are twofold: incentive and association. To stimulate the bring drive in a dog, you must provide a suitable incentive in the form of an object that your dog is able to fetch. In fact, the first stages of detector training are all about direct retrieving, followed by searching and fetching, and then training of the "alert" or response the dog gives when she has found the odor she is looking for. This alert can be active—for example, scratching—or passive—lying down or sitting. Whatever alert you train, your dog must learn that she is not allowed to touch any of the odorous substances she finds. She must also learn that her reward does not come immediately, as it does in other areas of dog training; she must learn to expect a delayed reward.

To train her to expect this kind of reward, ensure that every time you give your dog a reward during training, it is related to a drug odor. There are a variety of ways to teach your dog the association between the odors and the reward. One of the best ways, in our view, is to ensure the dog perceives the drug odor alongside the reward at an early stage of training. For example, at first hide the Hurley along with the cache of drugs so your dog can always take her reward upon finding the drugs she is searching for. Later on, only hide the drugs, and if your dog finds their scent, throw the Hurley from behind your dog, over her, so she can fetch it. Learning how to find caches in this way will help your dog focus her passions for searching and retrieving on the retrievable object that is also now strongly associated with the odor of drugs. We use the all-important retrievable object in four different parts of training: as a reward, a drive stimulator, an independence builder, and a way for you, the handler, to learn to read your dog's body language.

### THE REWARD

Use the retrievable object as a reward. Without it, your dog will lose her urge to search. Rewarding with a training tool at the end of each successful search exercise—finding an odor and giving the correct response—allows your dog to understand that she has completed the command, finished the job. Because the job always ends in a satisfactory way, she becomes receptive to further training.

### STIMULATING THE DRIVE TO BRING

At the end of each search, your dog can retrieve her reward and should be allowed to play with it. By encouraging your dog's ownership of the object and her play with it, you stimulate her bring drive.

### BUILDING INDEPENDENCE

During training, you need to help your dog develop independence so she is not entirely dependent on you as she searches. Such independence can be developed by using the training tool: every time you train, your dog will search more intensively for the tool, independently, to reward herself as quickly as possible.

## READING YOUR DOG

As you and your dog go through the many stages of search training together, you will come to recognize the meaning behind your dog's behavior and reactions. The retrievable object is a tool that allows you to observe everything your dog does, without interruptions; because she is driven to independently find the object, you will be able to observe her from a short distance, watching and learning her body language.

## Concentration and Distractions

Because curiosity is part of every dog's nature, during training you need to develop your dog's ability to concentrate on the task at hand and not get distracted by other, interesting things. To do this, you have to familiarize your dog with the many different environments in which she might later work. If you train your dog in many different locations, she will become used to a variety of surroundings, sounds, objects, smells, and experiences with others, and this familiarity will prepare her for work as a detector dog.

Of course, it is impossible to be prepared for every situation. However, in many cases, your dog will experience one type of environment in the same manner in which she views another. For example, working in aircraft hangars is similar to working in cargo sheds, warehouses, and other large, cavernous buildings.

Because every situation and environment can potentially be a search area, simulated search areas set up for training purposes should include indoor venues (in-use, empty, and dilapidated buildings; storage areas and basements; large sheds and hangars; public buildings; schools; and offices); open-air environments (parking lots, industrial sites, railways, public meeting spaces, and event grounds); and vehicles such as public trains and buses, cars and trucks, aircraft, and water-going vessels.

Agility training will help your dog work around obstacles such as boxes, steps, and vehicles, which are present in all these environments. Your dog must eventually be able to take on such obstacles

# BASICS OF DRUG-DETECTION TRAINING

Your drug-detector dog must learn to search various types of vehicles, including the forklift, shown here.

The reward!

without doubt or fear. If your dog is agile enough to jump over and maneuver around these obstacles, either on her own volition or on your command, she will be able to handle any environment without losing concentration. Of course, you must also train your dog not to jump around in a search area needlessly.

Here, we come back to the key idea that dogs concentrate better when they are not distracted. While training your dog, pay close attention to the most obvious distractions and familiarize her with them; make the distractions unworthy of her notice. Through structural repetition (possibly with rewards or corrections), your dog will eventually ignore distractions and accept them as simply part of the search area. Distractions can be of a direct or indirect nature, such as those listed below:

- Residual waste and food
- Unfamiliar situations
- Wild game or birds
- Pets
- Sudden noise or movement
- Objects that can be retrieved
- Varying climatic conditions
- Flooring or stairways of varying conditions
- Different types of vegetation
- Large crowds of people

A detector dog should have plenty of perseverance. The more perseverance your dog has, the less distracted she will be. You can help your dog develop this characteristic through gratification in the form of a delayed reward during training and operational deployment.

## Hiding Drugs

Regularly during training, you will need to make sure that your dog is not finding the hidden substance by searching for a human scent or any odors that might accompany the substance in question; she must find the drugs she is searching for by finding the odor of the drugs themselves. To do this, perform the sorting test. Hide an object (one that does not contain any drugs or has not been in contact with drugs) replete with human odor—perhaps your own or that of a helper—not too close to some hidden drugs. Then test your dog's odor-recognition skills by asking her to find the drugs, not the other hidden object. (We go into further detail about this sorting test later in this chapter.) Your dog's retrievable training object should not be positioned in the area around the hiding place for the drugs. Only reward your dog with her retrievable object if she demonstrates she can find the hidden drugs.

Generally speaking, during training, hidden drugs should be packaged in vials, bottles, plastics, or the like. But bear in mind that during the sorting test, you may need to remove the packaging from the drugs to decrease the likelihood of your dog sniffing for an accompanying smell (sometimes called an emitter) instead of the smell of the drugs themselves. If you need to do this, make sure you hide the drugs in a place where they are detectable but also where your dog cannot reach them (for example, in a closed closet, suitcase, or box). Also remember not to hide the drugs in plain sight; dogs can become used to responding to certain visual characteristics associated with "hidden" drug caches.

Five other rules you should follow when hiding drugs during drug-detector training follow:

1. Never leave hidden drugs unattended.
2. Always hide drugs in a safe place, or leave the hiding to a competent person, such as a colleague (fellow officer or trainer).
3. If you are training your dog to find more than one cache of hidden drugs in an exercise, remember to take note of the location and number of hiding places to prevent abandoning a package of drugs somewhere.
4. To avoid distracting your dog during search exercises, do not wear or hold anything that might contain drug substances.
5. When you begin training your dog to recognize different drug odors, do not mix different types of drugs together.

## Sterile Tools

To avoid disruption during training, as well as contamination and inadvertent planting of "clues" in hidden drugs, always use sterile tools (forceps or tongs) and/or gloves when handling drug packages. If you simply handle the drugs with bare hands, you will impart your own odor onto the drug packet; as well, some drugs are dangerous and should not be handled gloveless.

Detector dogs are always looking for clues about where a drug could be hidden. We cannot emphasize it enough: always work to prevent your dog from reacting to human scent during training. It really is of the utmost importance that you never hold or hide drugs packages without wearing gloves. In addition, make sure basic substances are stored separately. And, of course, be vigilant and watch for tracks you or a helper may have laid in the search area that might lead your dog to the cache. To avoid creating a track that leads to the prize, always ask a few people to walk around in a training search area before asking your dog to find the drugs.

## Detector Work Categories

Each type of detector work, both operational and in training, fits into one of the three categories we detail below. Handlers and instructors should fully understand the advantages and disadvantages of each category: controlled search, blind search, and operational search.

### CONTROLLED SEARCH

This type of search, wherein you, the handler, know the hidden location of the drugs, is conducted during the beginning stages of training a drug-detector dog.

#### ADVANTAGES

- Allows you to control the search and movements of your dog and to encourage her at the right moments.
- Enables you to learn and begin to recognize your dog's reactions to searching; allows you to prevent your dog's incorrect responses by reacting at the right moment. For example, if you see your dog wants to give an incorrect

response, you can say, "No" and "Search further" to avoid false alerts.
- Allows you to apply corrective measures without distracting your dog from achieving a positive indication.

**DISADVANTAGES**

- May lead you to indicating where the drugs are located.
- May encourage you to stand in one spot, which prevents your dog from learning to search systematically. A good dog handler should walk slowly with the dog and not simply stand in one place.

**BLIND SEARCH**

For you, of course, all searches in real life are conducted "blind." But for the dog, all searches are conducted blind, even during training. When conducting a blind search during training, the helper, instructor, or others who know the locations of the hiding places can be present.

**ADVANTAGES**

- Helps build the handler–dog team, giving each partner confidence in the other.
- Refines your concentration.
- Creates a need for the team to search systematically.

**DISADVANTAGES**

- You may not note the dog's important search reactions because you are not yet aware of what you have to look for.
- You may allow your dog to do unnecessary work. So your dog may end up searching the same area several times instead of moving on to the next area to search. (Sometimes this happens when a handler thinks he or she has seen a reaction in the dog and so sends the dog to search an area over and over again.)

- You may request confirmation from and encourage your dog at the wrong times, thereby causing confusion and even false indications.
- Attendees who know where the drugs are hidden may consciously or unconsciously give clues to the dog.

**OPERATIONAL SEARCH**

When you conduct an operational search during training, you, the handler, do not know the number of drug caches hidden in the search area. Indeed, there may be none. When performing an operational search in training, only you and your dog enter the search area. (Your instructor may choose to follow the search by means of a suspended camera or cameras.) You must ensure that your dog accurately scans the entire area. Mark all possible caches, as are indicated by your dog, with a stylus or otherwise. During training, you and your dog should perform more than one operational search in an area where no drugs are hidden.

ADVANTAGES

- Teaches you to place your trust in your detector dog.
- Confirms the need to work systematically, including low and high searches.
- Allows a busy dog to adapt. A busy dog will only be successful if she slows down and searches intensively.
- Search time increases, which helps develop your dog's concentration and control.

DISADVANTAGES

- You many feel unsteady without backup from colleagues who help you to systematically search and observe your dog's behavior.
- Too much search work without success may decrease the bring drive in some dogs.

## Training the First Drug

Always begin scent training with a drug scent that is not unpleasant or likely to elicit an adverse response in your dog. For instance, some dogs find that amphetamines sting their noses. But, just as different people experience scents in different ways, you can expect different dogs to have different reactions to the same odor. Try to discover a drug scent that your dog likes and start with that. Many dogs we have worked with like the scent of cocaine.

If your dog sniffs once at a certain drug and then physically avoids it, you know she doesn't like its smell because it is repulsive, stings the nose, or is otherwise too strong. Of course, do not use this scent when you begin scent training. Also consider that the first scent you train your dog on should not be one whose odor spreads too quickly in larger areas, such as hashish, because it is possible that too many objects in the search area will then take on the odor, making it difficult for your dog to pinpoint the exact hiding place of the drug.

When you practice searching for different drugs, you need to use original and clean products. At first, you should use only a small amount of the target scent, approximately 0.04 ounces (1 g).

When you use pure drugs, you have to make sure you protect them and your dog—make sure your dog cannot access them and that powder cannot enter her mouth or nostrils. We have found that small, re-sealable plastic bags provide fine storage for drugs used in training. As you prepare a drug cache for an exercise the next day, enclose the bag of drugs in an unused re-sealable plastic bag, making sure you don't touch either of them with your bare hands.

If you do not wish to use pure drugs in your search exercises, you may choose to employ scent-transfer objects, instead: cotton pads or a Teflon pipe with small openings in it (first without drugs inside, but later packed with well-sealed drugs) that are first positioned beside well-packaged drugs in a clean glass jar. The drugs

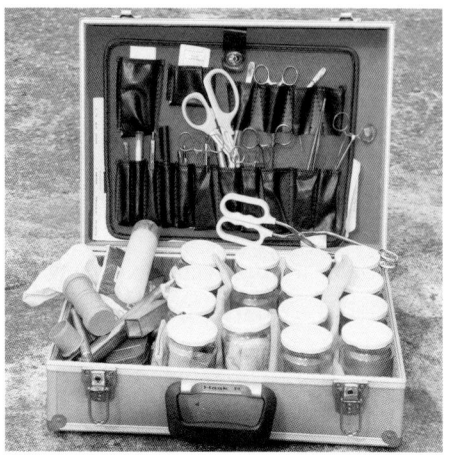

The training case, complete with pliers and different drugs encased in sterile glass jars.

(the scent source) must be in contact with the scent-transfer object overnight in the sealed glass jar. Shortly before starting the search exercise, use tweezers or tongs to remove the cotton pad or pipe from the jar, making sure you avoid contaminating it with your own odor. If you use scent-transfer objects, always remember to handle them as delicately as you would handle the original scent source; do not touch them with your bare hands! After one use, cotton pads should be disposed of.

At first, only scent the training tubes and cotton pads with one scent at a time. When you have finishing training your dog on a specific scent, you need new, clean jars and tubes. Do not use them for other scents because there is risk of contamination. For instance, glass jars that have been used for storing cocaine, and training tubes used as scent-transfer objects for cocaine, need to be discarded; washing and sterilizing them will not render them "clean."

### One Scent or More?

Some handlers choose to introduce their dogs to the different drug odors one at a time. As soon as their dogs do well with the first odor, they introduce the next one, together with the first one. It is possible to train your dog to recognize more than one scent at a time, and this surely is a faster method. However, the step-by-step method is more effective; when training your dog in this way, you can be sure she knows and recognizes each odor. The disadvantage to the "one at a time" method is that it takes more time to train than the concurrent method.

## The Response

The response your dog gives you when she has found the odor she is looking for is important. Make sure you teach your dog a response that suits your dog's behavior and character. If your dog has a well-developed drive to find the odor she is trained to find, you can always rely on her response. In drug-detector dog training, we see both active and passive responses.

### ACTIVE RESPONSE

Active responses mostly consist of scratching. The dog scratches in an attempt to penetrate whatever is covering the drug cache, the place that has the highest concentration of the odor she is trying

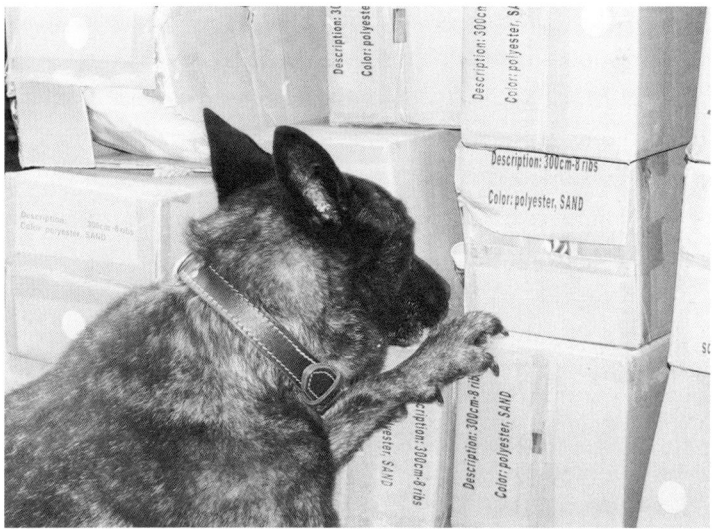

When displaying an active response, detector dogs often scratch at the surface of the cache.

to find. The type of scratching she employs should not be confused with so-called "orientational" scratching, by which the dog, to better smell an odor, scratches a covering away with her forepaw. She does this to open odor canals in the material she is scratching. The active-response scratching is different in that dogs employing this method scratch more intensively to reach the object they smell. Combined with the scratching, you may see your active-response dog biting at whatever is covering up the highest concentration of odor, attempting to pull the covering away.

Of course, this scratching and biting can be dangerous for your dog and result in her touching or ingesting some of the drug she has found. Furthermore, this type of response inevitably results in property damage. For example, once we conducted a search that involved a very expensive car; it turned out the drugs had once been hidden in the back seat, which was upholstered in leather. In the end, the dog demolished the expensive back seat without finding any drugs, which were no longer in their hiding place.

Another active response involves barking. If your dog does this, she will position herself near the scent clue she wants to alert you to and bark repeatedly or continuously without scratching. This type of response is suitable for dogs that bark easily on their own volition. Often dogs that alert with barking do so after scratching and becoming irritated when they cannot penetrate the find fast enough. In some cases, barking by itself is not enough, and the dog must indicate exactly where the highest odor concentration is coming from by putting her nose in or toward it.

*TRAINING THE ACTIVE RESPONSE*

To train dogs to display active responses, we choose to let them learn by playing, then later on turn the behavior they have learned into a duty. For training we use a Teflon pipe, or a metal tube, punctured with small holes; the open ends of the objects are firmly sealed.

First, teach your dog to play fetch with the tube. If she likes this game, place a well-packaged drug inside the tube. When she is retrieving the slightly odorous object well after you throw

# BASICS OF DRUG-DETECTION TRAINING

A detector dog in training finds a hidden Teflon pipe and retrieves it.

it right in front of her, start throwing it when and where your dog cannot see it, and ask her to "Search." She will search for it but will not be able to find it right away. When she does find it, reward her with a treat or by playing fetch with another object, such as a ball. She will quickly get the idea that searching and retrieving will result in a reward, and she will easily learn to find the tube by its scent.

When she is doing well with this game, change the terrain, conditions, and other surroundings, and continue playing the game until your dog has a real passion for searching. By this time, you should be using tubes made of different artificial materials (wood, iron, aluminum, leather, rubber), each containing its own drug scent. Do whatever you can to increase your dog's skill level and training. For example, slowly change your practice terrain to include places such as train stations, post offices, barracks, cars, trains, buses, and so on; and practice with all kinds of scent-filled tubes in these new environments.

At first, you and your dog should search in the open air with one hidden tube, and later on with more hidden tubes that you ask

The active response, with scratching.

her to find one after the other. After that, do the same inside buildings, placing one tube in various locations that are easy to find and accessible for your dog. Then, start training in other places with more tubes that each contain different drugs, or odors of drugs. Depending on how you train (one odor after the other, or a few odors together) make sure you regularly change the odors as soon as your dog shows she can find them easily.

ACTIVE RESPONSE TRAINING SCHEDULE

*Step 1:* Play fetch in the open air with a tube containing one well-packaged drug, or, if you are using the concurrent method, four kinds of well-packaged drugs at a time. After playing this game over the course of a few training sessions, initiate a game of hide and seek with your dog, hiding the tube in more and more difficult locations each time you play. You will want to have a helper on hand to make sure your dog cannot see where you've hidden the tube. In fact, you'll want more than one person around, because you also need to make sure your dog does not simply follow your track to the tube. Ask a few people to walk over the terrain and cross your own track several times. As the game progresses, make the hiding places more and more difficult to uncover, so your dog has to scratch to get the tube out. When your dog has found the tube, let her retrieve it and reward her with food or a ball or Hurley.

*Step 2:* Train your dog inside buildings using the same tube containing a well-packaged drug or drugs. Hide the tube in various locations that are not too difficult for your dog to find and get at. Praise your dog for scratching at hiding places in order find and retrieve the tube.

*Step 3:* Train your dog in a variety of places with the tube or tubes, and as you progress, bring in more and more distractions. Ensure the hidden tube is well covered so your dog must work to find and retrieve it.

*Step 4:* Repeat the first three steps, but now when hiding the tube in the different places, make sure you cover it with different kinds of wrappings (paper, plastic, fabric, metal).

*Step 5:* Beginning again at Step 1, start training your dog to find a second drug hidden together with drug she already knows; or, if you are training more drugs at a time, start training your dog with a new series of four drugs.

*Step 6:* After going through the above steps again with the new drug or series of drugs, hide only the second drug (or series of drugs) in a new tube and see if your dog can find its odor in all situations, from Step 1 to Step 4. Remember to conduct these exercises in various locations, such as houses, basements, and fields.

*Step 7:* Place a new drug together with the first or second drug in the tube. Try to pair the new drug with the one that was the easiest for your dog to find. Go through all the steps again. Complete the training in the same way, teaching your dog to recognize and find all sorts of drugs, in all sorts of wrappings and all sorts of places.

This detector-in-training has found the drugs under the hood of a car.

And, upon finding the cache, the dog indicates his find by scratching.

## PASSIVE RESPONSE

Some dogs demonstrate passive alerts by sitting, standing, or lying down (no barking or scratching) near the scent clue. This passive response may be accompanied by the dog pointing her nose into the spot that has the most concentrated drug odor.

Some years ago, handlers and instructors were somewhat skeptical about the passive response. With that type of alert, many reasoned, the dog's drives would decrease in intensity. But when dogs are trained correctly and rewarded the moment they respond to the odor of drugs, we have found that dogs like the passive response in searches for drugs. We have trained dogs to use this type of response quite successfully. The advantages are obvious. When the dog demonstrates a passive response, she poses fewer risks to herself (for example, contact with the drug or scratching at dangerous/sharp objects) and her handler (for instance, the possibility of the scratching breaking the packaging and dispersing the drugs, perhaps causing the handler to inhale those drugs). As well, the passive response can be used in searches for people, and it does not damage private property.

*TRAINING THE PASSIVE RESPONSE*

First, teach your dog to play fetch with the training tool (a tennis ball, Hurley, or other retrievable object). Then, put together a box that is about 12 inches wide, 12 inches long, and 8 inches high (30 × 30 × 20 cm). The top side of the box should have an opening into which you can fit the training tool. During the first session with the training box, it should hold the drug odor as well as the training tool. Practice this first exercise in a room where there are no distractions. Before starting, show your dog the training tool and let her see you put it in the box so she knows it's in there. Because your dog is crazy about her ball, she will go straight to the box to try to get it, sticking her nose right into the opening on top. When her nose is in the box, say, "Sit." If she doesn't sit, command her again and quietly bring her into the Sit, telling her she is a good girl.

Now point at the hole in the box, ensuring your dog stays sitting. When she puts her nose into the hole of the box from a seated position, enthusiastically praise her and, with your throwing hand behind your dog, throw a different ball or Hurley for her to retrieve. Make sure your dog does not see you throwing the ball, or she will pay more attention to you than to the box she is supposed to be smelling. Each time she sticks her nose into the hole on the top of the box, attempting to get her ball, your dog will smell the drug scent or scents.

After repeating this exercise many times over many training sessions, deepen the exercise. This time, don't place the ball in the box but keep the scent or scents in there. Immediately after your dog sniffs, sits, and pinpoints the opening in the box, throw her ball for her to retrieve and praise her for the good work. The next step is to slowly increase the amount of time your dog has to pinpoint, her nose in the hole, from one to five seconds (or even more), before you throw the reward.

If your dog understands what she has to do with the scent-laden box, bring another, identical box to the training place and put the boxes in a lineup. One should carry the scent of drugs and the other should not. Always use the same box for the odor substances, otherwise you run the risk of all your boxes acquiring the same scent, and your dog will end up pinpointing every box.

Begin passive-response training with a box that holds the odor of the drug you are training your dog to recognize. The lid of the box should have an opening through which you can place a tennis ball or other training tool. Your dog should be able to see the tool.

When displaying the passive response, the dog sits quietly and points.

Bring your dog over to the lineup in such a way that she first meets the box that does not have the drug scent and then the one that does. Now you will see if you have trained her properly. If your dog sits at the first box and brings her nose to the hole, you will have to go back to the initial training because she does not yet understand that she is not supposed to sit and bring her nose down to just any old box, but only with boxes in which she smells the odor of the drug or drugs.

If your dog worked out the mini-lineup well—she sniffed the first box and then moved on to the second, where she sniffed, sat, and put her nose to the hole—reward her by throwing the training tool. After a few training sessions with the two-box lineup, you can start asking her to investigate three or four boxes, or even more. Be sure to regularly change the position of the scented box in the lineup.

If everything goes well, you can progress to putting the boxes in corners of the room and asking your dog to search for the correct box, sit, and pinpoint. If she does this correctly, take out the container or wrapping that encloses the drug in the box and hide that in the same spot it was the last time you practiced. Your dog should approach the place where she can smell the hidden scent container or wrappings, and she should sniff, sit, and pinpoint.

Finally, you can practice this exercise in different rooms, using different hiding places: in other houses, cars, outbuildings, and places where your dog will have to work in her career as a drug-detector dog. Always build up the training slowly, making sure your dog understands each exercise, until she can find the substances anywhere and give a correct passive response every time.

### PASSIVE RESPONSE TRAINING SCHEDULE

*Step 1:* Place one training box containing one drug (or four different drugs if you are using the concurrent method) in a quiet place. Ask your dog to sit in front of the box. Now, making sure your dog can see what you are doing, insert the training tool into the top opening of the box. Allow your dog to go over to the box, but do not let her scratch at it. Instead, command, "Sit," and point at the opening. As soon as your sitting dog presses her nose close to the opening at the top of the box, throw another training tool as reward but in such a way that she does not see you throw it.

*Step 2:* If your dog understands that she has to sit in front of the box and pinpoint, place a second box without drugs in a row with the other box. Lead your dog to the boxes, ensuring that the first box she meets is the empty box. To pass from this step to the next one, your dog must correctly proceed to the second, scented box before giving the passive, pinpointing response. Reward her with the retrievable training tool.

*Step 3:* Bring in more empty boxes and regularly change the position of the scented box in the lineups you create. You can use all types of boxes when you create these lineups.

*Step 4:* Start training your dog to recognize the scent of a second drug, hidden together with the first drug in the box. If you are training four different scents at a time, begin training your dog to

## BASICS OF DRUG-DETECTION TRAINING

In Step 4 of the training schedule for passive response, hide a second drug together with the first drug your dog learned to recognize in the box. If you are training more than one drug at a time, in this step you should put a new series of four drugs in the box and go through Steps 1 to 3 of the training process with the new series.

recognize a new series of four drugs in the box. With these new scents, go through the exercises in Steps 1 through 3.

*Step 5:* Pair a new drug up with the first or the second drug in the box, making sure you use the drug that was the easiest for your dog to find. Go through Steps 1 through 3. Complete the training in the same way with all sorts of drugs. When your dog completes the exercises properly, make sure you reward her by throwing the training tool.

*Step 6:* Put a box containing one type of drug (or four kinds, depending on your training method) in the corner of a room. Let your dog search, sit, and pinpoint. If she does this correctly, remove the container or wrapping that encloses the drug(s) in the box and hide it in an accessible spot near where it was in the box the last time you practiced. Do this with all the drugs your dog has been trained to search for, find, and pinpoint.

*Step 7:* From this point on, hide the different drugs in increasingly difficult spots—low and high, in vehicles, in someone's coat, and so on. Always reward your dog for her good work by throwing her the training tool, making sure she does not see you throwing it.

This dog is learning how to investigate a scent-identification lineup. One of the containers holds the scent of the drug the dog is looking for.

The dog displays a passive response by lying down and pinpointing.

## Physical Response

Dogs constantly receive signals through their senses of smell, sight, and hearing, and you, the handler, may not even realize your dog is perceiving something. It is essential for you to understand

## BASICS OF DRUG-DETECTION TRAINING

your dog's behavior and know when she has received certain signals. Because your dog cannot talk, you must encourage her to signal you when something is up. At the same time, you must be careful not to influence your dog into signaling a false response. When handlers fail to recognize behavioral signals, dogs become confused, which in turn results in handlers becoming frustrated and operating on a hit-and-miss basis.

When a dog is searching, you will see the following behaviors:

- Normal steps: the movements and the pace of the dog during the search before she detects the odor of drugs
- Change of attitude: a difference in tempo and/or in behavior; movement of the ears, tail, or a sudden change of direction upon encountering an odor
- Lifting the head: the dog may lift her head and tilt it in a certain direction, or she may stand on her hind legs and raise her head to smell the air when she perceives the smell of drugs

When your dog knows how to search for drugs at ground level, teach her to find them in high-up and harder-to-reach places.

- Positive interest: body movements and behavior that indicate to the handler that the dog has detected the presence of drugs, but not yet the "hot spot"
- Response: the passive (sitting or lying down) or active (scratching or barking) alert the dog has been trained to demonstrate when she has actually found the location of a drug or drugs
- Confirmation: after the dog demonstrates the alert, the handler can confirm that drugs have been found by attempting to lure the dog away from the "hot spot" (giving additional search commands or trying to pull the dog away on leash). If the dog is sure of her find, she will continue to alert and will not leave her place.

A handler who does not read the reactions of his or her dog is like a person reading a book in a language he or she does not understand. You, the handler, must be able to understand, explain, and respond to your dog's reactions.

# 3

# Accidental Drug Uptake: First Aid for Your Dog

Dogs are naturally curious, licking and sniffing at everything, and, generally speaking, they are not terribly picky about their food. For many dogs, wallowing in an unknown substance is not a strange activity. If you ever see that your dog has picked up or licked a possibly toxic material, you should always take immediate action, following eight important steps:

1. Prevent further absorption of the substance into your dog's system via his mouth, tongue, nose, eyes, ears, coat, skin, and paws.
2. Separate your dog from the substance.
3. Protect yourself from the substance.
4. Control your dog.
5. Immediately rinse his mouth with plenty of water (the oral mucosa quickly absorbs substances).
6. Know whether or not you should induce vomiting. If the substance is caustic, acidic, or sharp, do not induce vomiting. If your dog has accidentally ingested drugs, induce vomiting.
7. Always, as soon as possible, contact your veterinarian.
8. Collect and preserve the substance affecting your dog in a plastic bag.

During training, always hide the drug cache in such a way that your dog can find it but cannot access it.

## Do Not Induce Vomiting

If your dog has come into close contact with a caustic or acidic substance, as by licking drain cleaner or mineral spirits, for example, or if he has ingested broken glass, do not induce vomiting. Vomiting would cause more damage, as the substance would pass through the esophagus a second time. In these cases, it is best to neutralize the poison or sharp object and to ease the pain in the throat and stomach. Never give milk to a dog that just has eaten, licked, or drunk caustic chemicals. Many toxins dissolve very well in the fat in milk, which allows them to move more quickly into the bloodstream. In other cases, give your dog milk or eggs, or a neutralizing agent containing magnesium. Give the latter at a dose of 1 teaspoon (5 mL) per 5.5 pounds (2.5 kg) of the dog's body weight. If you do not have time to calculate the exact amount, give him just a little to ease the pain. Bear in mind that you will have to administer this neutralizing agent under duress.

If corrosive substances are in your dog's eyes or on his coat or skin, directly flush the affected area/s with a lot of water.

## Induce Vomiting

Do not put salt in your dog's mouth, on his tongue, or in his throat to induce vomiting. Dogs have died through such administrations of saline. As well, if your dog is unconscious, do not induce vomiting. Wrap an unconscious animal in a blanket and position him so that his head is slightly lower than the rest of his body.

### INDUCING VOMITING WITH HYDROGEN PEROXIDE (3%)

Hydrogen peroxide (3%) is a safe alternative to salt. Pour the liquid into your dog's mouth, administering 0.4 teaspoons (2 mL) per 2.2 pounds (1 kg) of body weight, up to 9 teaspoons (45 mL). You can find hydrogen peroxide at the drugstore. Be sure to heed the expiration date on the bottle. When hydrogen peroxide expires, it loses its ability to induce vomiting.

After ingesting hydrogen peroxide, 90 percent of dogs vomit and, on average, 25 percent of the stomach contents are regurgitated.

### INDUCING VOMITING WITH APOMORPHINE

An injection of apomorphine is better at inducing vomiting than a dose hydrogen peroxide. An apomorphine injection liquid stimulates emesis in dogs that have been poisoned or have ingested a foreign object. Note that in many countries, only vets are allowed to handle apomorphine.

The dosage can be given intravenously: 0.03–0.04 milligrams per 2.2 pounds (1 kg) of your dog's body weight; or as an intramuscular injection: from 0.04 to 0.08 milligrams per 2.2 pounds (1 kg) of your dog's body weight. Onset of action when administered intravenously is within one to four minutes; with intramuscular administration, the onset of action is usually within five to 20 minutes.

If the recommended dosage does not provide the desired result, do not administer apomorphine again because of the risk of depressing your dog's central nervous system.

After having received an injection of apomorphine into the bloodstream, 100 percent of dogs vomit about 75 percent of the stomach's contents

### AFTER VOMITING

Because the stomach is never completely emptied after emesis, and because some of the substance your dog has ingested may already have made its way into the intestines, it is wise to follow up with the following three steps.

1. Give your dog activated carbon, also called activated charcoal or activated coal, which binds many toxins.
2. Give your dog a laxative formulated specifically for dogs. Consult your vet about this.
3. Take your dog to the vet so he can be under observation until the substance leaves his system.

## Accidental Uptake of Drugs by Dogs

Immediately induce vomiting in your dog if he accidentally takes in drugs. First, try inducing vomiting manually (i.e., by putting your fingers or the backside of a spoon into your dog's mouth, touching the back part of his tongue, deep in the throat—your dog may not allow this). If that does not work, induce vomiting by injecting apomorphine intramuscularly. Apomorphine should be given as soon as possible after poisoning if manually inducing vomiting does not work. Take the following steps before injecting:

1. Hold the ampoule in such a way that its point is away from your body.
2. Tap the ampoule until the liquid spreads out within its container.
3. Break the ampoule.
4. Suck the full contents of the ampoule into the syringe.
5. Inject the apomorphine perpendicular to the skin into the muscle of the upper leg or thigh.
6. Apomorphine works best if your dog has a full stomach.
7. Never administer a second dose.
8. In case of persistent vomiting, consult your vet about neutralizing the substance with naloxone (0.04 milligrams per 2.2 pounds [1 kg] body weight).

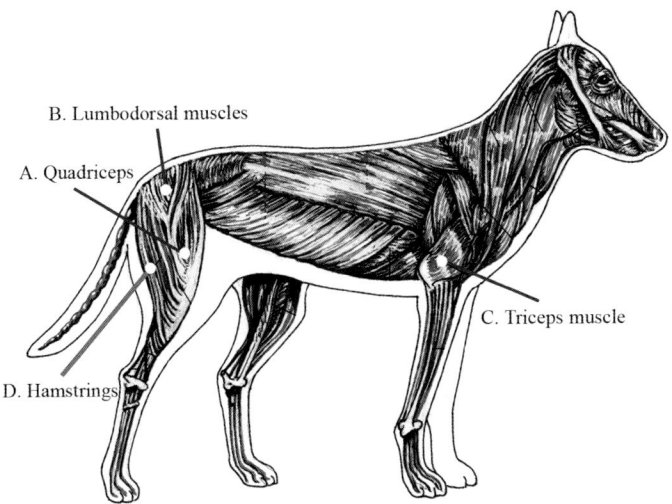

The musculature of the dog. Appropriate places for intramuscular injections are (A) the quadriceps (the muscle on the front of the thigh, (B) the lumbodorsal muscles (the muscles on each side of the lumbar spine, (C) or the triceps muscle (behind the humerus in the front leg. If you choose to inject medication into the lumbodorsal muscles, always inject away from the spine. Do not inject medication into the hamstrings (D, muscles at the back of the thigh) in order to avoid damaging the sciatic nerve, which runs through that area. Place the needle in the muscle and withdraw the plunger to create negative pressure. If no blood is aspirated, give the injection. After withdrawing the needle, massage the muscle to help disperse the medicine.

## The Effects of Drugs on Dogs

### CANNABIS: MARIJUANA, HASHISH

The effect of cannabis on dogs is similar to its effect on humans—symptoms occur within 30 to 60 minutes. The drug's effects reach their peak between two and four hours after ingestion and phase out slowly. Symptoms of poisoning can last for three days; THC is rarely fatal. Symptoms include the following:

- Changes in behavior
- Balance disorder, drifting, ataxia
- Weakness in muscles
- Apathy and even drowsiness

- Dilated pupils
- Vomiting, drooling
- Throbbing, rapid pulse, but a slow heartbeat
- Hypothermia or, rarely, overheating
- Hypersensitivity to touch
- Hyperactivity, tremors, or convulsions
- A rapid change of clinical symptoms

### COCAINE

Dogs rapidly absorb cocaine via the mucous membranes of the mouth, eyes, nose, or gastrointestinal tract. Within 60 minutes after uptake, the dog will achieve the maximum concentration of the substance in his bloodstream. Cocaine is rapidly degraded by the liver and excreted in the urine. Death due to cardiac arrest or overheating is possible. Symptoms, showing themselves within a few minutes, include the following:

- Nervousness, hyperactivity, anxiety
- Very fast pulse
- Tremors and muscle cramps
- Nervous-system attacks (similar to epileptic seizures)
- Overheating
- Difficulty breathing

### AMPHETAMINE

Amphetamine has a stimulating, uplifting effect on the dog's central nervous system. It is rapidly absorbed by the gastrointestinal tract. The duration of this drug's action after ingestion is four to 24 hours. Again, death due to cardiac arrest is possible (the likely fatal dose is 10–23 milligrams per 2.2 pounds [1 kg] body weight). Symptoms include the following:

- Restlessness, foaming at the mouth, panting
- Changes in behavior, hyperactivity

- Hypersensitivity to noise and pain
- Dilated pupils
- Overheating (fever)
- Raging heartbeat, and throbbing and rapid pulse
- Vomiting, diarrhea
- Cramps
- Breathlessness
- Cardiac arrhythmias, stroke

**OTHER HARD DRUGS**

The dog's gastrointestinal tract, like that of humans, is relatively slow to absorb hard drugs (maximum duration of absorption: two to four hours), and dogs only slowly recover from uptake of hard drugs (remnant amounts are present in the blood for 15 to 60 hours). Death due to pulmonary edema and low respiratory rate is possible within 12 hours of uptake (the dose needed for this effect depends on the drug and the dog). Symptoms include the following:

- Sleepiness
- Imbalance
- Ataxia
- Hypersensitivity to noise and pain
- Overreactions to stimuli
- Excited behavior
- Vomiting, foaming at the mouth
- Heavy breathing
- Delirium, cramps
- Constricted pupils
- Sharp drop in blood pressure
- Breathlessness
- Unconsciousness, coma, or death

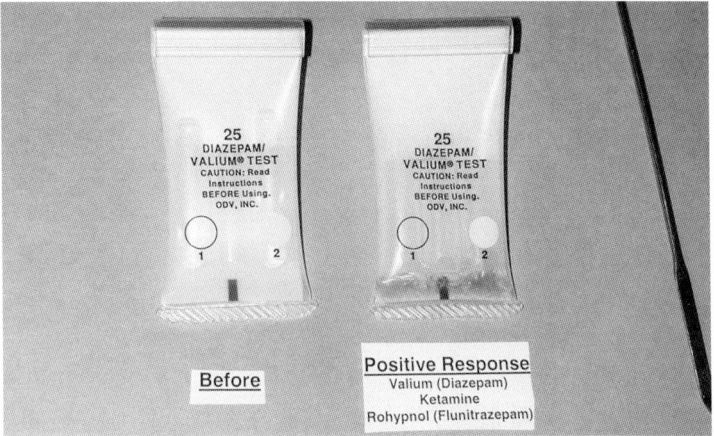

A field test for diazepam, ketamine, and rohypnol helps you quickly discover if your dog was in contact with those drugs.

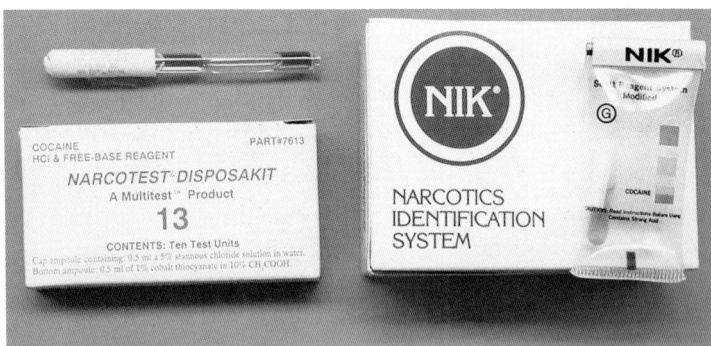

A field test for cocaine.

## Other Health Problems During Training or in Service

During drug-detection training and fieldwork, you and your dog may encounter other dangers to health besides accidently taking in drugs. For example, you may come across oil, tar, or dye, which could irritate your dog's skin, coat, or paws. Both you and your dog may become dehydrated during long searches in both hot and cold weather.

### CLEANING YOUR DOG'S COAT

You can always brush dry spots of dirt (clay, mud, or soil) off your dog's coat. If this does not work, use water or any dry dog-coat conditioner. Never use benzene, turpentine, paint thinner, white spirit, or other such products to remove diesel oil, tar, asphalt, dye, or similar substances from your dog's coat or other parts of his body. Such solvents dissolve the target substance into very small particles that can be absorbed by your dog's skin. After being absorbed, they can enter the bloodstream and cause severe damage, even death.

It is far better to use butter, olive oil, or another vegetable oil applied to a rag, newspaper, or paper towel to remove as much of

Never use benzene, turpentine, paint thinner, white spirit, or any other such products to remove diesel oil, tar, asphalt, dye, or similar substances from your dog's coat or other parts of his body.

Pay close attention to your dog's paws after a search action—make sure they didn't come into contact with anything dangerous.

the substance as possible. Use shampoo to finish the job, rinsing with plain water.

## DEHYDRATION

Dehydration as a result of heat can be a serious problem for operational detector dogs. Most cases of dehydration in working dogs result from stress and insufficient intake of water (dogs need two to three times the normal amount of water during periods of extended physical effort). When environmental temperatures reach 77–86°F (25–30°C), dogs lose a tremendous amount of fluids and electrolytes through panting, so dogs working in such conditions should have plenty of water to drink. They should also regularly drink an isotonic or hypotonic electrolyte mixture.

Your dog can also become dehydrated when it's cold. Dogs that become tired or stressed often refuse to eat and drink. In cold temperatures, your dog can become dehydrated in less than 12 hours, so increase his water intake at the earliest sign of dehydration. A simple dehydration test entails pulling your dog's skin up a little at the back of the neck or, even better, pulling the fold of skin at the side of the chest outward. The skin should return to its original position as soon as you let go. If it does not, your dog is dehydrated and you need to see a vet immediately.

The health and welfare of your drug-detector dog, both in training and during an operational mission, is of utmost importance. Without good health, it is impossible for him to make the strenuous efforts required to successfully perform intensive searches.

# 4

# Reading Your Dog

Your dog will display many physical reactions to her search work, and you, her handler, must be able to understand what these reactions mean. In other words, you must be able to read your dog. In practice, dogs react to a find with certain body attitudes or expressions that are unique to each dog. What is consistent about these expressions is that they clearly show that dogs feel stress when they locate clues.

The most important parts about your dog's behavior—the body language you definitely need to be able to understand—are the acts and expressions she shows while searching. This behavior is very complex; searching dogs display a wide range of expressions and body language.

To read your dog, you must pay attention to all the changes in behavior that she displays. You must know your dog well, how she reacts to things in everyday life, at home and in training. To read your dog, you must have a bond that exists as a result of many situations experienced together, during which you observed her carefully.

Being able to read your dog means recognizing and interpreting the many physical reactions she demonstrates during search work.

## Classification of Behavior

What do you pay attention to as you learn to read your dog? What follows here is only a short summary of the behavior and body language possibilities your dog might display. More details can be found in our book *K9 Behavior Basics* (Brush Education, 2013). Behavior can be defined, broadly speaking, as a combination of innate, acquired, and trained expressions.

Innate behavior includes all the acts determined by heredity and are already partially present at birth. At first, they include simple things, like puppies urinating and defecating when their mother licks them, or using the forepaws to knead the mother's nipple to help extract milk from the deeper regions of the mammary glands. Later, dogs will display various innate behaviors, ones they have never been taught, like turning around before they lie down, or scratching at the soil after they have answered nature's call.

Acquired behaviors are also determined by heredity, but dogs must learn them to display them properly. These special behaviors are learned during the socialization period of a puppy's life, between the fourth and 12th week after birth. In this period, the dog learns to react to her siblings, other dogs, people, odors, sounds, and sights, among other things in the environment.

Trained behaviors are the manifestation of strengthened or suppressed innate and acquired behaviors. These behaviors begin to develop in obedience training and are further strengthened during specialized training, for example, when your dog goes through the training and exercises required to become a detector dog. Note that if there is no hereditary tendency for a certain type of behavior, it will make no sense to your dog and so teaching and training it also makes no sense.

## Expressions of Behavior

A dog's behavioral expressions can be roughly divided into the following categories: confident, uncertain, anxious, submissive, aggressive, evasive, displacement, and stressed.

Your dog demonstrates confident behavior when she directs her ears forward, shows an attentive attitude, carries her tail at a normal to high level and, without hesitation or fear, looks in the direction of where something is happening.

She is uncertain if she displays restless ear movements, with the ears laid back; restless panting, sometimes slavering; or a low tail with uncertain, irregular wagging. If your dog is demonstrating this kind of body language, she will also be looking for your support and sometimes may even seek refuge behind you.

If your dog is anxious, she will panic, pull her tail between her legs, and try to escape.

Your dog shows submissive behavior (which should not be taken for anxious behavior) when, knowing her place in the pack, she submits to the will of one higher in rank. If your dog lies on her back, or crouches with her chest on the ground, offering her neck to a higher-ranking animal, she is displaying submissive behavior. (The latter of the two behaviors seems to arouse bite restraint in a higher-ranking dog.) Your dog is also showing submissive behavior if she pushes her nose out and licks it while standing at a distance from a higher-ranking member of the pack. We often see submissive behavior combined with uncertain behavior, although they don't consistently appear together.

You know your dog is acting aggressively when she threatens, lunges, and bites. Her neck and back hairs bristle.

With evasive behavior, you have to be able to distinguish between literal evasion (such as taking a step aside or walking around a difficult situation) and avoidance. Dogs showing avoidance behave as if they haven't seen something. They avoid awareness of a confrontation and walk along as though they are wearing blinders.

Most of the time, dogs display displacement behavior when uncertainty or frustration interrupts their natural drives. Perhaps your dog is unable to work out the situation at hand, so she switches to another behavior. She may scratch herself, shake, stretch, bite into her leash, sniff at something, or yawn, among other possible actions.

Your dog will show that she is under stress when she chews, blows out, pants restlessly, or licks her own snout. Combinations of stress behavior with other behaviors are also possible.

## Eyes

You should be able to assess your dog's mood and behavior by looking at her eyes. When a dog is satisfied, her eyes seem to shine; if she isn't satisfied, her eyes show a dull expression.

This dog is looking right at something that has aroused her interest.

In uncertain situations, your dog will look at you, her handler, questioningly, as if she is asking for confirmation or direction. She also does this when thirsty or tired. You've probably seen a panting dog, tongue hanging far out of her mouth, with a slightly questioning look on her face—this is the picture of an uncertain dog.

A search dog at work will sometimes look at her handler when the latter stays too far away, and a K9 will give her handler a disturbed look when the handler hinders the dog's search, perhaps by calling the dog's name, talking unexpectedly, or making noises or movements.

## Head and Ears

Dogs that are interested in a certain spot, or that hear or smell something interesting, often tilt their head toward the item of interest. In particular, a dog will turn her head to localize a sound.

Your dog's ears are extremely animated and can, in combination with the turning of the head, follow sounds. Even dogs with hanging ears show active ear play, although less than those with pricked ears.

When a dog smells something interesting, she will point her head toward it.

EAR POSITIONS AND THEIR MEANINGS
(DOGS WITH PRICKED EARS)

- Erect, pricked-up ears: the dog is self-confident, attentive, and interested.
- Ears turned in a certain direction: the dog is locating certain interesting sounds that attract her attention.
- Laid-back ears: the dog is showing doubt and uncertainty and, if her hackles are up and she is growling, she is ready to attack.

EAR POSITIONS AND THEIR MEANINGS
(DOGS WITH HANGING EARS)

- Loose, hanging ears: the dog is displaying a normal, relaxed attitude.
- Ears tensed so that they are open at the front: the dog is in a state of heightened attentiveness. If her head is also tilted or turned, she is attempting to locate interesting sounds.
- Ears carried low: the dog is showing submissiveness or uncertainty.

## Tail

Like the ears, the dog's tail indicates her emotional state:

- Horizontal tail: the dog is satisfied.
- Tail carried straight up: the dog has gone from a state of heightened attentiveness to a state of excitement.
- Tail pushed between back legs: the dog has gone from a state of reservation to one of fear.

Such signals have exceptions. For example, greyhounds almost always carry their tails between their legs, regardless of their emotional state. Of course, dogs with docked tails can't display these signals at all, which are often very important for handlers reading their detector dogs.

## Mouth

Have you seen your dog pulling her lips up and showing her teeth? This is not always an expression of aggression; in fact, when some dogs do this, they look like they are laughing. A happy dog may pull her lips up, showing her incisors. However, when the canine teeth are visible, you know your dog is signaling aggression.

When your dog holds the corners of her mouth in a normal position, she feels certain of herself. When she brings the corners of her mouth frontward, she is indicating depression or distrust. And if she pulls the corners of her mouth back, she is displaying fear, defeat, or defenselessness.

In addition to the above mouth expressions, handlers should pay attention to slanting, slavering, blowing, and the tongue hanging out restlessly. These are signs that your dog feels highly uncertain. Signs of stress include chewing, blowing, and the dog licking herself along her own snout. Remember that your dog's tongue hanging out and slanting does not always indicate fatigue, thirst, or extreme heat.

When your drug-detector dog suddenly opens the back part of her lips and makes a sniffing or blowing sound, she may be indicating that she has smelled drugs or at least has detected a trace odor of drugs. The same may be the case if your dog, with a closed mouth, brings her nose up high, as if trying to follow an odor. Often drug-detector dogs display this behavior when searching along walls, and sometimes you can hear your dog sniffing loudly at doors and along other openings in walls.

## Body Language

As soon as you can interpret your dog's normal behavior, you will begin to see the important, but often short and sometimes minor, deviations from normal behavior that occur during search actions. To read your dog correctly during an exercise or operation, you must pay attention to the whole picture of your dog's body language.

Your dog may be indicating she has found a scent clue, or at least the wafted odor of one, if any of the following occur:

- Suddenly during searching, she changes direction, makes a curve, or deviates more or less from a straight line.
- She changes tempo, either picking up or slowing down her pace.
- She shows interest in a specific area for somewhat longer than normal.
- She stands still somewhere, staring, or "pointing" like a hunting dog, sometimes standing with one leg off the ground.
- If she has been trained to display an active response and she begins to scratch or bite at a particular spot to uncover something. (Note that when dogs only scratch the ground once or a few times, they haven't likely found the cache. If you see this behavior, keep quiet, because your dog is orienting herself.)
- If she has been trained to display a passive response and she tries to sit or lie down, but does not entirely take up either of those positions. (In this case she is unsure about the situation and cannot decide how to signal you.)

Your dog may indicate she has found the scent she is looking for (or at least a trace of it) by suddenly changing direction, deviating from moving straight ahead.

## The Dog's World

The dog's range of interests is much more restricted than that of humans, limited as it is to what is of vital importance to her. Her world is not only different but also much smaller than ours. It is hard to imagine your dog's perception of the world, but it is important for every dog owner, and especially for K9 handlers, to be sensitive to their dogs' reality. That sensitivity can be crucial in assessing the dogs' performance.

Begin with the understanding that unlike humans, your dog lives in a world of smells. She gets an impression of her environment on the basis of the odors she perceives. Early on, dogs form an "odor print" (a term commonly used in the world of detector-dog trainers, which means the collection of smells that make up the specific complex of smells in any given environment) of their environment and immediately notice changes in this odor print. Your dog's keen sense of smell allows her to create this odor print, and her behaviors stem from disturbances to it. In order of importance to her are the senses of smell, hearing, and vision. Most people try to understand something new by looking at it

Dogs glean an impression of their environment by perceiving odors.

intensely, from all sides; dogs investigate new things by sniffing or licking them.

## The Nasal Cavity

The dog's nasal cavity is a maze of folds: the nasal turbinates. This labyrinth of nasal turbinates greatly increases the surface area of the dog's inner nose. In front of the nasal cavity are the *conchae dorsalis* and *conchae ventralis*, whose mucous membranes have little or no olfactory cells. The main function of these conchae is to warm and moisten incoming air. The conchae divide the nasal cavities into various nasal passages.

The dorsal nasal passage lies above the dorsal nasal concha, also called the "smell corridor" because it ends at the ethmoid where the olfactory mucosa is present. The middle nasal passage is located between the dorsal and ventral nasal conchae. In this passage, also called the "sinus corridor," the sinuses emerge. The ventral nasal passage is located between the ventral nasal concha and the nasal cavity floor (or palate). This nasal passage ends in an opening that forms the connection with the throat; called the "breathing corridor," it provides a direct pathway for breathing. The common nasal passage lies along the nasal septum. The previously mentioned nasal passages are well-connected to the common nasal passage.

Behind the dorsal and ventral conchae are the ethmoid conchae, which fill the rear of the nasal cavity. The mucous membrane of the upper ethmoid conchae contains a large quantity of olfactory cells that allow the dog to scan scents.

## A Smelling Animal

The dog's phenomenal ability to smell is well known. Odors in the dog's environment are easily detected by olfactory cells on the large surface area of her olfactory epithelium (that labyrinth of folds in the turbinates), and a thick mucous membrane.

To compare, the size of a typical adult human's olfactory area is 1.6 to 2 square inches (4–5 cm$^2$) and the thickness of the mucous membrane is 0.006 millimeters. Adult, medium-sized dogs have 36.2 to 66.9 inches (92–170 cm$^2$) of olfactory area that is about 0.12 millimeters thick. The average number of olfactory cells in a human amounts to about 5 million, while a Dachshund can have 125 million olfactory cells. The fox terrier has 150 million, and the German shepherd has about 220 million olfactory cells.

Also consider that in dogs, the olfactory bulb (the part of the brain that processes data scanned by olfactory cells in the nose) comprises more than 35 percent of the brain, while the olfactory bulb only takes up 5 percent of the human brain. Although there is no known direct relationship between the size of an animal's olfactory area and its sensitivity to odors, these numbers are very impressive and show how well dogs are equipped for odor perception.

The lifetime of an olfactory cell is about one to two months. When an olfactory cell dies, it is replaced by a new one, so reduced sense of smell due to damaged olfactory cells is only

The dog's nose specializes. Dogs trained to recognize certain smells have more olfactory cells for that particular odor than other smells.

temporary. The new olfactory cell does not always have the same type of receptor as that of the old cell. The receptor type is determined by the scents the dog regularly smells. So dogs trained to recognize and react to certain smells have more olfactory cells for those particular odors. Training, therefore, increases the dog's ability to perceive odors that untrained dogs may not be able to perceive.

## Search Dogs

Search dogs can be divided into three groups: tracking dogs, trailing dogs, and air-scenting dogs. Tracking dogs use their noses to follow a human-scented track on or near the ground surface. Trailing dogs first smell a scented article belonging to the person in question before discerning and following a track whose smell matches that of the article, alternately with the head up and down, depending on the wind direction. Air-scenting dogs search with their noses in the air to find the smell from an odor source they are trained to recognize—an example of this kind of dog is a drug detector. Drug-detector dogs do not find drugs by following a surface track but by perceiving the scent that moves along with the airflow. Of course, they can also perceive the odor in the air coming from the upper layer of the floor or ground surface. Air-scenting dogs follow the scent mostly with their heads up.

The odor of drugs, or whatever the dog is searching for, is, of course, most concentrated in the air closest to the source of the odor, and it moves in the direction the wind is blowing or via air currents and becomes more dilute the farther away it is from the source.

In 1997, researchers tried to establish dogs' thresholds for detecting drug odors.[1] In the experiment, four out of five dogs successfully detected the smell of illicit cocaine at 0.1 ppb, but they could not perform successfully when the smell of cocaine was below 0.05 ppb. Humidity was identified as ancillary variable.

Cocaine breaks down faster in humid environments, which results in the by-product methylbenzoate.

Drug detector dogs recognize the scent of a particular drug by comparing the odors they have learned with those in the area they are searching. Over time, the smell of the source cache spreads out so the environment or packaging around the drug cache will take up the smell of the drug. Even when drugs are packaged in several layers of plastic, rubber, or metal, are hidden in barrels and/or processed with special smells, dogs are able to find them. Detector dogs can even find drugs hidden in thick-walled steel tubes with bolted covers, or inside tin cans.

## Odor Print

To understand how a dog perceives an odor print, consider an image of an analog clock face divided into four sections, each section still recognizable as part of the clock. Detector dogs can recognize each single part of the whole as belonging to a complete odor. When the detector dog on a search finds drugs, she will encounter the following parts, which make up a complete odor print:

1. Main odor: the smell of the drug the dog is trained to find.

2. Accompanying odor: the smells of most objects in which drugs are packaged, or objects near hidden drugs, which are familiar to the detector dog. Recognizing accompanying odors begins in training: the smell of the Hurley or that of the training tube, or that of the packaging around drugs used in training.

3. Human scent: during training, you use sterile gloves or tools like tongs to handle drug packages to prevent human scent from influencing your dog's search for the scent of a drug—however, whether on the training field or in a real search, at least a trace odor of humans will exist in the area around a drug cache.

4. Odor of a disturbed area: this will mix up the odor print a bit, making it more difficult to pin down.

To prevent your training dog from focusing on human scent, accompanying smells, and/or odors of disturbance, instead of on the odor of drugs, always train her in different locations and with different objects.

## Influencing the Search Work

There are many factors that can influence the odor print of drugs. The most common include quantity, drug complexes, adaptation, type of drug, hiding time, age of drug, location, temperature, humidity, climatic conditions, and coverings.

### QUANTITY

It is logical to assume that the more hidden drugs there are, the greater the perimeter of the dispensed odor will be. But differences in *amount* of odor can be perceived by the dog as differences in *kind* of odor. If a dog can find a small amount, she may not automatically be able to find a large amount. So when you are training your dog to recognize an odor, vary the amounts of odor a lot and often, but do not expect immediate success. Your dog may perceive that a large amount of an odor is a completely different thing than a smaller amount of the same odor. When a dog is used to finding only small amounts, she may not recognize a large amount. It simply smells different from what she has learned.

### DRUG COMPLEXES

If a drug is presented alone during training, your dog is more sensitive to its odor than if it is presented as part of a complex of drug smells. So, if your dog is capable of finding a very small amount of a "pure" drug, she may still have problems when it comes to finding the same amount within a complex of drugs.

Differences in amount of odor may be perceived by the dog as qualitative differences. And discriminating between complex odors is more difficult than between single odors. Dogs can recognize a single odor in smaller amounts easier than when that same odor is part of a complex compound. So training on a single odor first may speed up the training on the complex.

It appears that dogs learn complex odors as units. A dog's previous experience with single components in a complex, for example, does seem to speed up the learning of the complex odor. Beginning training with single odors, it would seem, must then lead to a more rapid learning of the complex compounds containing these single odors. But a dog trained to recognize single odors will not always recognize these odors in complex compounds. You must train your dog on both single and complex odors.

**ADAPTATION**

If a sensory cell is continuously stimulated in a certain way, it will eventually cease to react to the stimulus. This kind of sensory adaptation can make it impossible for a searching detector dog to locate the source of a smell, since the environment she is searching may already be saturated with the smell.

The density of drug odor in a room where a lot of a certain drug has been hidden, for example, or where a smaller amount has been hidden for a long time, can be very high. In such an environment, a detector dog may have difficulty locating the exact source of the odor, especially if she has been in the room for some time. The dog's sensory cells have been stimulated so much that they no longer react to the smell.

Adjust your training and search method to take account of adaptation. Consider the following example. If you enter a room where people are smoking, you notice this when you come in, but after a while you don't notice it any more. If you go out and let your nose "rest" for a bit, or you "get a breath of fresh air," upon re-entering the room, you will smell the smoke again. Giving your dog's nose a rest can help her in the same way.

If a sensory cell is continuously stimulated in a certain way, it will cease to react to the stimulus. This adaptation can make it impossible for dogs to find hidden drugs, since the environment in which they are searching may already be saturated with the smell of the drugs. If you allow your dog to go out of the search area and let her nose "rest" for a bit, or "get a breath of fresh air," she will return to the search area able to smell the drug and find the cache.

**TYPE OF DRUG**

Any kind of narcotic has its own particular "spread" of odor, depending on its composition and consistency (pills, powder, or liquid). This field of odor may range from very small to large, depending on the drug's structure.

**HIDING TIME**

The longer something is hidden, the greater the odor picture becomes. Over a long time, of course, the scent of a drug cache will decrease. In technical jargon, this is called "soaking time."

**AGE OF THE DRUG**

As with hiding time, the age of drugs also determines the strength of their odor. Older drugs have a weaker odor.

**LOCATION**

The drug cache's location—underground, in a cupboard, underwater, in a plastic bag, in glass—affects the amount of perceptible odor available to your dog.

## TEMPERATURE

Up to a point, heat makes odors stronger, allowing them to rise from the source object and spread out. Cold has the opposite result. Generally speaking,

- a *warm* object in a *cold* environment provides a good odor print,
- a *cold* object in a *cold* environment provides a poor odor print,
- a *warm* object in a *warm* environment provides a poor odor print, and
- a *cold* object in *warm* surroundings provides a good odor print.

## AIRSTREAM

Air currents, inside and outside, move the odors of drugs. This may be advantageous in a headwind, but know that airflow can also cause your dog to become confused about the location of the odor's source.

## HUMIDITY

Along with temperature, humidity is a factor you need to consider when you and your dog are working in a search area. Low humidity together with a low temperature prevents odor molecules from spreading out enough to be detected. When the outside air is dry and hot, the odor print will be noticeable, and in moist and hot weather, the odor print is even easier for your dog to detect. When the air is cold and damp, your dog will find the odor print difficult to perceive.

## CLIMATIC CONDITIONS

Wind disperses the odor print, and the sun's warmth increases the smell of the odor print. Rain reduces the odor print's smell, and snow limits the odor print's smell but does not erase it altogether. Odor can be frozen in ice and will keep; when the weather warms up and the thaw begins, that frozen odor emerges and is noticeable.

## COVERING THE SCENT

Well-trained detector dogs can sense odors even if someone has tried to cover them up. Even if someone applied a strong odor to an area or a drug cache, your dog will still be able to recognize several odors that will help her in her search. It is possible to deceive you, the dog handler, but as a professional, you know you can trust your dog and her ability to "smell through" the cover-up.

Many factors may influence your dog's ability to perceive odor prints, but those mentioned above are the most important. Time and practical experience also play roles. In fact, the list of factors is unlimited; but, for the detector dog, the odor of drugs permeates that of most substances. Each odor print is different, but as long as drugs are or were present in a search area, the well-trained drug-detector dog will be able to find what she is looking for. Remember, because odors are invisible elements, you must learn to have absolute confidence in your dog.

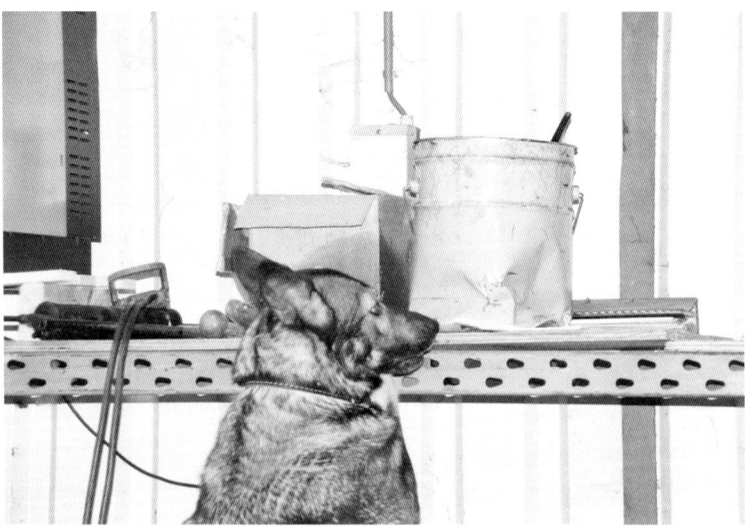

Odors are invisible, so you, the handler, must learn to have absolute confidence in your detector dog.

# 5

# Influence of Air Currents in Search Work

In K9 detector work, weather influences such as relative humidity, temperature, and wind are often greatly underrated or just ignored, even though knowledge about these factors can be a great help to you and, hence, your dog. If you can correctly assess these influences, you can also correctly assess your dog's search work. We often think we know better than our dogs, but our assessments are often based on snap judgments and bad information about temperature and wind conditions as we perceive them, higher above the ground than the dog's level of perception.

When your dog works through a search area on a warm summer day, his nose will be positioned just above the ground where the temperature may be over 108°F (40°C). You, the handler, will have a different picture than that of your dog, since you are experiencing the temperature as 68°F (20°C). Knowing your dog must work under much more difficult circumstances than many people think will give you more reason than ever to remark on your dog's amazing abilities.

For example, let's take a quick look at the tracking dog's work. Because of high temperatures during the daytime, warm air will rise from the track and lift up the odors of the track. This explains why, in such a situation, tracking dogs do not put their nose close to the ground and often amaze their handlers by working out the track very well with a high nose. But what is most amazing—what is absolute folly, actually—is that many trainers (and judges) persist in insisting that a dog in this situation should still be putting his nose close to the ground surface, because "a dog only tracks correctly with a deep nose."

## Relative Humidity

Humidity is highest early in the morning and in the early evening; it is low during the day. Indoors, the relative humidity can be very low. A low-humidity environment can influence your dog's nose. While searching under extreme circumstances, such as dry humidity, the dog's mucous membrane gets dry sooner than usual, which will translate into poorer than normal search performance. If you and your dog are working out a search area in such conditions, bring along a wet towel in a plastic bag that you can use to clean and moisten your dog's nose during the search.

The Three Categories of Relative Humidity

| | |
|---|---|
| **Dry** | 0–30% |
| **Normal** | 30–60% |
| **Moist** | 60–100% |

## Temperature

Some compelling facts about temperature come to us via micrometeorology, the science that investigates the atmospheric influences directly above Earth's surface, especially temperature in the first 5 feet (1.5 m) above the surface—the place where your dog conducts his search work.

One report records the temperature taken on a sunny day 4 feet (1.2 m) from the surface to be about 68°F (20°C).[1] At the same time, the air temperature just above the ground surface was 111.2°F (44°C). At 1 inch (2.5 cm) above the surface, the

# INFLUENCE OF AIR CURRENTS IN SEARCH WORK

temperature was already lower (93.2°F or 34°C), and at 12 inches (30 cm) above the surface, a temperature of 80.6°F (27°C) was measured.

Directly after sunset, the temperature just above Earth's surface dipped to 55.4°F (13°C), while at 12 inches (30 cm) it was still warm, 84.2°F (29°C). So, on a sunny day, dogs perform outside search work in temperatures between 86 and 104°F (30 and 40°C).

Air Temperatures Near Earth's Surface

| Height above Earth's Surface | Temperature During the Day | Temperature after Sunset |
|---|---|---|
| 4 ft (1.2 m) | ± 68°F (20°C) | Not recorded |
| 12 in (30 cm) | 80.6°F (27°C) | 84.2°F (29°C) |
| 1 in (2.5 cm) | 93.2°F (34°C) | Not recorded |
| 0 in (0 cm) | 111.2°F (44°C) | 55.4°F (13°C) |

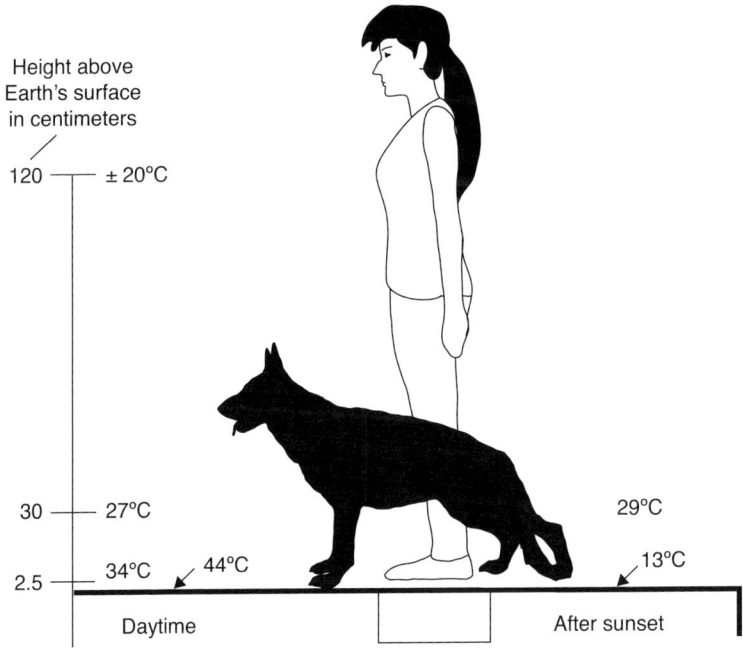

Air temperatures on Earth's surface.

## Wind

Handlers mostly measure the wind roughly, with a wet finger put up in the air to feel what direction the wind is blowing from. Although this is a common practice, it's a big mistake, as the micro-meteorology results make clear. The wet-fingertip measurement is taken at about 5 to 6.5 feet (1.5–2 m) off the ground. But the area where our dogs work is much lower. In general, the wind at our height blows harder than it does just above the ground. The ground surface inhibits the wind.

As well, ground formations, vegetation, and buildings also redirect the wind, and even on a windy day, the air may be still behind these obstacles. Consider driving a car as a strong wind hits the car broadside. You have to have a firm hand on the wheel and correct the car to stay on course, but if you drive past a building that blocks the wind or through a forest, the wind no longer pushes you, and again you must correct the car to stay on the road. Your dog may also experience these bursts of still air as he investigates a search area and encounters obstacles to the wind at his level.

## Environmental Influences on Outdoor Search Work

Because we work with detector dogs, we are interested in gauging the wind near Earth's surface, the bottommost meters of the atmosphere. In this layer of air, wind is strongly influenced by the terrain and small-scale meteorological processes, and often appears erratic.

For clarity, wind direction is the direction from which the wind is blowing—so a north wind moves from north to south. Wind speed exhibits rapid variations, with fluctuations in the order of seconds to minutes. Note that wind direction and speed change relative to the time of day. Just as tides have a daily rhythm, wind responds to the predictable, daily changes in solar radiation and temperature.

Changing wind conditions are mainly caused by obstacles that impede the flow of air, and these may be more numerous in one place than another. The surfaces of large bodies of water are fairly smooth, for example, so air flows freely over them, meeting few impediments. A grassy plain, however, has a much rougher surface than the lake it surrounds, jarring the flow of air over it. The plain, however, not only has grasses but also scattered, single shrubs and trees, and wind must go over or around these—creating turbulence. The plain becomes a different landscape as it approaches the mountains. Here, there are dense clumps of shrubs and trees, and different sizes of vegetation (in height, width, and length) present in each copse. The airflow is strongly hindered and slowed down among these groupings of trees and shrubs. The towns that dot the plain, replete with buildings, provide even rougher surfaces for the wind to travel over, obstructing airflow even more than copses of trees do.

Wind almost always behaves erratically because of surface features; sometimes fluctuations are strong, sometimes weak. Swirls of different sizes give wind a whimsical character. The size of swirls

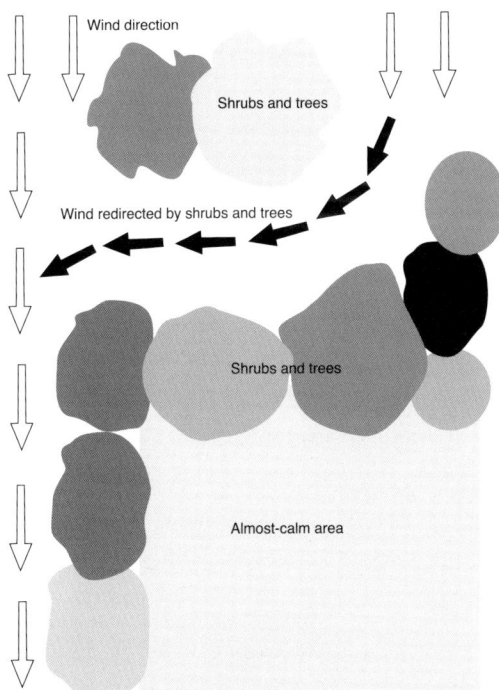

An aerial view of a hypothetical outdoor area. Air currents always follow the path of least resistance. Streets and roads, as well as natural features, can channel the wind in different directions. Such air currents, of course, have a great deal of influence on K9 search work.

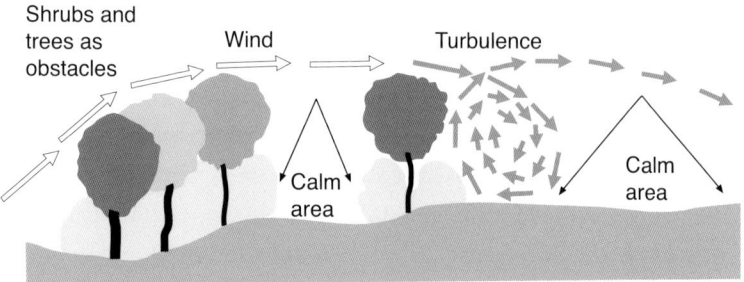

The first group of shrubs and trees that the wind encounters in this example (on the far left) create an obstacle, forcing the airflow up and over the second group of shrubs and trees, beyond which there is turbulence. Calm areas occur between the two groups of trees and shrubs, and after the area of turbulence. When working with your dog outdoors, you must always be aware of how obstacles can affect airflow.

varies from a few millimeters to tens or even hundreds of meters. The speed with which the vortices move and rotate varies greatly. For the most part, swirls of air are caused by the wind encountering obstacles on Earth's surface. The rougher the terrain, the greater and more volatile the swirls. Wind turbulence can also be facilitated by locally fluctuating temperatures. The greater the temperature differences over short distances, the more capricious the wind seems.

Wind at Earth's surface almost always fluctuates: the wind is gusty, but how gusty strongly depends on the nature of the terrain in combination with wind speed and the proximity of precipitation. Wind speed is measured in miles per hour and kilometers per hour, according to the Beaufort Scale. The table detailing the scale here also provides descriptions of the effects of different strengths of wind on Earth's surface.

The Beaufort Wind-Force Scale and Phenomena Associated with Wind

| Beaufort Number | Name | Average km/h | Average mph | Characteristics |
| --- | --- | --- | --- | --- |
| 0 | Calm | < 1 | < 1 | Smoke rises vertically |
| 1 | Light air | 1–5 | 1–3 | Direction of wind shown by smoke drift but not by wind vanes |
| 2 | Light breeze | 6–11 | 4–7 | Wind felt on face; leaves rustle; weather vane moved by wind |

# INFLUENCE OF AIR CURRENTS IN SEARCH WORK

| Beaufort Number | Name | Average km/h | Average mph | Characteristics |
|---|---|---|---|---|
| 3 | Gentle breeze | 12–19 | 8–12 | Leaves and small twigs in constant motion; wind extends light flags |
| 4 | Moderate breeze | 20–28 | 13–18 | Raises dust and loose paper; small branches are moved |
| 5 | Fresh breeze | 29–38 | 19–24 | Small trees in leaf begin to sway; crested wavelets form on water |
| 6 | Strong breeze | 39–49 | 25–31 | Large branches in motion; whistling heard in overhead wires; umbrellas used with difficulty |
| 7 | Near gale | 50–61 | 32–38 | Whole trees in motion; inconvenience felt when walking against the wind |
| 8 | Gale | 62–74 | 39–46 | Breaks twigs off trees; generally impedes progress |
| 9 | Strong gale | 75–88 | 47–54 | Breaks branches off trees; slight structural damage occurs, such as roof tiles removed |
| 10 | Storm | 89–102 | 55–63 | Trees uprooted; considerable structural damage occurs |
| 11 | Violent storm | 103–117 | 64–74 | Extensive damage to woodlands and buildings |
| 12 | Hurricane | > 117 | > 75 | Nothing remains standing |

The wind has a great influence on the temperature near the ground. Wind mixes up the air near Earth's surface and can easily disperse the heat generated by solar radiation during the daytime. At night, when Earth's surface cools down, the wind brings warm air to the surface, counteracting nocturnal cooling. If there is very little wind overnight, Earth's surface can cool considerably. This cooling process is exacerbated in an area with many obstacles that inhibit the wind.

## LAND, SEA, MOUNTAIN, AND VALLEY WINDS

In coastal areas, the uneven heating of land and sea creates a local wind: during daytime, a sea breeze blows, but at night, a land breeze blows. During the day, the air above land that has been warmed by the sun rises, creating an area of low pressure. The cooler air over the water, where there is higher pressure, then flows

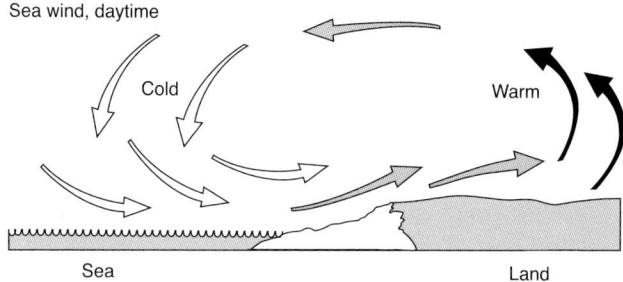

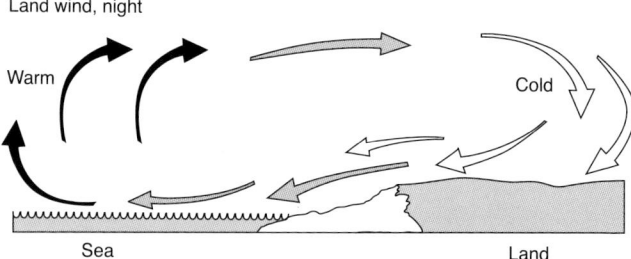

During the daytime in coastal areas, the wind blows from over the water, where there is higher pressure, to the lower pressure over the land. This creates the sea wind, which varies in strength as a result of temperature differences over the land and sea. At night, there is a change in wind direction, as the air over the sea is now warmer than that over the land.

into the lower-pressure area over the land. This sea breeze varies in strength, depending on temperature differences between land and sea. But at night, especially when it is cold, the sea is relatively warm compared to the land, and the situation is reversed.

Mountainous areas also have winds that follow this pattern: mountain and valley winds are local winds that occur as a result of changes in daily temperatures, and thus changes in pressure. The valley wind is a warm wind that blows during the day, uphill from the valley. It arises because during the day, the air closest to Earth's surface in the valley is heated more by the sun than the air layers above it. The warm air rises along the mountain slopes.

Mountain winds are the opposite of valley winds. The mountain wind is cold, and it blows downslope toward valleys during the

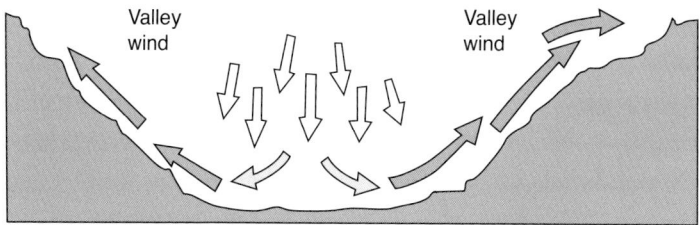

Valley wind created by heated slopes during the daytime

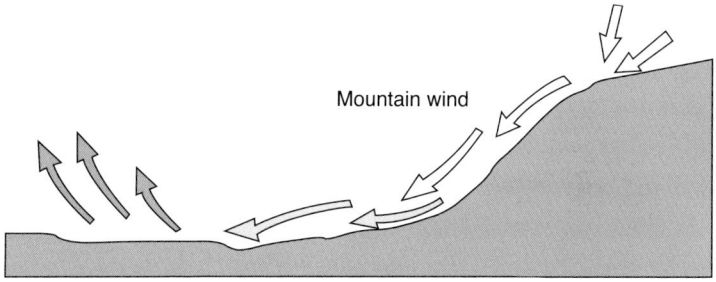

Mountain wind created by cooling at night

Mountain and valley winds are local winds that occur as a result of daily fluctuations in temperature. When the valley floor warms during the day, warm air rises up along the mountain slopes, creating the valley wind. In the evening, denser and colder air moves down the mountain sides and collects on the valley floor: a mountain wind.

evening, at night, and in the early morning. It occurs generally on clear, calm nights. After sunset, the air on mountain slopes cools quicker than the air at the same height just above the valley floor because the air in the valley is still warmer than that on the slopes. The colder air is denser than warm air and thus slides down to the valley floor. Mountain winds are often stronger late at night and early in the morning: during the course of the night, the air above the valley cools and the temperature difference between the air above the valley and that above the lower, and therefore warmer, ways out of the valley (or valley exits) increases. A relatively small anticyclone takes place above the cold valley and a relatively small area of low pressure forms over the warmer valley exits. Additional air flows from the high- to the low-pressure areas—from the valley floor to the valley exits—resulting in an increase in wind.

## THE SUN'S INFLUENCE

The solar radiation that reaches Earth's surface is partially absorbed by the surface terrain and converted into heat. The extent of absorption strongly depends on the nature of the terrain. Overgrown and dark areas, such as forests and asphalt, readily absorb radiation; white areas, such as snow and ice fields, bounce it back into the atmosphere. Of the radiation that is absorbed by the terrain, a small part slowly heats the deeper layers of soil. The rest of the absorbed radiation contributes to evaporation and heats the air just above Earth's surface. Most solar radiation reaches individual locations around the world during daytime hours at around noon, when the sun is at its highest relative to the area receiving sunlight.

Air temperature is measured at a height of 5 feet (1.5 m) above Earth's surface. This air temperature has a daily routine, reaching its highest value (maximum) in the afternoon and the lowest (minimum) shortly after sunrise. Closer to Earth's surface, however, the influence of incoming and outgoing radiation is greater. The temperature close to the ground, therefore, has an exaggerated daily routine compared to that at 5 feet, especially in clear weather. In the afternoon, the air closer to the ground is warmer and at around sunrise colder than it is at 5 feet.

Another thing to keep in mind when conducting a search with your dog is that temperatures mentioned in weather reports and weather forecasts are not representative of temperatures in urban areas. Especially in large cities, the difference between the weather forecast and the actual temperature can be significant. Stone and concrete buildings retain much of the sun's radiation during the day and only slowly cool down at night. In addition, people produce a lot of indoor heat in urban areas—by heating buildings, cooking, using computers, and so on—which may leak outside and further delay the fall of air temperature at night.

Sunshine influences Earth's surface temperature, which in turn affects your dog's ability to find caches during a search action. The effect of solar radiation on a drug cache at the ground surface in high air temperatures and low ground temperatures is interesting. When air temperatures are high near the ground, the scent of hidden drugs rises slowly or not at all because the temperature of the air surrounding the drugs is higher than that of the air in the hiding place, thereby hindering the updraft of the colder, heavier air containing the scent of the drugs. In this situation, only wind can carry the scent. Conversely, cold ground temperatures (in winter or on summer evenings and early mornings) facilitate the scent of hidden drugs to rise.

Another important situation you need to consider is that rain prevents scent from rising. Water can absorb the scent of hidden drugs, so rain on the surface of the cache acts like a cap, preventing the scent of the drugs from rising. At the same time, the rain cools the surface of the cache, resulting in the air around it becoming heavier and preventing the scent from rising. As soon as it has stopped raining, however, the situation with the cache will change back to the way it was before the rain began.

**THE WIND'S INFLUENCE**
Depending on the time of day anywhere in the world, Earth's surface and the atmosphere continuously receive and reflect solar radiation. While the surface of a location under the cover of nightfall does not receive direct solar radiation, it does continue to radiate heat and absorb radiation from the atmosphere. But that radiation is not enough to stop the nighttime cooling of Earth's surface. Nocturnal cooling is not only determined by radiation absorbed by and reflected from Earth's surface; wind and clouds also play a major role in this cooling.

The wind is a major factor in Earth's release of heat into the air. Air itself is a good insulator, so heat is not transferred if the air is not moving. Wind facilitates the transfer of heat (and moisture) from the soil into the atmosphere. The windier it is, the more effective the transfer of heat and moisture from Earth's surface into the atmosphere. During the day, when the sun warms Earth's surface, the wind carries heat off the surface, which means that the layers of air closest to Earth can heat up quite a bit. At the same time, the wind promotes evaporation, wicking moisture from the soil.

After sunset, the situation changes. Earth's surface cools by radiating heat upward, but the air above the surface remains warm. If the weather is clear and there is little wind, the temperature of Earth's surface drops quickly at night. In winter months in a cold climate, where the sun still warms Earth during the day (if for a short period), for example, the temperature of Earth's surface may be below freezing. But even during the winter, the air just above Earth's surface does not cool down quickly at night. The temperature at an altitude of 5 feet or so is still up to 5° warmer than the temperature closer to the ground.

### BUILDINGS AS OBSTACLES TO WIND

Turbulence, where the wind is constantly changing in direction and strength, is partly a consequence of the wind moving at different heights and correspondingly different speeds above the ground. Right on Earth's surface, air does not move; as altitude increases, however, so does the wind's velocity because the influence of friction from Earth's surface is less and less the farther up the wind is moving in the atmosphere. This principle applies in particular to air moving at 33 to 67 feet (10–20 m) above ground surface.

As a result of the above principle of air movement, an obstacle in the wind's path (a house or other building) affects the wind

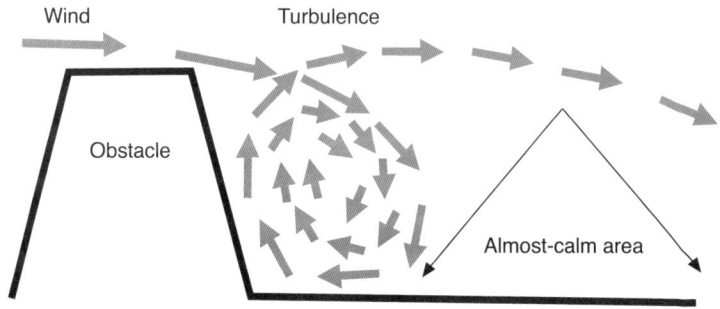

Wind speeds over 5 to 6 miles per hour (9 km/h) create turbulence behind obstacles like walls and buildings. Beyond those areas of turbulence, however, are almost-calm spots.

# INFLUENCE OF AIR CURRENTS IN SEARCH WORK

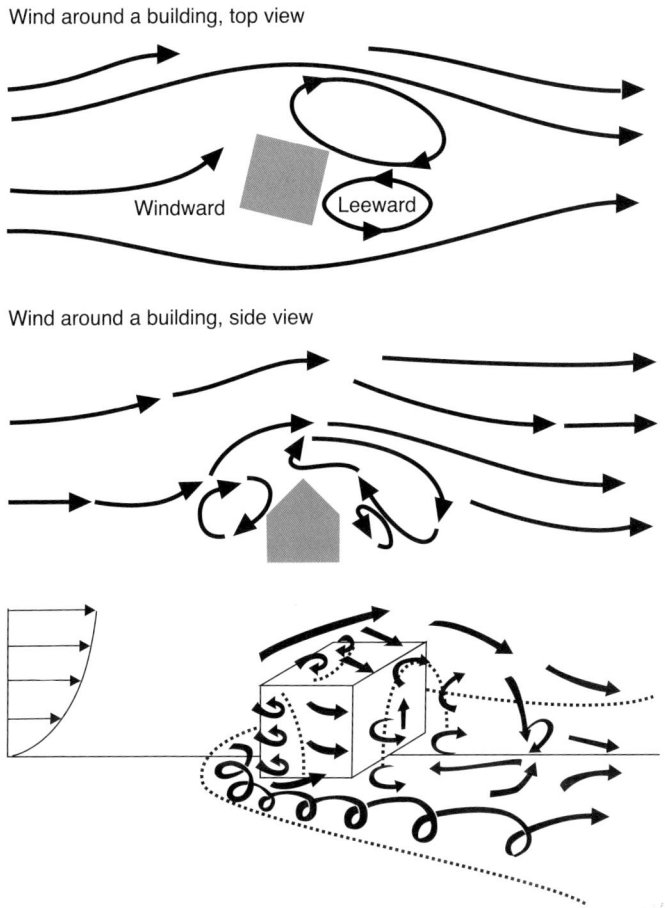

Whirling wind around buildings complicates K9 search work. The dotted lines in the bottom drawing represent areas where turbulence is likely.

at altitudes higher than the top of that obstacle. When the wind blows against the front of the obstacle, a weir effect takes place. This can be seen in the winter when snow is blowing into the side of a house, for example—the wind blows the snow against the house, causing snow to accumulate along the side of the house. The house blocks the wind, so it is not as windy behind the house, but wind passing beside the house toward the back of it draws air away, forming swirls, so snow can accumulate in the area behind the house. The size of this area where snow can accumulate is about 15 times the height of the obstacle.

### THE HIGHER YOU GO, THE MORE WIND THERE IS

Have you ever walked or cycled through a street where apartments or other large buildings stand, and just when you passed a large building you felt a sudden gust of wind? It can be very windy at the base of large buildings. And if a storm is in progress, it can even be dangerous to cycle around large buildings. The wind always blows harder higher up from Earth's surface, and the closer to the Earth's surface a wind blows, the more it is inhibited by surface friction. Tall buildings contend with more wind than low buildings do. When a high wind blows against a high building, the building stops the air and forces it to gust in different directions, including down. This explains why it is often gusty at the base of tall buildings. The windiness around these buildings is even more intense if open areas like parks or squares—places through which the wind can zip—are located adjacent to the buildings.

Breezes and strong wind gusts that play between neighboring high buildings are also strong. The air, after being redirected downward by the building is then, as it were, pressed through a kind of funnel, and wind speeds pick up as more air is forced into that funnel. This translates into strong winds and wind gusts moving through the narrow passages between tall buildings and is called the Venturi effect. Keep this effect in mind if you need to conduct a search around tall buildings. As well, consider the less dramatic upwinds and downwinds.

### UPWINDS AND DOWNWINDS

At the same temperature, dry air is heavier than humid air and, therefore, dry air sinks and humid air rises. At the same humidity, cold air is heavier than warm air and, therefore, cold air sinks and warm air rises. As a result, there are upward and downward air currents.

Sunshine heating Earth's surface will result in soil heating the air layer directly above it. Because warm air is lighter than cold air,

# INFLUENCE OF AIR CURRENTS IN SEARCH WORK

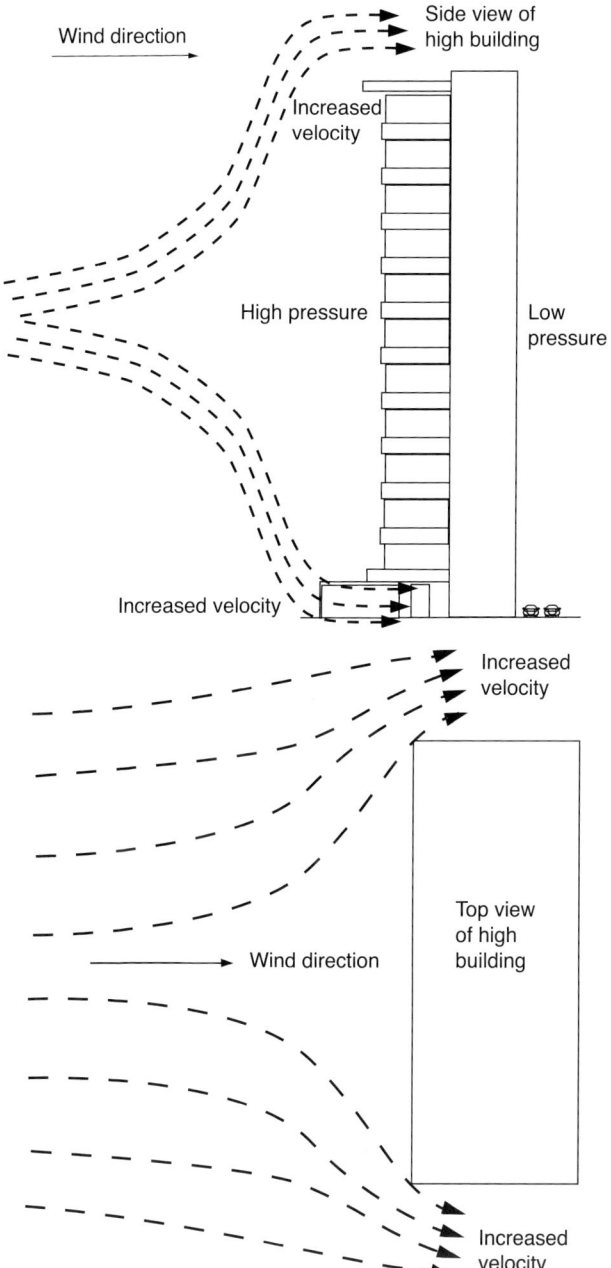

When the wind blows against a high building, the airflow is impeded and forced to take different routes in many directions with increased velocity.

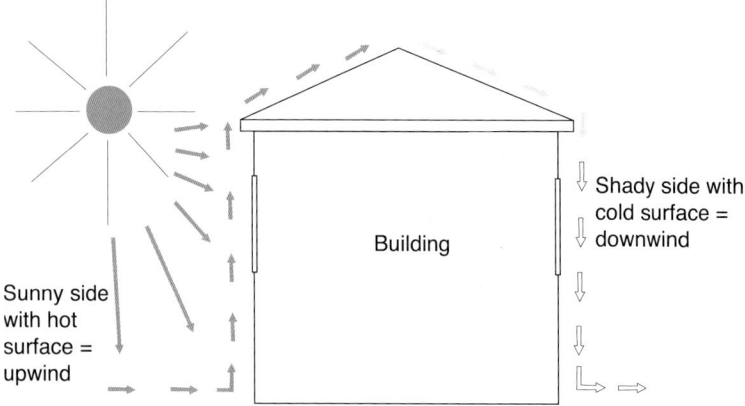

The effect of the sun on the outside walls of a building.

this process leads to upwinds. When air cools, it becomes heavier, and that process causes downwinds.

If the temperature of a wall surface is higher than the temperature of the air surrounding it, an upward airflow (buoyancy effect) will result. If the wall's surface is colder than the air, a downward flow of air results. So on the sunny side of a wall or a building, there is an upwind and on the backside of the same wall or building, in the shade, there is a downwind.

## Air Currents and Other Considerations Inside Buildings

Rooms inside buildings also experience air currents. The sunny side of a room will have an upwind, and the shady side will have a downwind. In effect, the air is rolling inside the room.

In much larger rooms or halls, you may encounter this rolling effect to a greater degree. On the sunny side is the primary air roller that, with its upwind, moves air to the top of the room. At the ceiling on the sunny side to about the middle of the room, the warm air from the upwind meets colder air from the shady side of the room. The cooler, shady side of the room develops a secondary air roller, with an upwind along the wall and a downwind in the middle of the room. As you can guess, your detector dog may

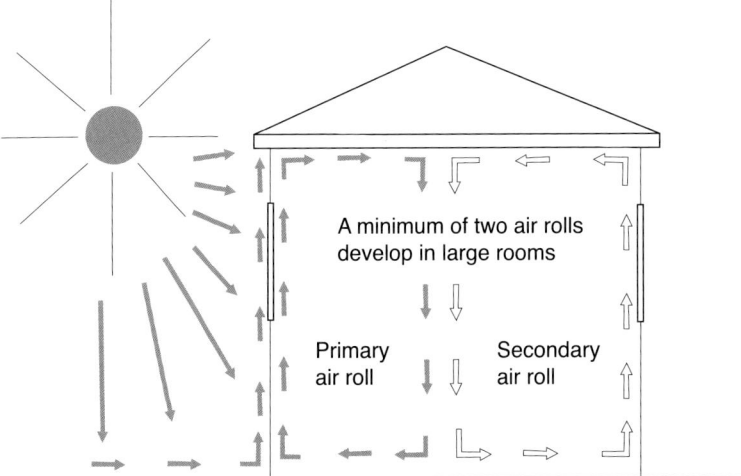

The effect of the sun inside a building.

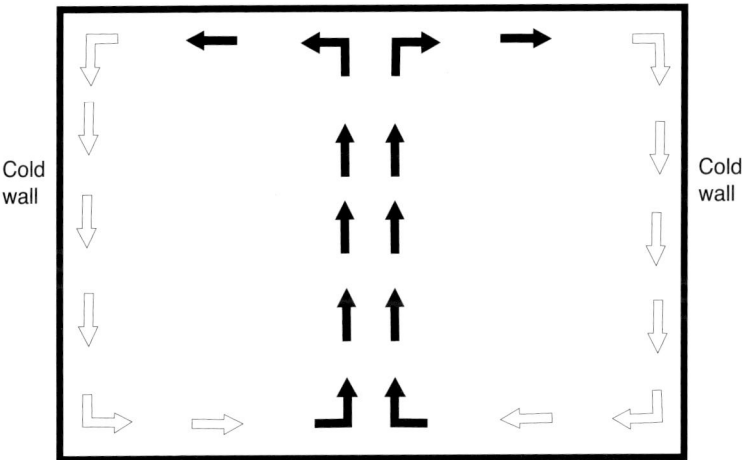

The effect on airflow of a warm room with cold walls. A downwind forms along cold walls.

find success when searching near walls, but the middle portions of rooms can cause problems.

Even when a building is heated, and warm on the inside, rooms may still have cold walls because of cold outside temperatures; this results in a different pattern of air currents than the one described above. The air travels downwind along the cold outside walls, but near the middle of the room the air becomes warmer and so an upwind develops.

Air always cools off near windows and outside walls when it is very cold outside. This creates greater airflow in a house, even if you can close all vents. An airflow always feels cold; this even applies to a flow of air that is 72°F (22°C), and even more to a stream of cooler air. Air currents are always at play inside buildings, and lower outside temperatures will always allow colder air to enter the place through the vents.

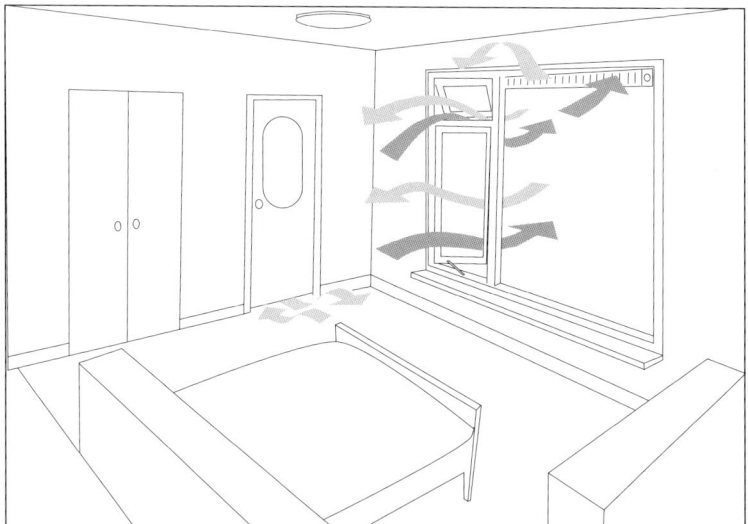

The airflow in a room.

Air currents can be made visible by squirting talcum powder into the air.

# INFLUENCE OF AIR CURRENTS IN SEARCH WORK

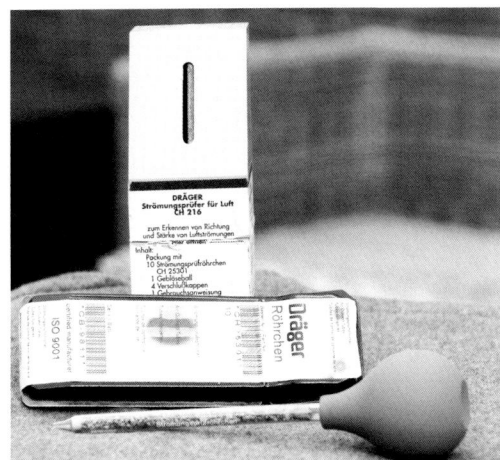

There are also special air current tubes that help detect the flow and strength of air currents.

At the micro-level in buildings you will also find air currents. For example, curtains on windows influence air currents: the layer of air between the window and the curtain is "trapped," and so an airflow arises. The thicker and more insulating the curtain is, the greater this effect. Buildings have many sources of heat, such as people, computers, all kinds of electrical appliances, and, of course, the sun shining in through the windows. Under the influence of these heat sources, warm air rises and sets air currents in motion.

## PRESSURE DIFFERENCES

When wind blows on a building, it creates a pressure on the building's facade. Air is forced through openings into the building on windward side, and air exits the building through openings on the leeward side.

Wind flow around a building causes positive pressure (inward) on the windward side and negative pressure (facing out) on the leeward side. This creates a pressure differential across the cross-section of the building, whereby a flow of air is formed. Cross-ventilation occurs when air enters the windward side of the building, flows through the building's interior, and leaves the building again on the other side, the leeward side.

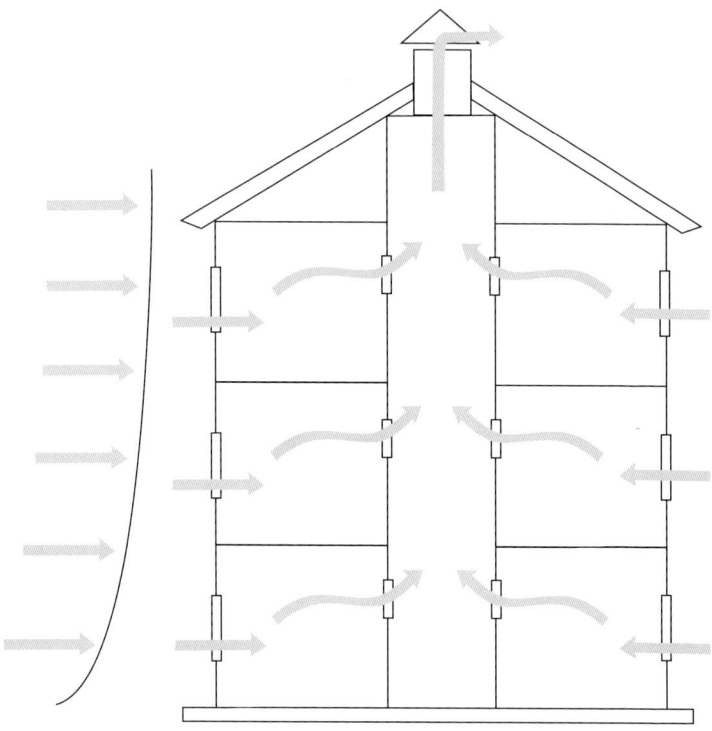

Wind flow around a building causes positive pressure (into the building) on the windward side of the building and negative pressure (outward from the building) on the leeward side. Usually, this would mean air entering on the windward side and exiting on the leeward side. In this example, however, the wind blowing against the left side of the building is flowing into a hall on the lower level. Rooms on the upper two levels are all connected to a wide staircase with a vent at the top. The vent sucks the incoming air upward. This creates a pressure differential across the cross-section of the building, and air flows into the building from both sides.

## CHIMNEY EFFECT

A shaft or chimney ventilation happens because of air pressure. When airflows are produced as a result of temperature differences between inside spaces and outside, the airflow inside moves in a vertical direction along the path of least resistance. Temperature differences cause a difference in air density that leads to an air-pressure differential, whereby an airflow is put in motion, with cold air (high density) sinking toward hot air (low density).

Consider the air in a vertical channel, such as a chimney. If it is heated, it rises. As a result, the air pressure at the bottom of the chimney becomes lower, so colder air from outside is sucked in, which keeps the flow of air in motion. This is called the chimney effect. In the winter season, the chimney effect is at work inside buildings, where the inside temperature is greater than the outside temperature. This effect can be described by the following seven conditions:

1. The inside temperature is higher than the outside air temperature.
2. Warmer air rises.
3. The upward movement of air causes a negative pressure within the bottom of the air shaft.
4. At the top, positive pressure arises.
5. As a result, the warmer air at the top of the building flows out of the building through whatever openings are available.
6. The air underneath the warm air is replaced by colder outside air, sucked in via cracks and seams in wooden floors, along window frames, and from exterior doors.
7. In summer, when the indoor temperature is lower than the outside temperature, the reverse happens.

The chimney effect in a staircase or elevator causes the pressure in the space below to fall. This causes the air to flow back in through existing openings (doors, windows, power outlets, air vents). Wind can increase this phenomenon, and the higher the building, the bigger the updraft.

The airflow in a conservatory, or a greenhouse, during the winter is determined by its glass outer wall(s). The extent of the cold trap that exists along the glass facade depends on the height of the glass. Near the floor, the airstream deflects toward the center of the conservatory, so that high air velocities at floor level may arise. In a conservatory that is not heated and that has a single glass outer

If air in a vertical channel, such as a chimney, is heated, it rises. As a result, the air pressure at the bottom of the chimney lowers, and colder air from outside is sucked in from any available opening (windows, cracks in walls or floor, and so on). This is called the chimney effect.

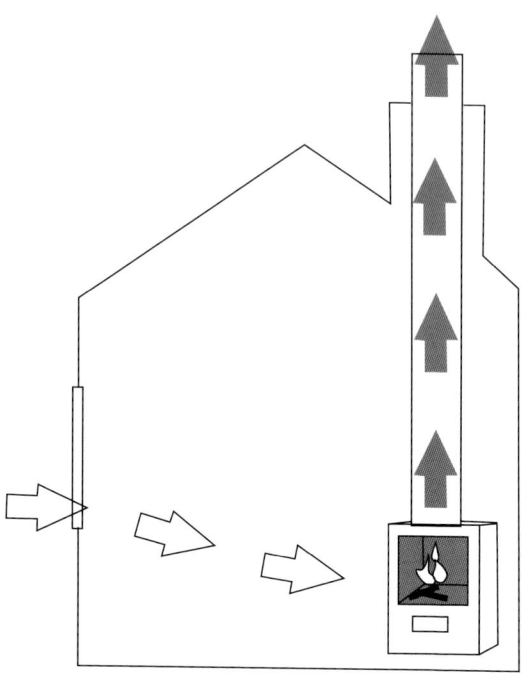

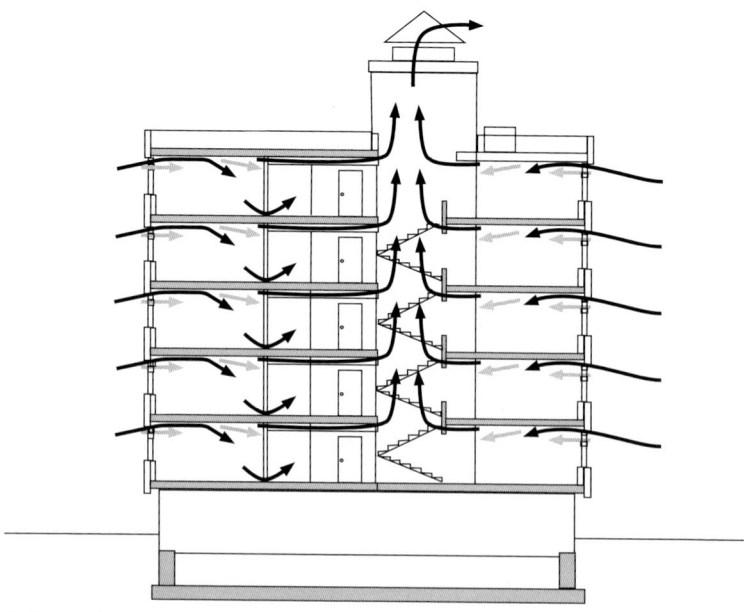

Airflow in the stairwell of an apartment building.

# INFLUENCE OF AIR CURRENTS IN SEARCH WORK

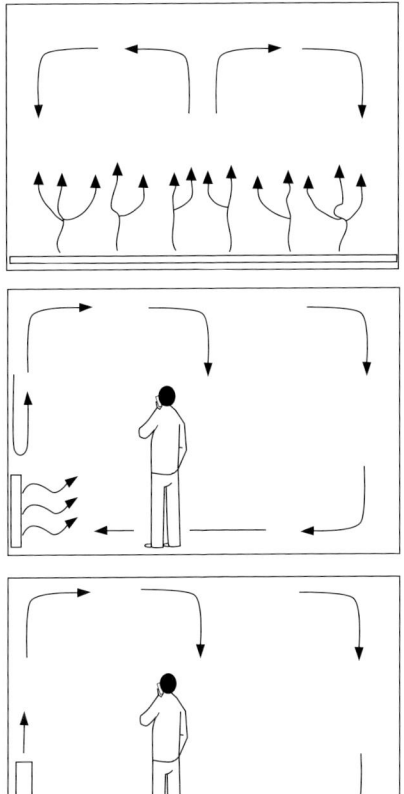

The airstream that results in a room because of various types of heating systems. Top: in-floor heating; middle: radiator heating; bottom: forced-air heating.

wall, air speeds can reach up to approximately 3.3 feet per second (1 m/s). The high air velocities at floor level can be prevented by placing convectors at the bottom inside of the window.

## AIRFLOW IS NOT CONSTANT

The airflow in homes and buildings is not constant. Ventilation can change quickly in each room. Also, the rate at which indoor odors release is changeable. Changing ventilation patterns and odor-release rates influence the concentration of odor available to your dog as he investigates an indoor search area. As well, the concentration of the odor in the air depends in part on the volume of the space itself.

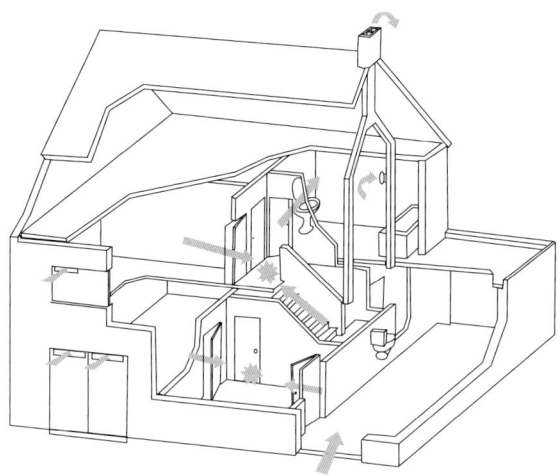

When searching a house with your drug-detector dog, you must always account for airflow and turbulence. The arrows in the figure represent airflow; stars indicate turbulence.

## DANGEROUS GASES

When conducting searches indoors, always be careful about gases, especially in basements. Pay attention to warning signs and get information about the area you are searching. Know that a lot of gases are toxic and heavier than the air by which they flow, often unnoticed, to the lowest point in the room. They can build up to become invisible "gas lakes" in shafts, basements, or recesses. These gas lakes can accumulate in the air layer in which your detector dog is operating.

Usually gases have a smell but are not visible. If your dog refuses to enter a room or a cellar, think of the possibility of gases. Gases are usually flammable and can explode with the presence of the smallest spark. Do not smoke inside of or in the area surrounding an indoor search area.

## OTHER DANGERS

Before approaching a search area, carefully assess it for all possible risks. Many searches are conducted in drug houses or in demolition buildings. In case of a partially damaged house or building,

Be alert for dangers such as scattered drugs, injection needles, and other drug paraphernalia.

consider the wind speed and direction; the direct or indirect danger of collapsing floors, walls, and rubble; the strength of the floors and beams; damage to staircases; loose hanging building materials, and so on. Always be alert for any situations and objects that might endanger you or your dog. Such dangers, especially for your dog, can include drugs scattered on the ground or in other places accessible to your dog, injection needles and other drug paraphernalia, and spoiled and hazardous food. Be on the lookout for human feces in or around buildings that you are searching for drugs. Dogs sometimes eat human feces, and those found around drug houses may contain drug residue, which can pose a danger to your dog's health. Furthermore, watch out for exposed electrical wires, sockets, and other related hazards.

Always be aware of the possible presence of radioactive materials, and find out if there are chemicals, such as oil, rodenticide, or acid (battery acid), in the rooms or basement. Do not be fooled into thinking that all fluid on a floor must be water, or all powder on the floor in the kitchen must be flour. If these fluids or powders

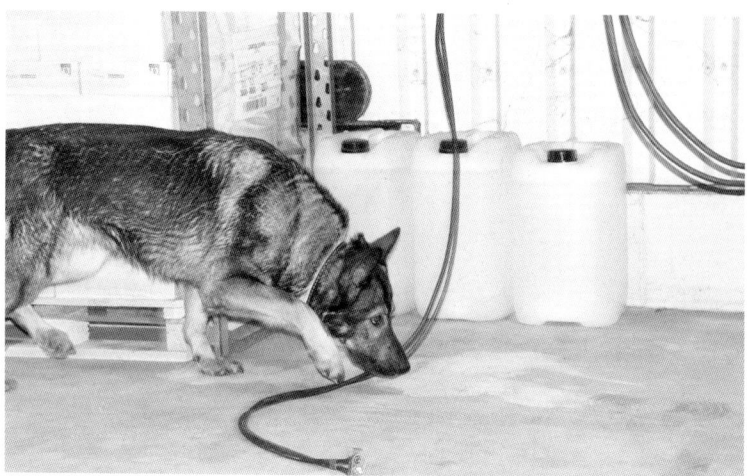

Don't believe that all fluid on the floor is water.

And don't believe all powder in the kitchen is flour.

are in fact acid or alkali, your dog's paws, coat, and nose are in danger.

*INTERNATIONAL SIGNS*

Dangerous goods or hazardous goods are solids, liquids, or gases that can harm people, other living organisms, property, or the environment. They are often subject to chemical regulations. In many countries, dangerous goods are more commonly known as hazardous materials (abbreviated as HAZMAT or hazmat). The containers and buildings in which dangerous goods are stored are often labeled with diamond-shaped signage. The color of the diamond indicates the hazard: for example, flammable is indicated by red, oxidizing agents are indicated by yellow, and explosive materials are indicated by orange, because mixing red (flammable) with yellow (oxidizing agent) creates orange. A nonflammable or nontoxic gas is indicated by green, and poisonous gases are indicated by white diamonds.

Not all countries use precisely the same graphics (label, placard, and/or text information) in their national regulations. Some use graphic symbols, but without English wording, or with similar wording in their national language(s).

The law related to HAZMAT Class 2 in the United States includes all gases that are compressed and stored for transportation. Class 2 has three divisions: flammable (also "combustible"), nonflammable/nonpoisonous, and poisonous. In Canada, there is also a Class 2.4 for corrosive gases. Gases are assigned to one of four divisions:

2.1 Flammable Gases (red-colored diamond): gases that ignite on contact with an ignition source, such as acetylene, hydrogen, and propane.

2.2 Nonflammable Gases (green-colored diamond): gases that are neither flammable nor poisonous. Includes the cryogenic gases/liquids (gases at temperatures below −100°C) used for cryopreservation and rocket fuels.

2.3 Poisonous Gases (white-colored diamond): gases liable to cause death or serious injury if inhaled.

2.4 Corrosive Gases (white-colored diamond, sometimes with a red border): corrosives are different than poisons in that they are immediately dangerous to the tissues they contact, whereas poisons may have systemic toxic effects that require time to become evident.

# 6

# Planning a Search Action

The drug-detector dog is used in many different circumstances and locations. Search locations can be broadly classified into three different areas: open air; indoors; and trains, vehicles, aircraft, and vessels.

EXAMPLES OF OPEN-AIR LOCATIONS

- Parking lots
- Fields
- Streets
- Parks or forests
- Railways
- Public meeting places
- Harbors and dockyards

EXAMPLES OF INDOOR LOCATIONS

- Houses, cellars, and attics
- In-use, empty, and dilapidated buildings
- Factories and labs
- Warehouses and hangars
- Public buildings

- Airports
- Railway and bus stations
- Cargo control rooms
- VIP areas, especially shielded areas
- Individual entrance control areas at events
- Schools, including lockers and storage compartments
- Prisons
- Greenhouse
- Animal barns

EXAMPLES OF TRAINS, VEHICLES, AIRCRAFT, AND VESSELS

- Passenger and cargo trains
- Individuals' cars
- Trucks
- Scooters, motorcycles, bicycles
- Public transport, buses, tramways
- Transportation for VIPs
- Airplanes, helicopters
- Private and public vessels
- Ferries

## Create Ideal Working Conditions

Your insight and expertise as a dog handler assists you to create ideal and safe working conditions for you and your dog. Each situation requires its own desirable working conditions.

When you start a search for drugs, some items in the area related to the drug trade may pose dangers (e.g., infection from HIV or hepatitis). These items include the following:

- Pipes, water pipes, crack pipes, and homemade devices (e.g., a test tube attached to a hose)
- Metal tubes, snuff tubules, razors, mirrors
- Nozzles, filters

- Scales
- Syringes and needles, silver paper, spoons, tourniquets, and lighters
- Pillboxes, film-roll containers

Before you start a search action, it is important that you follow procedures by which you will be able to search in an organized and systematic manner. Particularly important to these procedures are the quality of the search and the attention to the safety of humans and other animals present. Each situation will be different, so your application of the procedures to the search area involves some interpretation on your part. To achieve the best possible results, all your instructions and requests of colleagues, security personnel, and others must be followed as much as possible. Important to a safe and quality search are the follow examples of proper procedure:

1. Checking the room or area and especially the surface for the possible presence of potentially hazardous items such as the following:

   - Glass
   - Nails
   - Used syringes
   - Chemicals
   - Exposed power cables
   - Fragrance lamps
   - Food scraps
   - Open alcohol or other open liquids

2. Often you will find rubble, dirt, blood, excreta, and related matter, so always wear gloves, and make sure you watch your dog for coprophagia (some dogs like to eat human feces).

3. Create freedom of movement and a working space for your dog.
4. If necessary, adjust the goods or furniture to properly scan them and the area.
5. Streamline people's movements in the area, if possible.
6. Adjust light and, if possible, temperature and airstream by opening windows, doors, and so on.
7. As much as possible, prevent your dog from becoming restless and distracted.

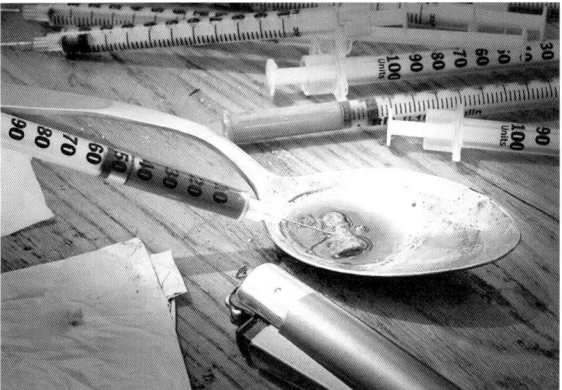

Used drug paraphernalia can indicate the presence of drugs.

A meth pipe.

## Check Before Searching

Before starting a search, you should first obtain all relevant information about the area, which will allow you to plan your dog's search action properly. Perform a survey and, where possible, move objects that may interfere with your dog's work. Before beginning, consider the following points:

1. Never do a search action alone; always have a colleague with you as backup.
2. Take a look at the search area and ascertain whether or not investigating the scene with your dog is (a) possible, and (b) has a chance of success.
3. Determine whether or not to deploy your dog.
4. If you have several dogs, decide which dog is most suited to the job.
5. Determine the appropriate method for the search.
6. Make sure you are fully equipped for the task at hand.
7. Look for dangerous objects when entering the area and immediately remove them.
8. Take note of the weather.
9. Take note of the wind direction.
10. Ascertain where a drift of scent might arise inside the building/area.
11. Let your dog lie down and relax so he gets used to the situation or becomes accustomed to the object he needs to search.
12. The final decision about whether or not to use a K9 to search rests with you, the handler. If you go ahead, make sure you also
    - figure out an appropriate search method for the situation;
    - ask a colleague to film the search action;
    - consult your colleague about what has been searched and what hasn't as you progress; and
    - use common sense.

No matter how good a detector dog is, he can only be successful when he is used according to his needs and character, and according to the right method. Through careful planning, you should be able to minimize the risks for your dog and at the same time carry out the investigation successfully.

## Search Methods

Because of the different situations that occur during search actions, you must be able to use different search methods and employ the most appropriate one according to the situation. You must know how each method is to be applied.

### FREE SEARCH

This is a method commonly used indoors or in a confined area before beginning systematic searching. The dog is not really working according to a controlled system, and he is encouraged to cover as large an area as possible. During deployment and training, this is also called a "quick scan."

### SYSTEMATIC SEARCH

This method, as the name implies, is used to perform a search action in a systematic way. With your voice and body language, you

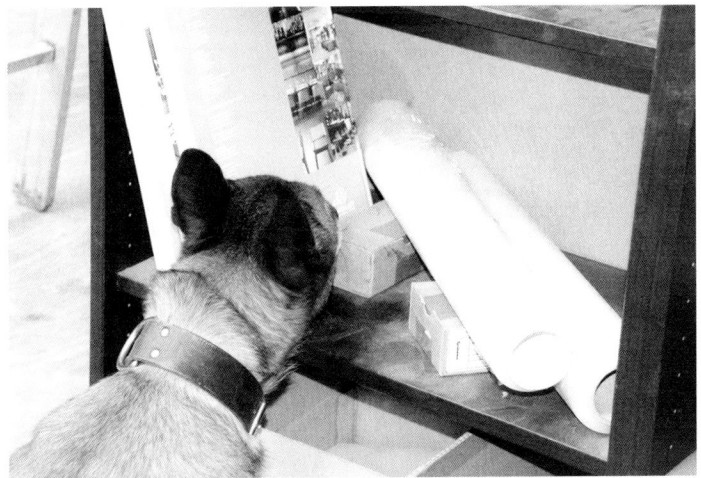

Allow your dog to conduct "quick scans" inside rooms to be searched.

encourage your dog to sniff and investigate an area in a controlled and thorough manner. A successful systematic search includes the following four procedures:

1. Choose a fixed point to start and always search in a clockwise direction.
2. Ask your dog to search from low to high, again in a clockwise direction.
3. Whenever and wherever possible, let your dog investigate high places in the search area.
4. Even if your dog goes away to search somewhere else, let him do so and then start again from the point where he seemed to have left off.

**SEARCH WITH A LONG LEASH**

In certain situations, you may conclude that your dog should work at some distance from you but should still be physically under your control. In these situations, use a long leash. You should know how to handle a long leash so your dog does not get tangled up or otherwise restricted. You may need to motivate your dog when you use this method.

**SEARCH WITH A SHORT LEASH**

If it is necessary to do a systematic search action in which your dog must be kept under full control, use a short leash, but make sure he is not hampered by it. Keep the leash in your left hand and lead with your right, moving your dog along the objects that need to be scanned.

The proper application of a method of investigation of an object or a region can determine the difference between a search action's success or failure. Remember that the methods discussed here are merely the tools for searching, to which you must apply your correct assessment of and appropriate reaction to the situation.

## Searching Open-Air Locations

Searching open terrain is most often not as easy as it seems. There are a lot of disturbances, including wind and weather. If there are no dangers and it is possible, you can start an investigation first with a "quick scan," wherein your dog goes through the area quickly to find some odor of hidden drugs. After that, the total search area can be divided into several sectors that your dog will search in detail, slowly inspecting all the places in a certain sector, including the following:

- Beside, under, and up in trees
- Under shrubs and stinging plants and bushes
- In and around hutches or sheds
- Near lampposts and flagpoles
- Around billboards
- Under paving stones or street tiles
- In flower boxes and pots
- In and around waste bins (Once, one of our dogs found drugs hidden in a sealed dog-feces bag lying close to a garbage can.)

Drug-detector dogs can search for buried containers and dig them up, when they are trained to do so. You cannot know how deeply your dog can smell into the ground for a given substance until you give it a try! Weather and soil conditions are very important in open-air searches and can affect the search in positive and negative ways, as does the strength of the odor, the packing material around the drug cache, and any other masking agents.

Big caches may also be located hidden in containers outside, around the building you are searching. One search turned up these cocaine bricks, which were hidden outside.

Your job as handler is to watch your dog's behavior and postures during the search work. Perhaps your dog is sniffing for a longer than normal time at a certain spot or is showing interest in something. In these cases, even if your dog has not alerted, use a thin probe to check beneath what your dog has been sniffing.

## Searching Indoor Locations

Search dogs work in a variety of different locations during their career. In many cases, however, one search area is the same as others, from his perspective. For example, working in a hangar may seem the same to him as working in cargo sheds, warehouses, and other large, open buildings.

During indoor searches, make sure you control your dog. You must curb your dog's natural tendency to explore and probe at random, and your dog must not be allowed to roam freely. You can only allow your dog to make "quick scans" inside rooms or other well-lit places indoors. Generally speaking, consider the following points when conducting an indoor search:

1. Make sure your dog does not do any harm. Check beforehand to find out where your dog may and may not climb up.
2. If necessary, open entrance doors and windows.
3. Before starting the search operation, your dog should first be allowed to become familiar with the surroundings and odors of the building.
4. Work systematically, and direct your dog to search rooms in a clockwise direction.
5. Work from the outside of a building to the inside.
6. Begin on the first accessible floor and then work upward.
7. After that, check the basement and crawlspaces.
8. Conduct the search at different heights:
    - start searching from the floor to waist height;
    - then from waist height to eye level; and
    - then from eye level to and including the ceiling.

9. Don't forget to search the air-conditioning or heating system.
10. Look for fire extinguishers and fire hoses, and let your dog smell them—drugs could be hidden inside.
11. Allow your dog to go outside the space (even outside the building) to get a breath of fresh air.
12. Search the garage and check the vehicles associated with the building.
13. Check the garden, including flower boxes and outbuildings.
14. Use common sense.

Air currents can be extremely difficult to assess when working indoors. Drafts, cross-ventilation, and heating and air-conditioning units all affect scent patterns. Try to control these conditions as much as possible by switching off air conditioners and heaters.

If your dog alerts downwind from the hiding place, you must be extremely careful in administering correction or praise. Where a draft is obviously present, encourage your dog to work back upwind in an attempt to pinpoint the source. This requires you to search all areas as you and your dog move back upwind. If you

Alerting a cache of drugs located in a desk drawer.

direct adequate verbal encouragement at your dog, this technique should be successful.

As you guide your dog through the search area, use initiative, never overlook the obvious, and show your dog each area to be checked. If a situation appears doubtful, follow your dog's instincts rather than attempting to rationalize it from a human point of view.

## SEARCHING IN HOUSES

After arriving at the search area, first start a survey and inquire about the owner, occupants, or tenants of the property. Also find out what the property is being used for.

Note for yourself the important things and points of concern. If possible, take pictures of the situation and make notes of all valuables and already damaged goods to avoid undue claims. Further points of special interest follow:

- If pets are present, remove them.
- Carefully check all furniture.
- Smaller drug caches may be hidden behind plinths, sockets or mirrors, clocks, picture frames, and tapestries hung somewhat higher on the wall. Also check in or under mantel clocks and cabinets placed high up, since these spots will be too high for your dog to reach.
- There are many hiding places in kitchens, including cupboards, the dishwasher, freezer, oven, range hood, refrigerator, and stove.
- Check in particular the bedrooms, places that would be private to individuals. The drug world is populated with unreliable characters who steal from one another. Most of the time, small amounts of drugs are hidden lower in the house and bigger amounts are stowed higher.
- Examples of storage places include ceilings, under floor boards, behind roof decking, or in specially made nooks.
- Consider measuring the rooms so you can figure out if there are false walls at play.

PLANNING A SEARCH ACTION                                                                111

- Often, bigger drug caches are hidden in containers in the ground around the house.
- Make sure you check places the house's occupant could easily see, places no one could get in or out of without being seen by the occupant.
- Most often, the greatest amount of a drug cache is hidden in one place; and often the entire cache is hidden in one spot.
- Be careful when you open up a hiding spot, and watch out for possible security measures that might injure you.

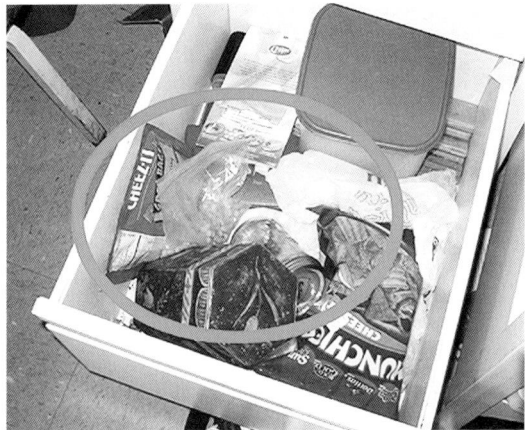

Sometimes, a small drug cache will be hidden in the lower parts of the house, while a larger one is stowed somewhere on the second floor.

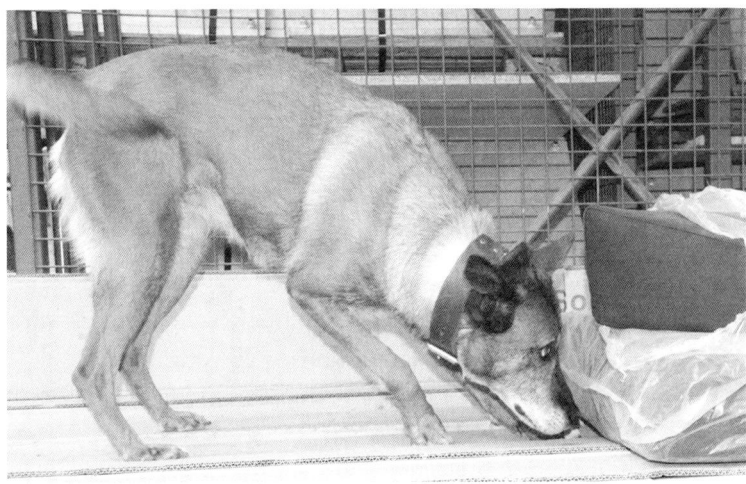

Garages and other storage areas should be searched thoroughly.

## SEARCHING IN ANIMAL BARNS

Searches in barns or kennels are not the simplest to conduct, but they can be done. In spite of the strong scents of fertilizer and animal manure, your dog should have no problem finding drugs in barns or kennels, or on farm grounds in general. Depending on your dog's reaction to them, cattle can stay in the barn. It is very interesting to watch a well-trained detector dog searching among cattle.

## SEARCHING IN PRISONS

When searching a prisoner's cell, also search in a clockwise direction, and be aware that amounts of drugs might be small, so take special interest in the following:

- Chair and table legs
- Bedframes
- Mattresses, bedding, and pillows
- Curtain and tablecloth hems
- Drainage basins
- Under or beside toilets
- Tennis balls
- Shoes
- Inside TVs or radios
- Behind sockets
- Inside or under cupboards
- Behind wall plates or pictures on the wall
- Inside air-conditioning or heating systems

Larger caches can be found in places where several inmates have access, such as changing rooms, kitchens, laundry rooms with washers and dryers, showers, washrooms, and workrooms.

## SEARCHING HUMANS

Often handlers and their dogs are indoors when they must search people for the presence of drugs, but sometimes these searches take place outside, where other people, traffic, foreign odors, other animals, loud noises, and strange objects can divert your dog's attention from the primary task. In some cases, you, the handler, may also be tempted to relax your vigilance in the face of so many distractions. However, your team's ability to function effectively under such circumstances is of paramount importance. Employ basic obedience, scent discrimination, and systematic techniques to reduce the impact of distracting influences. When searching people in populated areas, consider the following 14 tips:

1. If possible, eliminate or minimize distracting influences, such as other people.
2. When distractions cannot be reduced significantly, work slowly, exercise firm control over your dog, and encourage him to perform the task required.
3. Adhere to established search techniques and require your dog to do so, too.
4. When searching people for drugs, only work with dogs that alert with a passive response, by sitting or lying down. It's important that the dog does not behave aggressively or bark.
5. Don't rationalize the legitimacy of a particular situation. Everyone and everything is suspect. If there is doubt, your dog's instinct, not yours, should be respected.
6. Logic, common sense, and sound dog-handling practices are required at all times to successfully accomplish the search mission. If you employ these skills properly, working in populated areas will present no major problems for you and your dog.
7. When you check people for the presence of drugs carried on their person, consider that some people don't like dogs or are even afraid of them.
8. You, the handler, have to approach people with respect, and if you supply a good explanation of what is going to happen, that will help eliminate much fear in the person you are going to search.

9. When searching people outside or inside a nightclub, a relaxed atmosphere usually prevails, but the opposite can be true if you are searching people at a prison entrance. Regardless of the situation, stay focused on your job and look to your dog's behavior, as well as the behavior of the person being searched by your dog. Often, watching the person you are searching gives you a lot of information. The following behaviors are typical for people who are in possession of drugs or have used drugs recently:

    - Tough, nonchalant behavior (usually at nightclubs)
    - Aggression
    - Nervousness

10. When walking with your dog among the people you are searching, control him and make sure that if he is interested in a certain person, he gets the space and time he needs to thoroughly sniff that person from all sides (and from low to high). If you are investigating a lineup, make sure there is sufficient space between subjects.

11. Be careful—watch your dog constantly when he is thoroughly sniffing someone because he may already, or also, have smelled drugs on another person standing a little farther away than the one he is sniffing. You can tell that he has smelled something if he smells someone then looks around, or if he is standing between two or more people and sniffs around with a high nose.

12. Always check any baggage the person is carrying.

13. Stay friendly with any people your dog alerts to—remember that this person might not have anything to do with drugs and may just have been in an area where drugs were used.

14. If your dog tries to make a passive response and the person of interest walks away, let the dog follow the person and watch carefully to note if he continues to alert. He may, for example, alert beside a person who had been standing next to the person who walked away. If necessary, of course, stop the person in question, and have your dog investigate the individual again.

When searching humans for drugs, work with dogs trained to display a passive alert.

## SEARCHING VEHICLES

When searching inside vehicles, you are significantly impeded by the small space, but you also have to take account of the weather (certainly temperature and humidity) outside. After all, usually such a search is carried out in cars that are outside, in the open air. In addition to those factors, you must also take into account the presence of "less-than understanding" drivers and passengers. You must only let your dog do such a search if you can ensure a safe search situation for you and your dog.

When searching vehicles, you must exercise firm control on your dog at all times. Also, be careful not to read a false alert, as vehicles have much extraneous scent in and around them. Human- and animal-associated odors may confuse your dog and distract him from the search.

In searching for drugs in a vehicle, you will run into two possible situations, the first of which involves a car that has been stationary for a long time, and you are called in relation to possible drug smuggling. This situation usually portends favorable conditions as the vehicle is normally parked somewhere quiet, safely stowed away. The second situation involves a vehicle that has just been stopped because it is suspected that drugs may be present there. This kind of situation is more difficult—the driver and passengers will be involved, and there may be more distractions on the street for your dog to contend with.

Following are nine tips that may help you and your dog conduct a successful search in the second situation described above:

1. To work in a quiet area, have the driver stop the car on the side of the road, in a safe location.
2. Ask everyone to step out of and away from the vehicle.
3. Find out who was sitting where in the vehicle.
4. Leave the key in the ignition.
5. Check around the vehicle for dangerous items and drugs that may have been ejected from the vehicle before the search.
6. Check the vehicle for well-known drug-user items.
7. Before the dog searches ashtrays and glove compartments in stopped cars, you, the handler, should search them and then remove the ashtrays so you can search behind them.
8. Tell the driver that you and your dog will be investigating the car for drugs. Experience has shown us that people will often show you where the drugs are if you ask them. Mind you, they often only show you a small amount of drugs and don't indicate where a larger cache might be.
9. Know how a vehicle is built and where possible cavities might be. Any deviation from the norm should be considered suspicious. For example, know that a diesel-powered car does not have a gas tank in the back. Also, if there is a gas tank, check for a converter in the engine compartment. As well, know that most cars do not have complete spare tires but only simple ones; if a complete spare is there, check it for drugs.

When searching a personal vehicle and the owner is present, tell him or her that you and your dog will be searching the car for drugs. In our experience, people in this situation usually tell you where the drugs are hidden. However, even if you receive this information, still conduct your search to ensure the owner hasn't just told you about one, small cache.

When searching vehicles, first quarter your dog downwind of the vehicle. If he does not alert, proceed directly to the front of the vehicle and commence searching in a clockwise direction.

Take your time when searching bigger vehicles.

In general, vehicle searches should be conducted in exactly the same manner each time. This is not always possible with other types of searches. If you employ the following 13 techniques, you should not encounter any significant problems when searching vehicles:

1. Close all vehicle doors and open the hood and trunk.
2. First, quarter your dog downwind of the vehicle. If no alert occurs, proceed directly to the front of the vehicle and commence searching in a clockwise direction.
3. Search the bumpers and the front.
4. Search the lights.
5. Search the wheel wells.
6. Search the edges and seams of doors.
7. Search the cover of the fuel tank.
8. Search the fuel tank.
9. Search the vents and air intakes.
10. Search the spare tire if it is on the outside of the vehicle.
11. Make sure fenders, tires, hubcaps, quarter panels, and the undercarriage receive careful screening.
12. Search the trunk and engine compartment next. If the engine is still warm, put a piece of carpet over it. (The carpet gives your dog a comfortable, safe place to stand.)
13. Terminate the search with a careful examination of the vehicle interior. This includes seats, floorboards, dashboard, ashtrays, armrests, headrests, seat belts, and accessories. For this type of search, smaller detector dogs (such as spaniels) are very suitable. Try to operate with a fixed pattern at every car search so that nothing will be forgotten. Following is a possible order you could adopt:
    a. Put all the doors open, and start searching at the driver's side.
    b. Search the interior side of the door.
    c. Search the bottom left side of the dashboard.
    d. Search at and under the driver's seat.
    e. Search the console between the driver's and passenger's seats.

f. Search the covering at the inside top of the roof in the front of the car.
g. Search the passenger door.
h. Search the bottom right side of the dashboard, including the glove compartment.
i. Search the passenger's seat and under it.
j. Search the passenger door behind at the right side.
k. Search the front and top of the rear seat, including the floor on the right side.
l. Search the backside of the front passenger seat.
m. Search the covering on the inside top of the roof in the back of the car.
n. Search the trunk, undercarriage, and spare-tire space.
o. Search the passenger door behind the driver's seat, on the left side.
p. Search the front and top of the rear seat, including the floor on the left side.
q. Search the back side of the driver's seat.
r. Luggage may be removed from the trunk or interior of the vehicle and searched separately.

Vehicle searches are particularly difficult for some dogs because they must negotiate many obstacles to accomplish the mission. Encourage your dog to jump into the trunk, crawl under the vehicle, and search high into the engine compartment.

Remember that drugs may be hidden inside mechanical parts.

## SEARCHING MOBILE HOMES, RVS, AND TRAILERS

When searching mobile homes, RVs, and trailers, first look at potential hazards such as gas bottles. Shut off the gas and briefly scan the compartment or room.

When you search around the vehicle, pay attention to the following:

- Wheels and wheel wells
- Walls and externally accessible spaces
- Doors and entrances
- Under the vehicle
- Around the axles
- In trailers, the drawbar
- In RVs, the engine area and front—search these like you would a car

When searching the inside of a mobile home, RV, or trailer, always first do a quick scan from the vantage point of the entrance. Look at all seats, tables, cabinets, and beds. Then carefully search everything:

- Drawers and cupboards
- Windows and frames
- Seats, tables, cabinets, and beds
- Kitchen, toilet, and shower
- Lamps and other fixtures on the walls and ceiling
- Walls and ceiling: also knock on the walls and ceiling to listen for cavities
- Floor
- In RVs, the driver and passenger area

## PARCEL AND LUGGAGE SEARCHES

Railway and bus stations, seaports, and airports are handling centers for large quantities of goods, including all kinds of carry-on luggage, containers, handbags, luggage, and packages.

Excellent hiding places exist in scooters, motorcycles, and bicycles.

When you need to investigate larger objects, such as containers and cargo on pallets or airfreight pallets, search carefully around the objects first and let your dog smell all the openings, slots, and hinges. When searching smaller objects, such as bags, boxes, parcels, or suitcases, ask your dog to search these items after they are placed on a conveyor belt, or make a sorting lineup.

If you are creating a lineup, create a row of at least five and up to eight objects, preferably spaced 12 inches (30 cm) apart. Your dog can investigate this type of lineup either inside or outside. During sorting, have your dog conduct a "slow scan," in which he smells all the objects at a leisurely pace. This can be done by letting him search off leash, using signals to direct him to the different objects in the row. It is important that everything in the lineup is carefully searched:

- Fasteners and locks
- Hinges
- Zippers
- Suitcase edges
- Carrying straps;
- Support frames, especially those that have tube-like structures
- Name tags

Furthermore, keep in mind that one object could be contaminated by coming into contact with odor from another object.

## SEARCHING AIRPLANES

In a search action in and around a (passenger) plane on the ground, the presence of an airplane mechanic who knows the aircraft is required. A plane has many hidden and inaccessible areas, so take advantage of the mechanic's knowledge. She or he will be aware of all the less-obvious and hard-to-reach places. When examining a plane that is already loaded, ask for the help of a loadmaster. The loadmaster will be able to review cargo lists and will know details about the load in the plane. Start your search on the outside of the plane at the landing gear and work via the entrance(s) to the inside. In the investigation of the interior, the aircraft can be divided into compartments:

- Passenger areas, which can be subdivided into three search levels:
  - From the floor to the seat bottom
  - From the seat bottom to the upper side of the windows
  - From the upper side of the windows to the ceiling

Start your search on the outside of planes at the landing gear and work via the entrance(s) to the inside.

- Bathrooms
- Kitchen units
- The cockpit
- Baggage compartments

Work from a starting point at the entrance to a specific end point so your dog leaves no space unsniffed. Mark each controlled area on a map, and register the route you walked. Your final check of the plane should be under the floor, above the ceiling, and in all other hard-to-reach areas.

### SEARCHING SHIPS AND FERRIES

It can be difficult to take control of a ship or ferry to conduct a search, mostly because the vessels are large and complex. There are a lot of hiding places, rooms, cabins, and passages, and it's difficult to stay oriented and remember where your dog has already searched. Passing through all of a ship's spaces is often hard going

It often is a huge job to search ships or ferries because they are so big and complex. But a thorough search can yield results like this one: the products of a successful search conducted by the DEA and US Coastguard.

and requires some adjustment and special effort on the part of you and your dog. Having to crawl under and over pipes, walk on open stairs, and negotiate insecure footing and cramped working conditions may create problems for your dog. Dogs also have to deal with the fact that the ship doesn't stay still; however, they will get used to that after a while. Such conditions can be overcome only by concentration, patience, repetition, and your encouragement.

During a search action on ships, it is advisable to recruit a crew member such as a mechanic, an engineer, or the captain—someone who knows the subdivision of the ship and also knows what "belongs" to the ship and what does not. Especially with larger vessels (tankers, freighters, and ferries), you simply cannot work without the help of crew members, since those ships have many hard-to-reach areas and hiding places.

In larger vessels, a search will take a lot of time, so you may decide that several search teams should be available. We certainly recommend the deployment of more than one detector-dog teams when conducting a search of a large vessel.

Start your investigation at the most easily accessible deck and go on searching to the top deck. Search the rest of the ship from that same most easily accessible deck to the bottom of the ship. Make sure you have a system to your search route. We suggest using a map to make sure you've searched every room. Mark each controlled area and register the route you have walked during the search.

# 7

# General Information on Drugs, Drug Laws, and Penalties

The objective of this chapter and the next one is to increase your knowledge regarding the search object: drugs. You, the handler, must be aware of many types of illegal substances, how they work, and their effects on drug users. Handlers should be up to date on drug-use trends and developments, as well as the laws that prohibit their sale and use. Knowing as much as possible about this subject will ensure that you and your dog perform as well as possible during a search action. And don't forget that if you know about the drugs you are searching for, you will also be able to handle them safely and make sure your dog is safe.

In the broadest of terms, a drug is a chemical substance that alters the central nervous system, brain chemistry, or bodily functions, and has known biological effects on humans. In this book, the term "drugs" (also variously—depending on the type—called narcotics, stimulants, intoxication agents, hallucinogenic drugs, illegal chemicals, or dope) is used as a collective term for substances that have a more or less narcotic, stimulant, and/or hallucinogenic effect and that can lead to addiction and habituation and that may cause side effects. The word "narcotic" is often used for judicial purposes and by the police when they refer to illegal drugs.

The term "narcotic" comes from the ancient Greek *narkō*, meaning "stupor" and originally referred to a variety of substances that dulled the senses and relieved pain, or to any psychoactive compounds with sleep-inducing properties. Though some people still refer to all drugs as narcotics, today that term refers specifically to opium, opium derivatives, and their semi-synthetic substitutes. Another, more current term for these drugs is "opiates" or "opioids." When used in a legal context, the word "narcotic" refers to drugs whose use is prohibited by law, or that are used in violation of government regulations.

In English, the noun "drug" is thought to originate from *drogue* (Old French), which possibly also gave rise to the term *droge-vate* (Middle Dutch), meaning "dry barrels," referring to medicinal plants preserved in barrels during the process of refining pharmaceutical substances from them.

In ancient Greece, a cripple or beggar or criminal (the *pharmakos*) was cast out of the community, either in response to a natural disaster, such as a plague or famine, or in response to an invasion or a predictable calendrical event, such as the year end. The ritualistic sacrifice or exile of humans was believed to bring about purification. The victims, whose sacrifice was believed to prevent disasters, illness, or death, were called *pharmakoi*, and from this the pharmaceutical industry takes its name. In the past, religion and medical science were closely connected, so the people who were in contact with the higher power also advised on illness. Indeed, these people were skilled at preparing all sorts of medicines, using leafy plants, roots, and spices.

The Greek god Asclepius (in Latin, Aesculapius) was believed to be able to bring people back from the realm of the dead, and because of that he was also considered the god of medical sciences. In Ancient Greece, just as sacred dogs were employed to lick the wounds of sick people, a particular type of non-venomous snake was often used in healing rituals. The snake is a symbol for the medical arts because it sheds its skin and is "reborn," and also

## THE DREAMLIKE STATE

Herbs have always played an important role in non-medical areas of life, too. From the earliest times, people have yearned for happiness and have used derivatives of various leafy plants, roots, and mushrooms to become intoxicated and experience a kind of happiness, a dream-world kind of joy.

There is a big difference between a normal dream, experienced during sleep, and the drug-induced, dreamlike state. In normal sleep, pleasant and unpleasant things can go only as far as the dreamer can endure. Waking up, perhaps due to a violent dream, generally solves the problem in the dream.

The intoxicated dreamer, however, stays ensnared in his or her drug-induced dreams until the drug used to initiate intoxication has left his or her system. After repeated use, chasing that dreamlike state, the drug user finds that attaining the high isn't as easy, and when achieved isn't as intensely felt as when he or she first used the drug. The dreamlike state is shorter and the feelings of happiness and freedom are diluted. Most of the time, the user tries to attain a "higher" high by taking more of the drug. Chronic users of some illegal drugs can build up a tolerance to them, which means their bodies require larger and larger doses to achieve the same effects.

because its bite can bring death. Thus Asclepius is usually depicted with a snake-encircled staff; Asclepius's staff is still the symbol of medicine and pharmacy.

In the Middle Ages, European monks collected and passed on knowledge about medical drinks and spices. Their pastoral work hence became intertwined with the practice of tending to the sick with various "cures." In old drawings, you can still see that monastery or hospital herb gardens were located close to the physician's office and warehouse of dried herbs, also called the apothecary (*apotheca* in Greek, meaning "pharmacy").

Modern humans look to the power of chemicals to cure diseases, prevent epidemics, and even prevent poor harvests (by means of insecticides). The sheer number of pharmaceutical prescriptions and over-the-counter medications taken annually clearly shows

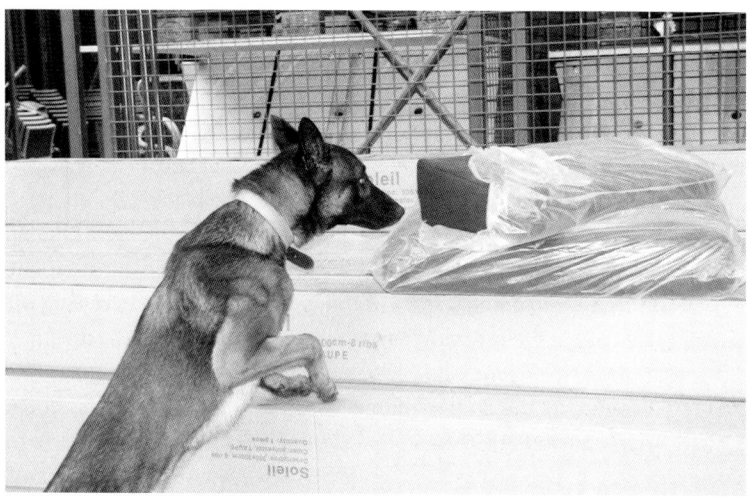

A young dog training to be a drug detector.

the important role of chemical products in our modern society. Modern pharmaceuticals not only cure and prevent physical disease but also can correct psychological problems that sometimes result from the stresses of modern life. Hundreds of pharmaceutical products are available to the anxious, depressed, and stressed. Many other products are designed and marketed to help people deal with everyday pain or pain resulting from injury or medical intervention. Sometimes it seems that there are more people using and even addicted to legal, prescribed pharmaceutical products than so-called drug addicts or junkies with their illegal drugs, such as morphine, cocaine, heroin, and/or synthetic opiates. Not surprisingly, the pharmaceutical industry has created solutions for drug addiction, with all sorts of new drugs (such as methadone) that compare with synthetic morphine, which can help people break the habit of using dangerous drugs.

## Drug Schedules

It can be difficult to organize all the information out there about illegal drugs. Until 1961, there were two lists of drugs: List I for hard drugs, and List II for soft drugs. Sometimes substances were known by other names than were listed, which led to the UN Single Convention on Narcotic Drugs of 1961. Ratified in New York, the convention was an international treaty for prohibiting production and supply of specific (nominally narcotic) drugs and drugs with similar effects except those under license for specific purposes, such as medical treatment and research. The Single Convention was an update to the Paris Convention of 1931, and it includes the vast number of synthetic opioids invented in the intervening 30 years, as well as a mechanism for more easily including new drugs. Earlier treaties had only controlled opium, coca, and derivatives like morphine, heroin, and cocaine. The Single Convention consolidated those treaties and broadened their scope to include cannabis and drugs whose effects are similar to those of the drugs specified in the convention. The Single Convention created four schedules of controlled substances and a process for adding new substances to the schedules without amending the treaty. The schedules were designed to have significantly stricter regulations than the two soft- and hard-drug groups established by previous treaties. As of February 2015, the Single Convention has 185 state parties and the Holy See, and almost all member states of the United Nations are state parties.

## The Netherlands

Drug enforcement varies widely between nations. Many European countries, including the United Kingdom, Germany, and, most famously, the Netherlands, do not prosecute all petty drug offenses. Dutch coffee shops are allowed to sell small amounts of cannabis to consumers. However, the Dutch Ministry of Health, Welfare and Sport notes that large-scale production and trafficking are dealt with severely under criminal law, in accordance with the UN Single Convention.

The Opium Act (*Opiumwet*) of the Netherlands prohibits the production, possession, trade, sale, and transport of drugs covered by the law. Drug use alone is not punishable. The Dutch Opium Act contains two lists. List 1 includes drugs with an unacceptable health risk (hard drugs), such as amphetamines, cocaine, ecstasy, GHB, heroin, and LSD. List 2 includes drugs that are to a lesser extent harmful to health (soft drugs), such as hashish and marijuana, hallucinogenic mushrooms, and medicines like barbital, diazepam, mazindol, pemoline, phenobarbital, and so on.

From 1960, the popular use of cannabis in the Netherlands increased. In 1972, the first coffee shop opened. In 1976, the Opium Act was amended and a distinction was made in both Lists 1 and 2. The law was interpreted in such a way that coffee shops could sell hashish and marijuana under certain conditions. The number of coffee shops greatly increased, but in 1995, the guidelines were tightened and the number of coffee shops reduced. Since 2003, it is possible to get cannabis—used as a painkiller by MS and AIDS patients—by prescription at the pharmacy.

In addition to the Opium Act, the Netherlands also has the Medicines Act and the Chemical Abuse Prevention Act. The preparation of synthetic drugs requires substances called precursors and pre-precursors. These chemicals are almost always listed under the Chemical Abuse Prevention Act (*Wet Voorkoming Misbruik Chemicaliën*). Examples of these include the following:

- Benzylmethylketon (BMK), for the preparation of amphetamine
- Piperonylmethylketon (PMK), for the preparation of ecstasy/MDMA
- Ephedrine, for the manufacture of methamphetamine

The trade in these chemicals is strictly regulated and punishable under the Chemical Abuse Prevention Act.

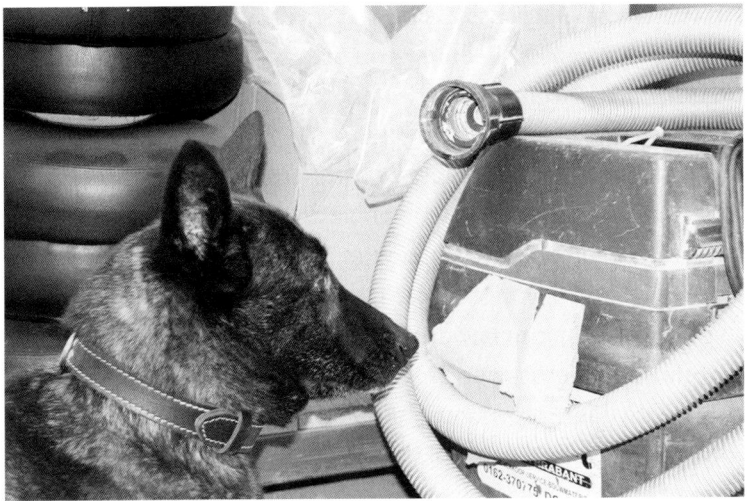

A detector dog will only become as good at her job as her handler permits.

## POLICY OF TOLERANCE

A lot of people mistakenly think that the use and sale of cannabis is not a criminal offense in the Netherlands. The Netherlands has a so-called policy of tolerance, which means that certain behaviors in violation of the Opium Act not will be prosecuted. This means that the possession and sale of hashish and marijuana are still criminalized, but policing of those acts no longer occurs, and the public prosecution service will not prosecute individuals who possess or sell those drugs.

It is worth noting that we are only talking about small amounts of hashish and marijuana sold to consumers in coffee shops. And these coffee shops must meet certain criteria in marketing and selling these goods: no advertising other than a mark on the wall; no hard drugs available or sold in the coffee shop; no alcohol allowed in the coffee shop; no noise, litter, or loitering customers near the coffee shop; coffee shops must be at least 383 yards (350 m) away from schools; and no sales to youth under 18 years and no access to the coffee shop to people under 18—identification is mandatory.

The law tolerates possession of a small amount (up to 5 grams) of soft drugs from List 2 for personal consumption; this means only 5 grams per person per day from a coffee shop. The coffee shop may have a maximum of 500 grams in stock, but production and trade of cannabis is prohibited. The Netherlands has had a great deal of trouble with drug tourism as a result of its tolerant policy, and other countries have suffered as a result. Citizens of neighboring nations—Belgium, France, and Germany, for example—come to the Netherlands to buy drugs and then take them back home.

Since 2011, drug tourism and the production of strains of cannabis with higher concentrations of THC have challenged the former policy in the Netherlands and led to a more restrictive approach, including the ban on selling cannabis to tourists in coffee shops. In October 2011, the Dutch government proposed a new law to Parliament that put cannabis with 15 percent THC or more onto the list of hard drugs. However, at this writing, about 80 percent of the coffee shops still sell, among their products, this kind of cannabis.

## The United Kingdom

The Misuse of Drugs Act 1971 is the main body of legislation concerning illegal drugs in the United Kingdom and was enacted with the intention of preventing the non-medical use of certain drugs. The act therefore covers all kinds of drugs, even those without medicinal uses. Drugs subject to the act are known as "controlled substances," the use of which are illegal. These illegal drugs are placed into one of three classes: A, B, or C. The classification system is broadly based on the harms the drugs cause either to the individual or to society when they are misused. The class into which a drug is placed corresponds with a schedule of penalties for offenses involving the drug. For example, misuse of Class A drugs attracts the most severe penalties, as they are considered likely to cause the most serious harm. Drugs controlled under the Misuse of Drugs Act are illegal to have, produce, give away, or sell.

Class A drugs include cocaine (including crack), ecstasy (MDMA), heroin (diamorphine), LSD, magic mushrooms, methadone, methamphetamine (crystal meth), and any Class B drug (for example, amphetamine) if prepared for injection.

Class B drugs include amphetamines, barbiturates, cannabis, cathinones (including mephedrone), codeine, and synthetic cannabinoids.

Class C drugs include anabolic steroids, benzodiazepines (tranquilizers), benzylpiperazines (BZP), gamma hydroxybutyrate (GHB/GBL), and ketamine.

Not all drugs are illegal, but that doesn't mean they aren't harmful. New, "legal highs" have been developed to mimic the effects of illegal drugs like cocaine and ecstasy but are structurally different enough to avoid being classified as illegal substances under the Misuse of Drugs Act. However, they can still have dangerous side effects.

The United Kingdom recognizes that some drugs do have legitimate uses as medicines, in research, or in industry. To use, import, or produce these drugs, people must obtain a license from Britain's Home Office.

An intensive vehicle search conducted during training.

## Canada

In Canada, illegal drugs fall under the Controlled Drugs and Substances Act, which includes the sentencing and fines for each category of offense (selling, production, use, and so on) in accordance with each type of drug. While at this writing cannabis is still an illegal substance in Canada, the Canadian government is working toward legalizing marijuana.

The Controlled Drugs and Substances Act includes eight schedules, listing the drugs and substances (and their derivatives, intermediates, preparations, salts, and/or alkaloids) that are prohibited in Canada. Schedule I, for example, includes what have been called "hard drugs," such as opium, coca, fentanyls, methamphetamine, amphetamines, and flunitrazepam, among others. Schedule II includes cannabis (for now) and synthetic cannabinoids, and Schedule III includes hallucinogens like LSD, psilocin and psilocybin, and mescaline. Schedule IV includes

In this case, the trainer hid a cache of drugs in the center console of a car for the prospective detector dog to find. However, during some exercises, there should be nothing to find, which prepares the dog for some search actions in real life.

A hiding place containing 36.5 pounds (16.6 kg) of methamphetamine.

GENERAL INFORMATION ON DRUGS, DRUG LAWS, AND PENALTIES   135

## MARIJUANA AMONG THE HERBS

Regardless of the different and often overwhelming odors encountered in a search area, a well-trained drug-detector dog can still do her job perfectly. This was clearly demonstrated during a training session conducted by the Rotterdam Police in a warehouse in that city's industrial district. The air in the warehouse, owned by the company Verstegen Spices & Sauces, was heavy with the scent of various herbs and spices, and we wanted to test whether or not the dogs were capable of finding a minimum of 5 grams of marijuana hidden among the stores of herbs and spices. Many employees of the company were coming and going, working in the production hall, and so it was impossible for the dogs to follow a familiar human track to the cache. Moreover, the small bag of marijuana was hidden by the warehouse keeper, who was a stranger to the dogs. Once again our Malinois dogs Eva and Speedy, our German shepherd Eros, and the other dogs present belonging to our colleagues, proved they could find that small amount of marijuana even among the other heady smells in that hall. Theirs was an incredible achievement—and after that trial, we have never doubted the dog's truly phenomenal sense of smell.

"downers" like barbiturates, benzodiazepines, and steroids. At this writing, Schedule V includes propylhexedrine, a stimulant, and Schedule VI includes Class A and Class B precursors, preparations, and mixtures (chemicals necessary to the production of illegal drugs and substances). Finally, Schedules VII and VIII are related to specific amounts of cannabis resin and marijuana.

The drugs included in Schedules I through IV, and Schedule VIII, of Canada's Controlled Drugs and Substances Act are listed in Appendix A at the back of this book. Appendix B consists of the punishments people can expect to receive in Canada related to possession of and/or trafficking in these controlled drugs and substances.

## United States of America

The Controlled Substances Act (CSA) is the statute prescribing federal US drug policy under which the manufacture, importation, possession, use, and distribution of certain substances is

While training your dog, make sure she must find caches that are hidden high up so she learns that she must search both low and high.

regulated. Since its enactment in 1970, the act has been amended several times.

As stated by the Drug Enforcement Administration (DEA) of the US Department of Justice, the CSA consists of two subchapters. Subchapter I defines Schedules I–V, lists chemicals used in the manufacture of controlled substances, and differentiates lawful and unlawful manufacturing, distribution, and possession of controlled substances, including possession of Schedule I drugs for personal use; this subchapter also specifies the dollar amounts of fines and durations of prison terms for violations. Subchapter II describes the laws for exportation and importation of controlled substances, again specifying fines and prison terms for violations.

**THE DRUG SCHEDULES**

Drugs, substances, and certain chemicals used to make drugs are classified into five distinct categories or schedules, depending upon the drug's acceptable medical use and the drug's abuse or dependency potential. The abuse rate is a determinate factor in the scheduling of the drug; for example, Schedule I drugs are considered the most dangerous class of drugs with a high potential for abuse and potentially severe psychological and/or physical dependence. As the drug schedule number increases—Schedule II, Schedule III, and so on—the abuse potential decreases, with Schedule V drugs representing the least potential for abuse. Like in the Canadian Controlled Drugs and Substances Act, these lists describe the basic or parent chemicals and do not necessarily describe the salts, isomers, and salts of isomers, esters, ethers, and derivatives that may also be classified as controlled substances. Please note that a substance need not be listed as a controlled substance to be treated as a Schedule I substance for criminal prosecution. A controlled-substance analog is a substance intended for human consumption and is structurally or pharmacologically substantially similar to or is represented as being similar to a Schedule I or Schedule II substance and is not an approved medication in the United States. See Appendix C to view Schedules I–V. Note that the lists are intended as general references and are not comprehensive listings of all controlled substances.

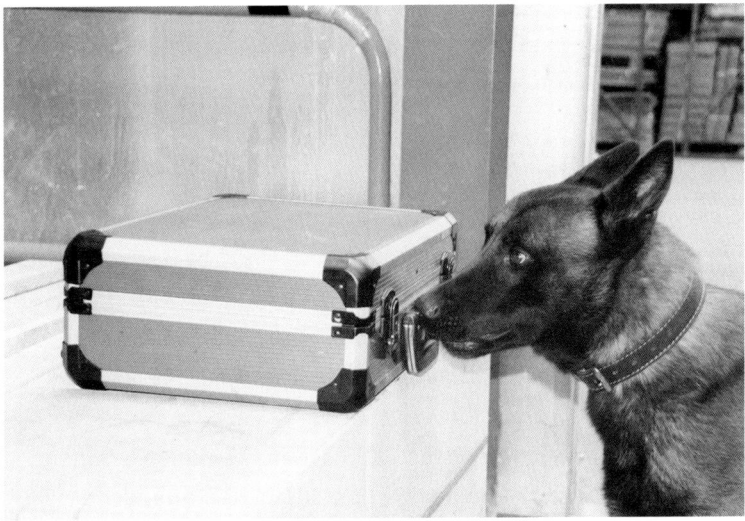

When searching luggage for drugs, remember that some bags could be contaminated by coming into contact with other luggage containing drugs.

## DISPENSING TO PATIENTS

Schedule I drugs are those that have no currently accepted medical use in the United States, so they may be used in the United States only in research situations.

Whether or not any drug may be placed on prescription is decided by the FDA. Unlike other prescription drugs, however, controlled substances are subject to additional restrictions. Schedule II prescription orders must be written and signed by the prescribing practitioner; they may not be telephoned in to a pharmacy, except in an emergency. In addition, a prescription for a Schedule II drug may not be refilled. For Schedule III and IV drugs, prescription orders may be either written or given orally (by telephone to a pharmacy). In addition, the patient may (if authorized by the practitioner) have the prescription refilled up to five times and at any time within six months from the date the prescription was issued.

Schedule V includes some prescription drugs and many narcotic preparations, including antitussives and antidiarrheals. Even here, however, the law imposes restrictions beyond those normally required for over-the-counter sales. For example, the patient must be at least 18 years of age, offer some form of identification, and have his or her name entered into a special log maintained by the pharmacist as part of a special record.

## PERSONAL USE PENALTIES

On November 19, 1988, the American Congress passed the Anti-Drug Abuse Act of 1988. Two sections of this act represent the US government's attempt to reduce drug abuse by dealing not just with the person who sells the illegal drug but also with the person who buys it. The first section is titled "User Accountability," and the second includes details related to "personal use amounts" of illegal drugs.

This second section of the 1988 act allows the government to punish minor drug offenders without giving the offender a criminal record if the offender is in possession of only a small amount of drugs. This law is designed to have an impact on the user of illicit drugs while simultaneously saving the government the costs of a full-blown criminal investigation. Under this section, the government has the option of imposing only a civil fine on an individual who possesses only a small quantity of an illegal drug. Possession of this small quantity, identified as a "personal use amount," carries a civil fine of up to $10,000.

In determining the amount of the fine in a particular case, the drug offender's income and assets will be considered. This is accomplished through an administrative proceeding rather than a criminal trial, thus reducing the exposure of the offender to the entire criminal justice system and, again, reducing the costs to the offender and the government.

The value of this section is that it allows the government to punish a minor drug offender and gives the drug offender the opportunity to fully redeem him- or herself and have all public record of the proceeding destroyed. If this were a drug offender's first offense, and the offender had paid all fines, could pass a drug test, and had not been convicted of a crime after three years, the offender could request that all proceedings be dismissed. If the proceedings are dismissed, the drug offender could lawfully say he or she had never been prosecuted, either criminally or civilly, for a drug offense.

**OTHER PENALTIES**

The Controlled Substances Act provides penalties for unlawful manufacturing, distribution, and dispensing of controlled substances. The penalties are basically determined by the schedule of the drug or other substance and sometimes are specified by drug name, as in the case of marijuana. As the statute has been amended since its initial passage in 1970, the penalties have been altered by Congress. See Appendix D for a detailed breakdown of federal trafficking penalties in the United States. The charts included in this appendix provide an overview of the penalties for trafficking or unlawful distribution of controlled substances. This is not inclusive of the penalties provided under the CSA.

This dog is learning how to display the active alert with a Teflon pipe as a training tool.

When training your dog to display a passive alert, make sure she learns to approach the object she has identified and then to pinpoint.

## Personal and Setting Factors

The effect of any given drug on a person can be difficult to predict. For example, one evening you may have a glass of wine and not feel impaired. Another time, you may drink the same amount and feel unwell or impaired. Personal and environmental factors exert influence on the effects of drugs (including alcohol) on a person. The ecstasy pill a person takes at a boring party may have a different effect than the one taken at the most fantastic music festival of the year.

By personal factors, we mean the answers one would give to the following questions:

1. Do you feel well?
2. What do you expect from the drug you are taking?
3. Are you physically and mentally healthy?
4. Are you using prescription medication?
5. Have you eaten and drunk enough in the past few days?
6. Did you combine alcohol and drugs, or combine different drugs?
7. Are the clothes you are wearing appropriate for the temperature and other environmental factors of the place you are in? (Are you too hot, too cold, wearing breathable fabric or tight clothing?)

By setting, we mean the environment, or the answers one would give to the following questions.

1. Is the weather cold, hot, or humid?
2. Are you surrounded by noise and many people?
3. Do you have access to drinking water?
4. Is there adequate assistance from front-line medical practitioners (first-aid helpers, nurses, doctors, EMTs) available?
5. Did you use drugs in a familiar environment?

6. Were you alone when you took drugs, or were you with friends, or perhaps with people you barely know?
7. Was the area where you took the drugs crowded or very quiet?

## Dependency

When drugs are used in a manner or amount inconsistent with the medical or social patterns of a culture, it is called drug abuse. While pharmaceuticals that are prescribed and used by patients for medical treatment are legal, the use of these same pharmaceuticals outside the scope of sound medical practice is drug abuse.

Drug dependence or addiction may occur when a person continues to use drugs—legal or illegal—even though the drug use causes them significant problems. Many regard drug abuse as a medical condition or a disorder because drug abusers are to some degree controlled by the drug they use. When a person's drug use becomes the most important activity in his or her life, compulsive drug-seeking behaviors can be observed. Those dependent on drugs will continue to use them despite serious medical and/or social consequences. (We use the term "dependent" here because in some countries the term "addict," with its negative implications, is no longer used.)

Some drugs are more addictive than others. Dependency on a drug can correspond to how quickly one is habituated (how quickly one's body tolerates a certain dose and so needs more and more of the drug to achieve the same, initial effect in subsequent sessions) and whether or not one experiences physical withdrawal symptoms when cutting down or stopping use. The manner in which a drug is taken can also influence how addictive it is. Smoked or injected drugs lead to dependency more quickly than other methods. Of course, how often the drug is used also influences dependency.

When searching large objects like containers and cargo on pallets or airfreight pallets, allow your dog to smell all openings, slots, and hinges.

## Methods of Intake

All drugs must enter the brain before they can exert an effect. Drug users employ a variety of methods to expose their central nervous systems to drugs.

### INHALATION

One can inhale a drug in a variety of ways: smoking a cigarette, joint, or crack cocaine; inhaling vapors of heroin ("chasing the dragon"); sniffing glue; inhaling cannabis smoke with a vaporizer. When it is inhaled, a drug's active substance ends up in the lungs. Many capillaries are found in lung tissue and so the drug is quickly absorbed into the blood, which is pumped through the heart and thence through the body.

Inhalation is the method that provides the fastest highway to the brain: within seven to 10 seconds of inhaling a drug, it reaches the central nervous system. Because effects are felt so quickly, a user can regulate intake efficiently. For example, one stops smoking marijuana when one is adequately "stoned." Drug inhalation damages lung tissue.

## INJECTION

Injection provides another fast track to the brain. For example, one might inject heroin, cocaine, or speed into a vein; or inject ketamine into a muscle. Injecting a drug results in a rapid and intense effect. When a drug is injected into a vein (intravenously), one feels the effect within 15 to 30 seconds; feeling the effects of an intramuscular, or under-the-skin (subcutaneous), injection of drugs may take three to five minutes.

Because injection allows a large dose to enter the bloodstream at once, and nothing of the drug is lost, intravenously injected drugs often result in a "flash": an intense feeling of pleasure that lasts a few seconds, after which a daze effect follows. Other methods of intake cause euphoria but no flash (except for the smoking of crack cocaine or crack). Injection, however, is the riskiest way to take drugs, as injecting directly into muscles or the bloodstream allows the drugs to bypass all three of the body's safety barriers: the skin; the activities and actions of white blood cells, namely macrophages, granulocytes, and natural killer (NK) cells; and the specific defenses B cells and T cells activate to combat particular pathogens.

Many drug users, ashamed of their dependency, stop injecting drugs into their arms because of the telltale scars, and some stop injecting because they simply cannot use the veins in their arms after a while: injecting drugs repeatedly collapses veins. Other veins employed by drug users include those between the fingers or toes, above the eyes, and sometimes those in the legs or abdomen. We have also seen drugs applied to open wounds by inveterate drug users who cannot find usable veins. They wound themselves and keep the wounds constantly open to serve as sites for applying drugs by hand.

## INTRANASAL (SNORTING)

When sniffing a drug—such as cocaine, speed, or ketamine—one feels the effect after only a few minutes. The nasal mucosa has many capillaries that can easily absorb drugs into the bloodstream, the highway to the central nervous system. Regular drug intake using this method can cause inflammation of the nasal mucosa. In extreme cases, this results in chronic rhinitis and/or reduction in the senses of smell and taste.

### ORAL

Swallowing drugs—swallowing an ecstasy pill or drinking alcohol, for example—represents a slow method of drug intake. The acidic environment in the stomach breaks down a certain portion of the swallowed drug. The rest of the drug is absorbed into the bloodstream via the stomach and especially the small intestine. Blood in the small intestine flows to the liver, where drugs are partially broken down. Then, the blood flows to and through the heart and out to the rest of the body, at which point the swallowed drug can reach the brain. This long road to the central nervous system means effects from swallowed drugs can only be felt after 30 to 90 minutes (depending on the contents of the stomach).

Because swallowed drugs are broken down in the stomach and the liver before reaching the brain (the "first-pass effect"), one must take a higher dose of the drug when using this method (as opposed to other methods of intake). The disadvantage of eating or swallowing drugs is that it is difficult to regulate intake. One can easily, and mistakenly, take too much because of the delay between intake and effect.

### CHEWING

This is one of the oldest ways to consume drugs. The drug, usually a plant—like the stimulant khat—is chewed so that the active substance is released from the leaves and is swallowed or absorbed through the mucous membrane.

### RECTAL OR VAGINAL INSERTION

These two methods of intake are not commonly used by recreational users because they are not enjoyable means to a pleasant end. Drugs may be inserted into the vulva, from which point they pass through the bladder wall into the blood. Or, drugs such as MDMA may be inserted into the anus, from which point they are absorbed through the mucous membrane of the rectum into the bloodstream. Blood in the rectum does not flow to the liver before flowing to the heart, so there is no first-pass effect with this method. As a result, the dose for rectal administration is lower than that for oral intake. One can feel the effects of drugs taken in these ways after 15 to 20 minutes.

### ORAL-MUCOSAL ADMINISTRATION

LSD is often taken on a strip of paper held in one's mouth for about half an hour. In this way, the drug is absorbed by the buccal mucosa, and it passes into the bloodstream. Effects from drugs

A full hiding place in a truck.

When your dog searches vehicles and other areas systematically, she will have more of a chance at successfully finding the cache.

taken in this manner can be felt quicker than if taken orally; effects from oral ingestion can be felt within 30 to 60 minutes.

## Secretion

The liver plays an important role in the degradation of drugs. The degradation products (or metabolites) enter the blood and are excreted by the kidneys through urine. Many drugs (for example, cocaine, ecstasy, LSD, speed) are excreted after two to three days and are no longer detectable in blood or urine. GHB, on the other hand, is rapidly degraded in the body and is not detectable in blood or urine after a very short time. Even if one takes a large dose, GHB cannot be found in the blood after eight hours, 12 hours in urine. For this reason, GHB drug tests are only conducted in the case of acute poisoning.

Another exception to the two- to three-day excretion rule, but this time on the other end of the spectrum, is THC (the active ingredient in cannabis). After a single use, traces of cannabis can remain in the blood and urine for up to five days. With regular use (over six months, three times per week), it can take up to three months before all THC is flushed from the body. THC is fat soluble and stored in fatty tissue, from which it is only slowly and in small amounts released into the blood and then excreted. Most drugs are fat soluble and also water soluble, and so only take two to three days to be excreted.

# 8

# The Different Drugs

Psychoactive drugs are divided into three groups: psycholeptics, psychoanaleptics, and psychodysleptics. Some psychoactive drugs fall into more than one category.

Psycholeptics are also called "depressants" or "downers" and slow down the activity of the central nervous system (the brain and spinal cord), reducing a person's alertness, and also slow down functions such as breathing and heart rate. Examples of depressants are alcohol, cannabis, heroin, the prescription drug group of benzodiazepines, and other prescription tranquilizers.

Psychoanaleptics are also called "stimulants" or "uppers" and increase the activity of the central nervous system, making a person more alert and aroused. Stimulants have a temporary energizing effect. Examples of stimulants include caffeine, cannabis, cocaine, ecstasy, methamphetamines such as speed and crystal, and nicotine.

Psychodysleptics, also called "hallucinogens" or "psychedelic drugs," have a "mind-altering," disruptive effect on the activity of the central nervous system. Perception changes, making a person see, hear, smell, or feel things that aren't there. Examples of hallucinogens are cannabis, ecstasy, LSD, and magic mushrooms.

As you may have noticed from the examples of the different drugs listed above, cannabis spans all three categories. Depending on which cannabinoid receptors these chemical compounds activate in the brain and spinal cord, cannabis can produce depressant, stimulant, and hallucinogenic effects in those who use it.

## Cannabis

Marijuana and hashish are produced by the hemp plant (*Cannabis sativa L.*), which grows wild in many parts of the world. "Cannabis" is the genus name of hemp and "sativa" (which means "sowing") is the name of the species. "L." concludes the species' official Latin name because Linnaeus, the plant expert, described this plant in detail in 1743.

The hemp plant likely originates in central Asia and may have been brought to central and northern Europe during the seventh century through southern Russia. Since then, it has spread the world over. Cannabis can grow in tropical, subtropical, and moderate climates, and in dry and poor soil. But the type of soil and climate in which the plant grows determines its characteristics. In cold and moderate areas, the hemp culture will be fibrous with little resin, but in warm areas, the plant produces a lot of resin and less fiber.

The plant's success worldwide has much to do with its practical applications. The male of the species has long been valued as a producer of the fiber needed to make strong rope and hearty paper products. The hemp seed is also nutritious, eaten by people and songbirds everywhere. The oil is high in essential fatty acids and can also be used in industrial applications, such as paint and varnish. A full-grown, year-old plant can reach a height of between 3 and 16 feet (1 and 5 m), depending on the soil and climate, which explains why hemp is used as a windbreak in many areas.

In the hairs on the bracts of the flowers, the female plant produces a sticky, light-brown substance called hemp resin. This resin is the substance that affects such a miraculous change on the human spirit. In many countries where the plant is cultivated, people separate the resin from the rest of the plant because the resin is the most effective ingredient. When taken as a drug, the resin is called hashish, while the dried tops and leaves of the plant are generally known as marijuana.

Cannabis is normally smoked, but it is sometimes incorporated into foods, for example, in "space cake," or dissolved in boiling water or warm milk. The plant has different psychoactive agents, also known as cannabinoids. The main one is tetra-hydrocannabinol (THC); the more THC in the marijuana or hashish, the stronger its effect on the human body.

### HISTORY

An ancient Chinese text, the *Lu Shi*, suggests that legendary Emperor Shen-Nung (2500 BCE) taught the Chinese people to cultivate hemp for its fiber. It is believed that the Chinese people of that time knew about cannabis and the effects that came with its ingestion, particularly in terms of the plant's curative abilities and the accompanying euphoria. As well, one can read of the use of cannabis as a stimulant in the Arabic translations of the *Materia Medica* by Greek physician, pharmacologist, and botantist Dioscorides, and *De Simplicium Medica: Mentorum Temperamentis ac Facultatibus Liber VII* by Greco-Roman physician Galen. These Greek and Roman texts influenced Arabic cultures to experiment with the use of cannabis. In religious ceremonies in India, cannabis was included in a "divine" drink. In ancient Roman times, guests were offered hemp cookies after a meal.

Cannabis has been used by humans in different ways: as medicine, raw material for rope and bags and, of course, a drug because of its psychoactive properties. The import and export of cannabis has been illegal in the Netherlands since 1928. The United States also banned cannabis in 1937 because of the belief that its use led to murder and madness. During World War II (circa 1942), however, the United States allowed the cultivation of cannabis, but that nation banned it again when the war was over.

## MARIJUANA

Marijuana is a mind-altering (psychoactive) drug. It is a dry, shredded green/brown mix of flowers, stems, seeds, and leaves from *Cannabis sativa L*. The mixture resembles tobacco but is made more or less fine by the inclusion of the flower tops of the female plant among top leaves and fragments of leaves. Marijuana is also called *cannabis* (Australia, Canada, England, United States), *banga* (Sanskrit), *bhang* (India), *dagga* or *boom* (South Africa), *maconha* (Brasil), *momea* (Tibet), *hsien ma tze* (China), and *kiff* (Morocco). The percentage of THC in marijuana varies depending on the plant's origin, species, and subspecies.

Marijuana is usually smoked as a cigarette (called a joint) or in a pipe or bong. It is also smoked in blunts, cigars that have been emptied of tobacco and refilled with marijuana, sometimes in combination with another drug. Marijuana is also mixed with food or brewed as a tea. Common street names include Aunt Mary, BC bud, blunts, boom, chronic, dope, gangster, ganja, grass, hash, herb, hydro, Indo, joint, kif, Mary Jane, mota, Nederweed, pot, reefer, sinsemilla, skunk, smoke, weed, and yerba.

Common varieties of marijuana include the following:

- Haze: a type with a strong, spicy flavor and aroma; very high in THC; varieties include Silver Haze, Purple Haze, Lemon Haze, Amnesia Haze, Cheese, and Buddha Haze.
- K2: a well-known cannabis species, popular in Europe, and mainly used for mass production.

Marijuana.

- Northern Lights: the strongest weed species, with THC levels up to 39 percent.
- Power Plant: a popular species, mainly obtained by taking cuttings.
- Skunk or Nederweed (Dutch weed): a marijuana variety developed in the Netherlands in the 1970s.
- Thai or Thai Stick: a tropical weed with a relatively low THC content. The original Thai Stick was popular during the late 1960s and 1970s. It consisted of premium buds of seedless marijuana that were skewered on stems. Several rows of fiber found in the stalk of the marijuana plant were then used to tie the marijuana to the stem to keep it in place. Thai Stick bud may also be tied around bamboo sticks with a piece of string known as a "Rasta hair." The Thai weed is often so sticky, however, that it easily adheres to the pole against which it is grown, without need for thread.
- White Widow: this was the first of the THC-rich white varieties.

**HASHISH**

Hashish consists of the THC-rich resinous material the cannabis plant produces, which is collected, dried, and then compressed into a variety of forms, such as balls, cakes, or cookie-like sheets. Pieces are then broken off and placed in pipes, or mixed with tobacco and placed in pipes or cigarettes, and then smoked.

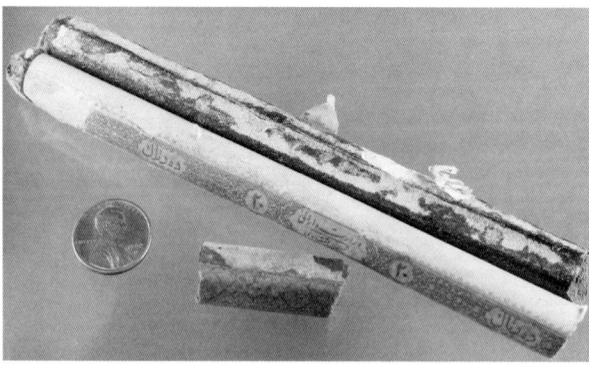

Thai Stick marijuana.

The areas that produce the most hashish are the Middle East, North Africa, Pakistan, and Afghanistan. The higher the percentage of resin, the denser the hashish. Hashish from Nepal and India is characterized by its density, while the Turkish "ezrar" is a loose powder. The resin from the plant was traditionally gathered by naked or leather-clad people, who walked through the hemp field. The resin would stick to their bodies or leather clothing. After their walk through the fields, other people were employed to scrape the resin off their clothes or bodies.

The percentage of THC in hashish, of course, varies. During preservation of this drug, levels of THC slowly reduce. When hashish becomes damp or moldy, THC decays into products of oxidation and so THC levels in the substance reduce quickly.

Common varieties of hashish include the following:

- Afghan: pure, dark brown; popular in the Netherlands in the 1970s and 1980s.
- Casablanca: a very strong hash species from Morocco, also produced in the Netherlands.
- Charas: hand-rolled hash from India, Nepal, and Pakistan. The difference between Charas and other hashish is that most hashish is made from a dead weed plant and Charas is made from a live one.
- Ice-O-Lator: a very pure, oily, light-colored hash created from frozen weed or cut waste mixed together for a few minutes in a bucket of cold water and ice. When chilled, the plant is placed in a coarse-sieve bag, which is inside a fine-sieve bag. The resin crystals fall through the coarse sieve bag, leaving only the purest resin crystals behind on the fine sieve. This sort of hashish is also called Bubble Hash or Ice Hash, but it is usually simply called Ice.
- Lebanon: a potent, yellowish product that was also very popular in western Europe in the 1970s, but with such a superior quality that it became unavailable for export in the 1980s—the people of the wealthy Gulf states prefer this hashish and kept the stocks for themselves.

- Maroc: divided into Zero, Zero Zero, Primera, Ketama, Sputnik, and many other species.
- Nepal: a very strong, "black" hashish. Previously hand-rolled, nowadays often sieved. This "pollen" or "dry sieve" is low quality and dry, but the smoke is quite strong, almost psychedelic. It is smooth to smoke, not harsh, but earthy and dusty. Many people, however, say Nepal "pricks" the throat.
- Skuff: cutting waste, often from the interior part of the plant, is frozen and then the THC crystals are sifted through the sieving method used for Ice, as described above.

**HASHISH OIL**

Hashish oil (hash oil, liquid hash, cannabis oil) is produced by extracting the THC from the plant material with a solvent that has a low boiling point (for example, butane, ether, or alcohol). The color and odor of the extract varies, depending on the solvent used. A drop or two of hash oil on a cigarette has the same effect as a single marijuana joint. Hash oil is so strong that it appears on the Netherlands's List 1 (hard drugs).

**THC EXTRACTIONS**

A THC extraction or marijuana concentrate is a highly potent THC mass that is most similar in appearance to either honey or butter, which is why it is sometimes referred to as "honey oil" or

Hashish.

"budder." These concentrates contain extraordinarily high THC levels that could range from 40 to 80 percent. One dangerous method used to extract THC involves highly flammable butane.

THC extractions can have up to four times the amount of THC in high-grade marijuana, whose THC levels are normally around 20 percent. The extractions are known as 710 (the word "OIL" flipped and spelled in numerals, backward), black glass, butane hash oil, butane honey oil (BHO), dabs, ear wax, errl, shatter, or wax.

Because extractions are so potent, the effects upon users may be more psychologically and physically intense than those resulting from marijuana use. People may consume extractions by infusing

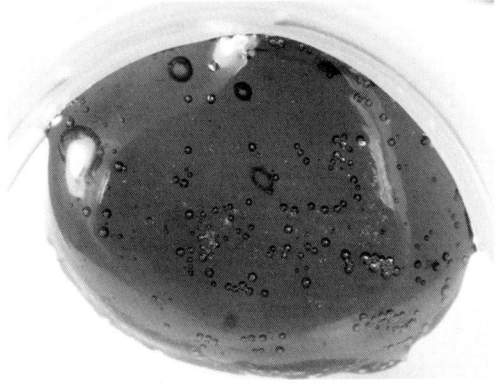

Butane hash oil.

THC extraction.

foods or drinks with them, but smoking remains the most popular form of ingestion. People use water or oil pipes, electronic cigarettes (also known as e-cigarettes), and vaporizers. The user takes a small amount of the extract, a "dab," then heats the substance using the vaporizer, which produces vapors that the user then breathes in, giving the user an instant "high." Using an e-cigarette/vaporizer to ingest marijuana extracts is commonly referred to as "dabbing" or "vaping."

## SYNTHETIC CANNABINOIDS

A whole range of drugs called synthetic cannabinoids have been created to mimic the effects of THC. Synthetic cannabinoids are often called "spice" and are usually sold in "herbal" smoking mixtures. Other street names for these drugs include black magic, blaze, crazy clown, demon, dream, fire, genie, K2, Mr. Nice Guy, ninja, paradise, redx dawn, sence, serenity, skunk, smoke, Yucatan, and zohai.

Most synthetic cannabinoids are manufactured in Asia, and their production is not held accountable to manufacturing requirements or quality-control standards. These chemical compounds are first purchased in bulk powder form, and then they are dissolved in solvents, such as acetone, before being sold to the user. The user will then either apply the dissolved drug to tobacco and smoke it, or put it in the "juice" designed for an e-cigarette and "smoke" it that way. Dealers in these synthetic drugs may also spray the dissolved drug onto dry plant materials before selling it (often called "potpourri" or "herbal incense") to the user.

One can never be sure what is in a smoking mixture, and sometimes these mixtures have been found not to contain any synthetic cannabinoids. The problem here is that the user cannot be sure what he or she is smoking, and how dangerous the substances may be. Overdose deaths—including death by heart attack—have been attributed to the abuse of synthetic cannabinoids. As well, users smoking synthetic cannabinoids have been known to suffer acute kidney injury, which requires hospitalization and dialysis.

Synthetic cannabinoids.

## THE MODES OF ADMINISTRATION

### SMOKE

Usually hashish is smoked as a joint, which is a cigarette containing tobacco and some crumbled weed or hashish. You can also smoke it "pure" (i.e., without tobacco) or use a hash pipe. Sometimes a water pipe is used. A water pipe (also called a "bong") is a cooling system. The weed is burned, and the smoke enters the water in the pipe. In the water, the smoke cools so the user inhales cool smoke, rather than the hot smoke inhaled by those smoking joints or hash pipes. Hash oil is usually dripped onto cigarette paper to which tobacco is added. It is also sometimes mixed directly with tobacco before being smoked.

### EVAPORATION (VAPORIZING)

When placed in a vaporizer, hashish or marijuana is not burned but heated at a temperature between 356 and 392°F (180 and 200°C). Only the active substances are released and inhaled by the user. When smoked, marijuana in its various forms introduces tar and carbon monoxide to the user's body—not so when a vaporizer is used.

### IN FOOD

Cannabis can be eaten, for example, in a space cake or hashish bonbon. A space cake is a cake containing hashish or marijuana. During preparation of such baked items, a bit of hashish or marijuana is added to melting butter, which, when introduced to the mixture, allows the drug to be evenly distributed throughout the batter. The effect of eating cannabis is generally much more intense than the effect of smoking cannabis, but the effects take longer to be felt (at least 45 minutes from the moment of ingestion). If users do not know about this delay and think the cake "didn't work" and thus eat more, they may easily ingest too much. In addition, users never know how strong a space cake is. Inexperienced users and tourists in the Netherlands often go wrong when eating space cake.

**IN DRINK**
Hashish and marijuana can be consumed as a "tea," steeped in a tea ball. Some prefer to steep the drug in warm milk, however, because THC dissolves quicker in fat than in water. The risks to drinking marijuana tea are the same as those related to eating marijuana: it takes at least 45 minutes to 1.5 hours before effects are felt. Again, users can take in too much quite easily.

**DOSAGES**
Hashish or marijuana strengths vary considerably, and therefore it is difficult to estimate dosages. The cannabis plant contains more than 85 substances, the cannabinoids. The most famous of these is tetrahydrocannabinol (THC), responsible for the psychoactive effects, by which you get high and cheerful. Cannabidiol (CBD) is another major cannabinoid and induces a calm, anti-anxiety, "stoned" feeling in users. If there is a lot of THC in the marijuana, and less CBD, a user will likely experience feelings of fear and unease. The THC levels in Dutch hashish and marijuana are much higher nowadays than that in hashish and marijuana produced elsewhere.

**EFFECTS**
Hashish and marijuana usually give a relaxing, pleasant feeling to users. But they can also cause restless or anxious behavior. Below are the known effects of cannabis products, organized according to mental and physical effects.

### MENTAL EFFECTS

- Relaxation, reduced stress levels
- More creative, philosophical thinking: ideas come easily to mind
- Enhanced sensory perception: music sounds intense, food tastes better, touches feel more welcome
- "Kick laugh," or uncontrollable laughter
- Confusion
- Anxiety or paranoia
- Panic attacks (in sensitive users of very high [often oral] doses)

### PHYSICAL EFFECTS

- Increased appetite (THC mimics the action of a neurological chemical called anandamide. The human brain, especially in the hunger center, has receptors that can bind to anandamide. Normally, when one hasn't eaten for a while, anandamide is released. It then binds to the receptors, which causes one to feel hungry. THC can bind to those same receptors, making users hungry.)
- General lethargy
- Fatigue
- Red eyes
- Dry mouth
- Relaxation of facial muscles
- Nausea (especially in combination with alcohol)
- Cough, asthma attack, respiratory irritation
- Reduced short-term memory
- Increased heart rate, agitation, feelings of tension
- Lowered blood pressure
- Headache

**SHORT-TERM RISKS**

In the short term, the biggest risk in using cannabis is becoming sick or faint (especially when cannabis is combined with alcohol). When a user consumes a high dose of cannabis (especially in food), he or she risks so-called "cannabis psychosis," in which the user is suddenly totally confused and also can be very afraid and experience hallucinations. These effects almost always disappear after the cannabis is spent. Because THC does not influence the areas of the brain where heart rate and breathing are controlled, users cannot die from an overdose of cannabis.

**LONG-TERM RISKS**

Marijuana smoke contains three times more tar and five times more carbon monoxide than tobacco smoke; the smoke produced during combustion of cannabis is more harmful than the smoke of tobacco. Smoking a joint is roughly equivalent to smoking four regular cigarettes. Passive smoking, or secondhand smoke, is also harmful; it is sometimes said that spending 40 hours with someone who chain-smokes cigarettes is comparable to smoking five joints. Intense cannabis use increases the risk of chronic bronchitis and cough, and the combination of tobacco and cannabis (in a joint) overtaxes the lungs. Some studies suggest that heavy users of cannabis increase their risks of contracting cancer of the mouth, throat, esophagus, and lungs. Cannabis also temporarily affects brain function. However, according to current research, cannabis has no lasting impact on brain function.

**ADDICTION AND COMBINATIONS WITH OTHER DRUGS**

The risk of psychological dependence on cannabis increases with prolonged and extensive use. The potential for physical dependence is less, although long-term users who stop may well suffer from withdrawal symptoms. The user who tries to quit may feel irritable and restless and be unable to sleep well. The user trying to quit may also suffer from chills, headaches, shaking, and sweating.

The withdrawal symptoms are mild compared to those associated with alcohol or heroin.

Heavy users sometimes develop tolerance to the drugs they take; they need more and more to feel the desired effects. An accelerated heart rate can accompany upping dosages to get the desired effects.

Combining cannabis and alcohol increases the risk of nausea and vomiting. Most users don't drink a lot of alcohol. Some users, however, combine cannabis and ecstasy, because the latter can reinforce the intoxicating effects of hash or marijuana.

If a cannabis user starts smoking dope during a mushroom trip, he or she may feel anxious or confused.

**DETECTABILITY**

Cannabis can be detected in the user's urine for one to five days (if use is occasional) or two to three months (if use is chronic). In contrast with the dissolution time of most other drugs discussed in this book, the degradation of cannabis in the human body is extremely slow. THC is stored in the fatty tissues and is not directly broken down by the liver; ecstasy, speed, and cocaine are all broken down by the liver. THC is first deposited by the bloodstream into fatty tissue, and later it slowly releases from the adipose tissue back into the bloodstream. Even though THC can remain in the body for a long time, users will not feel the effects of THC for that length of time. The effects of cannabinoids can only be felt for four to six hours after use.

## Hallucinogens

Hallucinogens, also called "psychodysleptics" or "psychedelic drugs," alter brain chemicals and create intense psychological effects, including extreme emotional reactions, hallucinations, and other sensory and perception distortions. Hallucinogens are found in plants and fungi or are synthetically produced, and they are among the oldest known group of drugs used for the purpose of altering perception and mood. There are many different types

**TINY TRACES**

The Vienna police once arrested a young man who was suspected of drug trafficking. He had traveled to Damascus, and the police knew he had returned with hashish, but the evidence was lacking. Police found nothing in his house, and the young man denied the allegations. An emergency call brought the drug-detector dog to the scene, and a search began for the hidden drugs. Without much hesitation, the dog indicated a suitcase under the bed. The suitcase was empty, no trace of hashish. Even so, the dog could not be redirected from the suitcase, so officers began to inspect it in greater detail. Still, they could find no drugs inside. The suspect denied even having taken a suitcase to Damascus, and he claimed that the suitcase belonged to his sister. However, officers discovered a small barcode sticker on the suitcase that proved it had indeed gone to Damascus, and the sister confirmed that her brother had taken the suitcase on his trip. The case was confiscated. In parallel experiments, gas chromatographic investigations revealed that drugs had been transported in the suitcase. The search dog was right and had been able to detect the tiniest traces of hashish with his formidable sense of smell.

---

of hallucinogens, and while some are more "natural" and may possibly be less harmful than others, they all may cause dangerous side effects in users, especially frequent users.

The group of hallucinogenic drugs that occur in nature and, in many cases, have been used for centuries by those hoping to experience religious or mystical epiphanies, include psilocybin, or magic mushrooms, and peyote, a spineless cactus with small protrusions called "buttons" that are used for psychoactive hallucinogenic purposes. Peyote grows in very few places, and its principal compound is mescaline, an amphetamine that causes hallucinogenic effects. Another natural hallucinogen is *Salvia divinorum*, a type of sage plant native to Mexico. The Mazatec people of southern Mexico once used it in their religious rituals.

Other hallucinogenic drugs are created in a lab instead of found in nature. Some of these substances were originally made for medicinal purposes, while others were always meant to be illegal drugs. Lysergic acid diethylamide (LSD), for example, was first synthesized in 1938 to treat everything from schizophrenia to sexual perversions, until the 1970s when it was recognized that the drug causes extreme side effects that make it unsuitable for medicinal use. Another lab-created hallucinogen, phencyclidine (PCP), was synthesized in 1926 as an anesthetic for animals. And 3,4-methylenedioxymethamphetamine (MDMA or ecstasy) is similar to both the stimulant amphetamine and the hallucinogen mescaline. It was synthesized in 1912 and later used in psychotherapy and marriage counseling until it was found to be dangerous.

## MAGIC MUSHROOMS

When people take magic mushrooms (also called fungus delight, magic, mush, mushrooms, and shrooms), they see, hear, or feel things that are not really there. Users may also experience other effects such as anxiety, nausea, and muscle twitches.

Magic mushrooms contain the substances psilocybin and/or psilocin. Psilocin is the most active substance and is responsible for the hallucinogenic ("trip") effect. Human metabolism converts psilocybin into psilocin. Different types of mushrooms contain different amounts of active substance. Some types of mushrooms, including Copelandia, Psilocybe, and Stropharia, are found worldwide. The best known are *Psilocybe cubensis* (sometimes called Mexican magic mushrooms), *Copelandia cyanescens* (termed the "Hawaiian"), and *Psilocybe semilanceta* (pointy bald heads, liberty caps). Mushrooms with psilocybin grow in many parts of Europe in the wild (bald heads especially).

*Psilocybe tampanensis* (philosopher's stone, tubers trip) are a type of sclerotium, a kind of truffle that grows underground and contains psilocybin and psilocin and thus has the same effects as magic mushrooms.

Psilocybin is also synthetically, and illegally, produced in labs and sold either as a white powder, or in tablets and capsules.

*Psilocybe cubensis*—magic mushrooms.

*Sclerotia tampanensis*—magic mushrooms.

## HISTORY

People have used psychedelic mushrooms for thousands of years. During excavations in Mexico and Guatemala, thousand-year-old statuettes of mushrooms were found. In the 16th century, the Spanish conquered Mexico and banned what they perceived to be the "devilish" use of magic mushrooms. American ethnomycologist R. Gordon Watson visited Huautla de Jimenez, Oaxaca, in 1955, where he met Maria Sabina, a shaman, who used psilocybin in her practice. Watson brought spores to Europe, where it was cultivated by Swiss chemist Albert Hofmann in 1958.

In 1976, a guide on how to grow mushrooms, *Psilocybin: Magic Mushroom Grower's Guide*, was published in the United States. The book was a huge success. The first "smart" shop in the Netherlands to sell magic mushrooms did so in 1993. However, the sale of magic mushrooms was banned by that country in 2008, following several incidents in Amsterdam involving the use of mushrooms by foreign tourists between 2006 and 2008.

### THE MODES OF ADMINISTRATION

Magic mushrooms may be sold as either dried, whole mushrooms or as a brown powder. They are generally eaten raw or cooked, although smoking dried or powdered mushrooms is also possible. Because they have a nasty taste, some users like to prepare a tea or soup, or mix the powder with fruit juice—consuming the mushrooms in a tea ensures easy absorption of the active substances because components of the fungal matter are released into the boiling water, and residual psilocybin accumulates. When slowly chewed, the oral mucosa absorbs part of the active substance in magic mushrooms. Powdered magic mushrooms can also be snorted.

### DOSAGES

Potency can vary greatly. One mushroom may have very different psilocybin content compared to another. In most cases, the dose for a good (strong) trip is 15 to 30 grams of fresh *Psilocybe cubensis*, which corresponds to 1.5 to 3 grams of dried, or 10 to 30 milligrams of psilocybin (0.6–1 percent psilocybin per gram of dried mushrooms). The dosage for a normal trip using sclerotia (truffles) is around 5 to 9 grams, for a strong trip, between 10 and 15 grams. Most users wait for a few weeks or months after taking mushrooms before planning their next trip. Thus, the experience remains special.

### EFFECTS

The effects of mushrooms are unpredictable, and results may vary from one person to another. On average, the first effects are felt about 20 to 40 minutes after ingestion. Depending on dose and the user's stomach contents, initial effects may not be felt for up to an hour. Between 1 and 1.5 hours after consumption, the peak phase begins and lasts between three and four hours. The average trip takes four to six hours, with effects coming in gradually diminishing waves. Although the change in sensory perception appeals most to the imagination, hallucinogens like magic mushrooms have other important effects, similar to those of LSD.

MENTAL EFFECTS

Emotions and senses may be heightened, and users may feel happy and creative. They may laugh or giggle a lot and experience a sense of mental and emotional clarity. Magic mushrooms can also cause hallucinations and affect the brain in the following ways:

- Distorting users' sense of reality (they see and hear things that are not there)
- Mixing up the senses (users believe they can see music or hear colors)
- Altering users' sense of time

Other negative mental effects of taking psilocybin include the following:

- Changes in mood
- Lightheadedness and loss of coordination
- Anxiety and panic attacks
- Confusion and disorientation
- Fear or paranoia

PHYSICAL EFFECTS

- Numbness, particularly in the face
- Increased heart rate and higher blood pressure than normal
- Dry mouth, sometimes leading to nausea and vomiting
- Muscle weakness and twitching, or convulsions
- Exaggerated reflexes
- Sweating and high body temperature, often followed by chills and shivering
- Loss of urinary control

SHORT-TERM RISKS

The main physical risk to using magic mushrooms is ingesting the wrong mushroom if, for example, a person decides to go into nature and pick them him or herself. There are all kinds of poisonous mushrooms that look very similar to psilocybin-containing mushrooms. Other short-term risks include nausea and vomiting, psychosis, and what is called a "bad trip," wherein the user believes he or she is being tormented by external forces or has a panic attack.

*LONG-TERM RISKS*

Little is known about the long-term consequences of using magic mushrooms. However, their use is linked to psychosis, or losing contact with reality, which can arise even if one has only used magic mushrooms a few times. Common symptoms of this include the following:

- Changes in thinking patterns (disconnected thoughts)
- Delusions (false beliefs that have no basis in fact)
- Hallucinations
- Changes in mood
- Disorganized behavior
- Problems seeing. Some users have trouble with their vision even after the drug should have worn off. These people may see variations in color, contrast, movement, shape, and so on, that are not normal.

*ADDICTION AND COMBINATIONS WITH OTHER DRUGS*

Physical dependence on psilocybin does not occur. The body becomes accustomed to the effects of magic mushrooms quickly, generally over the course of one or two sessions. This tolerance is, however, reduced after a few days. Because of the major effects that magic mushrooms impart, the chance of developing a psychological dependence on this drug is slim. Most users take magic mushrooms only once or a few times per year.

That said, consuming magic mushrooms with other drugs or with alcohol may increase the risk of experiencing serious negative health effects.

If one uses cannabis while on mushrooms, for example, the cannabis could prolong and exacerbate the mushroom trip and may make that trip unpredictable, which certainly isn't always a pleasant experience. Combining magic mushrooms with other drugs like cocaine, ecstasy, GHB, or speed, increases the user's chances of becoming anxious or panicky.

*DETECTABILITY*

Psilocin and psilocybin are fast-acting, unstable substances that enter the bloodstream in low doses. Magic mushrooms are detectable in the human body from 24 to 48 hours after ingestion, depending on the method of analysis.

## PEYOTE

Peyote is a small, spineless cactus. The top of the peyote cactus is referred to as the crown and consists of disc-shaped buttons that contain the active ingredient, the hallucinogen mescaline. Common street names for this drug are buttons, cactus, mesc, and peyoto.

*HISTORY*

Peyote has been used by indigenous peoples in northern Mexico and the southwestern United States as a part of their religious rites for thousands of years. Mescaline can be extracted from peyote or produced synthetically.

Peyote.

## THE MODES OF ADMINISTRATION
The fresh or dried buttons are chewed or soaked in water to produce an intoxicating liquid. Peyote buttons may also be ground into a powder that can be placed inside capsules to be swallowed, or it can be smoked with cannabis or tobacco.

## EFFECTS
Users may experience euphoria, which is sometimes followed by feelings of anxiety. Users of peyote and mescaline experience the same effects as those imparted by other hallucinogens like LSD, or magic mushrooms (psilocybin).

## MENTAL EFFECTS
The effects of using peyote include varying degrees of altered perception of space and time, altered perception of body image, hallucinations, and illusions.

## PHYSICAL EFFECTS
Following the consumption of peyote and mescaline, users may experience the following effects:

- Intense nausea
- Vomiting
- Dilation of the pupils
- Increased heart rate
- Increased blood pressure
- Rise in body temperature, causing heavy perspiration
- Headaches
- Muscle weakness
- Impaired motor coordination

## ADDICTION AND COMBINATIONS WITH OTHER DRUGS
Tolerance to peyote or mescaline typically develops rapidly with repeated daily use, generally over the course of three to six days. Once a user has tolerance to this drug, he or she must abstain from taking hallucinogens, including those that have cross-tolerance with peyote (such as LSD and psilocybin), for several days before

one can restore the desired sensitivity to the hallucinogenic effects. As of this writing, no physical or psychological dependence on peyote or the natural chemical mescaline it contains has been reported.

*DETECTABILITY*

Determining how long peyote is detectable in the body depends on many variables, including the individual's age, body mass, health, hydration, level of physical activity, metabolism, and so on, making it almost impossible to determine the general window within which peyote will show up on a drug test. The following is an estimated range of detection windows during which peyote can be detected by various testing methods. Peyote can be detected in the urine for two to three days, and some data indicates that peyote can be detected in the blood for up to 24 hours. A saliva test can detect peyote one to 10 days from ingestion. Finally, peyote, like many other drugs, can be detected by means of a hair-follicle drug test for up to 90 days.

**LSD**

LSD (lysergic acid diethylamide) belongs to the group of hallucinogens and consciousness-altering substances. It is a semichemical stripping agent that originates from a fungus. Often a drop of this product is applied to a piece of paper that is then

LSD in capsule and powder form.

ingested (blotter, paper trip) or processed in small pills (microdots). One can also obtain LSD in liquid form. Some street names for LSD include acid, blotter acid, dots, mellow yellow, and window pane. LSD is a potent hallucinogen; you only need to take a small amount of it to feel something. LSD is dosed in micrograms (whereas many other hallucinogens are dosed in milligrams).

*HISTORY*

LSD is a semi-synthetic compound made from ergot, a toxic substance. Ergot is produced by the fungus ergot (*Claviceps purpurea*), which grows on rye and other grasses. In the Middle Ages, regular outbreaks of ergotism (long-term ergot poisoning) wreaked havoc on human populations, especially the poor. This gangrenous poisoning was also known as "holy fire" or "Saint Anthony's fire," for monks of the Order of St. Anthony, who were particularly successful at treating the ailment. Those struck down by ergotism experienced intense hallucinations. Ergotism also constricts the small blood vessels, denying oxygenated blood to extremities. As a result, those affected often lost circulation in their fingers and toes, which became gangrenous and dropped off.

Toward the end of the Middle Ages, ergot gained a medical application when midwives began using it to induce childbirth and abortions, and to stop maternal bleeding after childbirth. Ergot alkaloids cause vasoconstriction and so induce strong uterine contractions.

In the early 20th century, chemists became interested in ergot and isolated several compounds from it. In 1918, the substance ergotamine was found and used for the treatment of migraines. It helps with the pain because the substance contracts the superficial blood vessels in the brain. In the 1930s, lysergic acid was discovered in ergot, which led to the discovery of LSD-25 or the "trip" substance LSD. In 1938, LSD was first created in a lab, and in 1943, the Swiss chemist Albert Hofmann accidentally discovered its psychoactive effects. While studying the drug on April 19, 1943, Hofmann took 250 micrograms. Shortly afterward he decided to pedal home on his bicycle and found himself "transported to other worlds," and thus he became the first person known to take LSD.[1] This day has become known as Bicycle Day.

In the 1950s, LSD was used to treat depression, and the Central Intelligence Agency in the United States began using it in mind-control experiments. It gained popularity as a recreational drug in the 1960s when—due to its ability to produce changes in consciousness, mood, perception, and thought—it became part of the psychedelic cultural movement. LSD became a "poster" drug in the worldwide spread of hippie culture. Perhaps the most outspoken proponent of the psychedelic revolution was well-known American psychologist Timothy Leary. The mainstream character of LSD has since disappeared, but in certain scenes it is still very popular.

### THE MODES OF ADMINISTRATION

The manner in which users take LSD depends on the form, but it is usually administered orally. When LSD is dripped on a paper strip or blotter, the user places the paper on or under the tongue to receive a portion of the active substance via the oral mucosa; alternatively, the user eats the strip of paper. A user may also swallow LSD in capsule or pill form. The liquid form of this drug allows the user to drip it directly into the mouth or mix it with water and drink. Also the user can drip one or a few drops on his or her hand and lick that. Liquid LSD is also sometimes dripped on sugar cubes, which are then consumed. Absorption through the skin is only possible with very strong concentrations, so holding an LSD-affected blotter in your hand will not lead to an LSD trip.

### DOSAGES

As LSD is a highly potent drug, the user needs very little to feel its effects. The first effects are noticed after consuming a dose of 20 micrograms, but these effects are not considered by users to be a real "trip." To experience a normal to strong trip, one is required to take between 50 and 150 micrograms. This is normally the amount on a paper trip, or blotter. Microdots are often stronger, between 100 and 250 micrograms. Remember that one microgram is one millionth of a gram; 1000 micrograms is 1 milligram (mg). It makes no sense to use LSD two days in a row, because after one dose, your body immediately develops a tolerance to it. One must wait at least three or four days before taking a subsequent dose of LSD. Most users wait a few weeks or months after taking LSD before they plan their next trip.

*EFFECTS*

Generally speaking, the action of LSD is very similar to that of other hallucinogens like magic mushrooms and peyote. The effects are felt 20 minutes to one hour after ingestion. The intensity of the trip increases over the course of the first two hours after ingestion. The peak phase, during which the psychedelic effects are the strongest, lasts three to six hours. This is followed by a "coming down" phase, which lasts between three and five hours. Depending on the dose, a complete LSD trip can take six to 12 hours. LSD causes an altered state of consciousness and changes in sensory perception and thought processes.

MENTAL EFFECTS

- Changes in sensory perception. The centers in the brain involved in processing sensory input (hearing, sight, smell, taste, and touch) are disrupted. The user becomes hypersensitive to sensory impressions.
- Changes in mood. Positive and negative feelings may alternate.
- Changes in perception of time. One's sense of space and time changes; time sometimes seems to stand still.
- Changes in thought processes. During a trip, thinking processes become more associative, and unusual cross-connections and linkages are made. This can lead not only to surprising insights but also to nearly psychotic ideas.

PHYSICAL EFFECTS
- Dilated pupils
- Mild increase in heart rate and blood pressure increase
- Sweating
- Dizziness
- Sometimes nausea

SHORT-TERM RISKS
- Nausea and vomiting.
- Psychosis. In people who are predisposed, LSD can be a trigger and start or worsen a psychosis. A combination of genetics and environment influence whether or not one is predisposed to suffering from psychosis. Stress, for example, has been shown to be an important factor in increasing the chances of experiencing psychosis in persons with a genetic predisposition. Most often big life changes (like starting university or changing jobs) or serious events (like having surgery or a death in the family) trigger the first symptoms of psychosis.
- A bad trip. The greatest danger of LSD lies in not judging situations properly while high. Inexperienced users, especially, can become fearful and suspicious. Users can also get a sense of megalomania that can lead to dangerous behavior. As well, users can start to worry and become completely caught up in negative thoughts.

LONG-TERM RISKS

Little is known about the long-term consequences of using LSD. We do know that users may experience what has been called a "flashback," wherein they will suddenly become caught up in an experience from a previous trip. The use of cannabis, fatigue, or situations that are similar to those in which one previously took LSD can cause these flashbacks.

ADDICTION AND COMBINATIONS WITH OTHER DRUGS

Psychological dependence on a drug means one longs for the drug and cannot really feel good without it. The likelihood of psychological dependence on LSD is slim, and most users take it only a few times in their lives or just a few times a year. Physical dependence also does not occur because the body quickly becomes accustomed to LSD and then over the course of a few days loses that tolerance.

*DETECTABILITY*

LSD is detectable in the urine up to 48 hours after ingestion.

**ECSTASY/MDMA**

Ecstasy is a derivative of methamphetamine and the active ingredient is 3,4-methylenedioxymethamphetamine, abbreviated to MDMA. Common street names are Adam, beans, clarity, disco biscuit, E, eve, go, hug drug, lover's speed, peacep, STP, X, and XTC. Besides its stimulatory effect, MDMA also has a mind-altering effect, expressed in feelings of love and empathy, with much need for contact with others. MDMA usually comes in pills, powders, and crystals.

*HISTORY*

MDMA was first synthesized in 1912 by Merck Pharmaceuticals, a side product in the synthesis of a new blood-coagulation-promoting agent created to replace hydrastinine, whose parent plant was becoming rare and expensive. Merck started looking for alternatives and eventually settled on using the substance 3-methylhydrastinine as a substitute for hydrastinine, expecting it would have the same efficacy. In creating 3-methylhydrastinine, MDMA emerged as an intermediate substance, but at first no one was interested in it.

It was not until 1927 that Dr. Max Oberlin at Merck showed interest in the pharmacological properties of MDMA. For economic reasons, however, Oberlin's study was stopped and shut down for several decades. In the 1950s, American and German armies tested various psychoactive substances, including MDMA, and a laboratory notebook from 1952 describes how MDMA killed six flies after 30 minutes of being exposed to the drug. In 1959, Dr. Wolfgang Fruhstorfer was researching psychostimulants, and one of the substances with which he worked, H671, was found to be MDMA. The first scientific article on MDMA was published in 1960, written in Polish and virtually unknown. It describes, among other things, the substance's synthesis.

In the late 1960s, MDMA was "rediscovered" by chemist Alexander Shulgin, a scientist who made all kinds of psychoactive substances in his own laboratory and then tested them on himself and a group of friends. He experimented with MDMA and was surprised by the warm and communication-enhancing effects of the drug. He distributed it among friends who were psychotherapists. They were enthusiastic about this new medium because it made their patients more open and took away emotional inhibitions. In these circles, MDMA was used chiefly to help people get in touch with their deeper "selves." MDMA then became popular among those interested in spiritual matters and yoga. The global spread of MDMA, however, began in the 1980s, when the drug gained the street name "ecstasy" or "XTC." The first underground house parties to champion the drug began in about 1987, and from 1990 the dance scene began to use the drug. A small number of clandestine

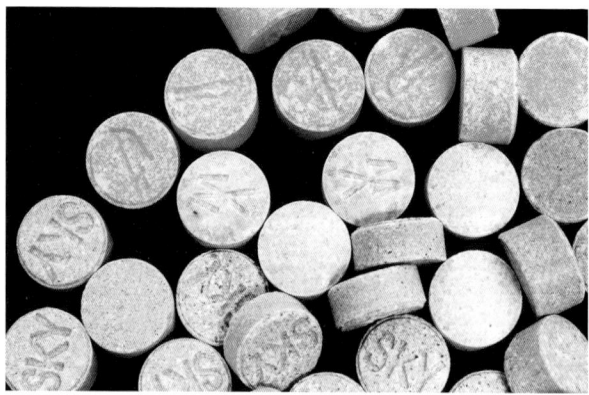

Ecstasy/MDMA.

## THE SEARCH GOES ON

Once everything outside the building was systematically searched, the handler took his detector dog, Ann, into the warehouse. In the semi-darkness, Ann moved around, seemingly randomly, guided by concise, invisible instructions she was finding on the antiques that were tightly packed and stacked throughout. She lingered in a few places, intensively searching, but not alerting. She then climbed the rickety staircase and waited impatiently for her handler to allow her to search the first-floor room. As soon as he opened the door, Ann's excitement was palpable, which made us think that she knew, before climbing the stairs, that she would find what she was looking for in this room. Despite the length of time she had been intensively searching this location, her enthusiasm and perseverance had not diminished. She put her nose in every corner, even jumped onto the sofa (although chairs blocked the way). She searched the sofa meticulously, ignoring the sound of a chair falling down behind her as she worked. Then, beside the stove, a basket filled with firewood on a wooden pedestal attracted her attention. She sniffed it, barked shortly, and began to disassemble the pedestal by scratching. Her handler helped her by carefully lifting the pedestal a little higher so she could scratch the basket forward with her paws. Her handler threw her toy, causing her to back away from the basket. Proudly the handler uncovered a handful of ecstasy pills. Now, her work proceeded anew, and things happened in quick succession. Within a few minutes, Ann found other caches: three Coke cans with screw-top lids, all brimming full of ecstasy tablets. It was a great success.

At the end, the dog handler commented, "Many people think that a drug-detection dog must be addicted in order to detect drugs. Of course, this is not true. Everything the dog learns is as a result of her game and prey drives. An addicted dog is seriously ill and could never perform such a search as this one." Full of pride, Ann looked at him. We were sure she understood every word he said.

MDMA laboratories have been identified in the United States, and the drug is also manufactured in Canada and smuggled into the United States from there. The Netherlands, too, has its share of MDMA labs.

## THE MODES OF ADMINISTRATION

MDMA is available in capsules, crystals, pills, and as a powder. One can also get it as a drink—MDMA dissolved in a beverage (Blue69)—but this is not common. MDMA is usually swallowed as a pill. Some users take a whole pill at once, while others break it in half or into quarters. Those who take MDMA as a powder, or small crystals, lick the powder and that way slowly build up their dose. Others put the powder in a capsule or roll it into a piece of cigarette paper (MDMA bomblet) to swallow it. Sometimes users dissolve a dose of powder into a drink. MDMA powder is sometimes snorted and (rarely) smoked.

MDMA has a negative influence on tooth enamel, so taking it as a drink or licking the powder risks damage to the teeth. Another downside to MDMA in powder form is that it is easily adulterated by dealers, which can change its potency and introduce others dangers. One cannot be sure of what is in a packet of MDMA powder. MDMA can also be administered rectally, often as powder in a capsule. Because the drug bypasses the digestive system in this method of administration, the effects are more quickly felt than if one were to take a pill orally. Sniffing is possible but extremely painful. Just as in rectal administration, the effects are felt faster and a lower dose is required. Both rectal and nasal administration are rare.

## DOSAGE

MDMA pills exist in many colors with different logos. The dose in MDMA pills can vary greatly. For example, some pills contain almost nothing, and others three times the normal dose. Moreover, some MDMA pills look identical to other MDMA pills but contain different drugs, such as PM(M)A or mCPP, substances that can be more harmful or have more unpleasant side effects than MDMA. A recreational oral dose for women is between 1 and 1.5 milligrams of MDMA per kilogram (2.2 lb) of body weight per occasion (maximum once every six to eight weeks). So, for a woman weighing 60 kilograms (132 lb), a recreational dose is between 60 and 90 milligrams of MDMA for a night. For men this dose is between 1 and 2 milligrams of MDMA per kilogram of body weight, so 60 to 120 milligrams if the user weighs 60 kilograms (132 lb).

*EFFECTS*

MDMA actually has two effects because it is both a stimulant and an entactogen. The stimulatory effect is similar to that of speed, only weaker. The user feels awake, sharp, and that he or she can think very quickly. The entactogenic effect can be described as a relaxed feeling; the user feels open and connected to others. Approximately 20 to 60 minutes after taking MDMA, the user feels the first effects: tingling sensations throughout the body, a warm glow, and rapidly emerging euphoria (feelings of intense love). The effects quickly become stronger and may overwhelm the user, causing him or her to become nauseated and vomit. After about two hours, the effects start to diminish, and after about four to six hours, most users feel normal once more. Many users try to take more after one dose, trying to hold onto those first feelings of intoxication. This does not work. The feeling gained by taking that first dose of the evening will not come back that night. Only the physical effects increase, such as dry mouth, muscle tension, and teeth grinding. As a result, users sometimes think there is speed in their pills.

MENTAL EFFECTS

- Euphoric, amorous feelings
- Empathy
- Strong sense of connectedness
- Need for contact, talk, and intimacy
- Energy
- Dance movements feel better
- Increased alertness
- Intense experience of music

- Desire to touch others, massage, and hug (hence the street name, "hug drug")
- Difficulty concentrating
- Forgetfulness
- In high doses, confusion or fear

PHYSICAL EFFECTS

- Tingling in the body
- Loss of appetite
- Increase in blood pressure and heart rate
- Increased body temperature
- Airways expand
- Difficulty urinating
- Dry mouth
- Large pupils
- Tense muscles
- Rigid jaws, clenched teeth (users may bite their own tongues)
- Difficulty sleeping
- Sometimes blurred vision
- Quick back-and-forth eye movements (nystagmus) and therefore difficulty with reading
- Sometimes dizziness, headache, nausea, shivering, and vomiting
- Sometimes sweating

SHORT-TERM RISKS

Severe, acute health incidents are rare but, when they do occur, they can be fatal. Serious problems or death from use of MDMA usually result from the combination of the pharmacological properties of MDMA and the circumstances in which the drug is used (temperature, water intake, physical activity, and use of other drugs, including alcohol).

Problems with concentration and memory are possible in the week after MDMA use. More serious psychological problems such as depression, flashbacks, hallucinations, and panic attacks may also occur, even after using MDMA one time.

Other short-term risks for MDMA include the following:

- Increased risk of heart problems (cardiovascular problems)
- Epileptic seizure
- Acute state of arousal
- Liver damage
- Psychological problems: Tomcat (Terrible Tuesday or Suicide Tuesday). Many people who use MDMA on the weekends have psychological problems during the week that follows. They feel depressed, down, irritable, sad, sensitive, or crabby, and sometimes suicidal. These feelings usually occur two to three days after using MDMA.

Serious short-term risks that are also associated with the use of MDMA include overheating, water intoxication, and serotonin syndrome.

OVERHEATING (HYPERTHERMIA)

When using MDMA, the user's body temperature rises. When MDMA is used in a hot environment, such as at a club or party, or in the sun at an outdoor festival, this rise in body temperature can be dangerous. Overheating can also occur if the user dances for a long time and does not drink enough water. Symptoms of incipient overheating are confusion, dizziness, headache, and stiff muscles. These are all symptoms that are also the "normal" side effects of MDMA. But if the user's body temperature does not drop, the following symptoms may occur: fainting, increased heart rate, nausea, pallor, shivering, and vomiting.

If the body temperature rises to 104 or 106°F (40 or 41°C), the user's life is in danger. Muscle tissue will begin to break down. Blood will start to clot throughout the body. Kidney and liver function will become impaired. Epileptic seizures will result.

## WATER INTOXICATION (HYPONATREMIA)

Because overheating is one of the most serious acute risks of the use of MDMA, many MDMA users think they need to drink plenty of water. Some users suggest that when using the drug you have to drink "lots" of water. Unfortunately, however, some users have died because they drank too much water while taking MDMA; they died of water intoxication. Drinking a lot of water causes an increase in blood volume and a reduction in the concentration of salts (sodium) in one's blood. In the meantime, MDMA causes the kidneys to excrete less water through urine (one cannot urinate or will have difficulty doing so). Furthermore, after using MDMA, users are not hungry and, because of reduced saliva production, may in fact find it difficult to eat. So the user does not take in any sodium. As a result of this low concentration of sodium in the blood, too much water in the blood flows into brain cells, making them swell. Swollen brain cells lead to edema, and swollen tissue fills the limited space inside the skull and creates pressure that may lead to seizures, coma and, eventually, death. Symptoms of water intoxication include fear, headache, nausea, malaise, and vomiting, followed by seizures, reduced consciousness, and coma.

## SEROTONIN SYNDROME

This side effect of MDMA use is caused by a dangerously increased level of serotonin in the central nervous system. Serotonin is a neurotransmitter that affects emotions, hunger, sexual function, and thirst. After using MDMA, the serotonin stock in the brain is considerably decreased. With regular MDMA use, the body may consume its entire store of serotonin because serotonin is not created quickly enough to replace what is being used while the user is under the influence of MDMA.

Should the MDMA user have the following symptoms, which are related to serotonin syndrome, he or she should get immediate medical help:

- Fever
- Restlessness or excitement

- Anxiety or confusion
- Unusual, spasmodic muscle cramps in the arms and/or legs
- Stiff muscles

*LONG-TERM RISKS*

- Brain damage. Experiments on lab animals suggest that MDMA can cause damage to certain brain cells. MDMA users who use the drug a lot display similar damage. It is not yet clear what the damage is and if that damage can be remedied.
- Impaired short-term memory
- Increased risk of cardiac arrhythmias, myocardial infarction, and stroke
- Fatigue, exhaustion
- Reduced physical resistance to infection
- Reduced physical fitness
- Weight loss
- Damaged teeth

*ADDICTION AND COMBINATIONS WITH OTHER DRUGS*

Users can become mentally dependent on MDMA. This is mainly reflected in users' desire not to attend a party without taking MDMA, or perhaps they find it hard to say no to the drug, even if they did not intend to use that evening. Physical dependence does not occur with MDMA. With regular use, the typical MDMA "love" feeling lessens, but users always feel the invigorating effects of the drug. However, if the user stops taking MDMA for two to three months, then takes it again, he or she may regain that "love" feeling.

If users combine MDMA and cocaine, they exert a lot of extra pressure on their cardiovascular system, which can seriously deplete the body. When MDMA and cocaine are combined, the body's adrenal glands are stimulated, which can result in an increased blood pressure and heart rate that, in turn, can lead to acute cardiovascular system problems. The combination of MDMA and cocaine also stimulates to the point of exhaustion those nerves that are involved in the release of serotonin and adrenaline, causing a feeling of emptiness in the user for a few days after use. The hangover from taking this combination of drugs is often much worse than the typical "Tomcat" resulting from taking either of these drugs on their own.

Speed works against the "love" effect of MDMA.

Alcohol flattens the effect of MDMA, which means that the user may take more MDMA to get the desired effect. This behavior increases the deleterious effects of MDMA. In addition, this combination can cause headaches and nausea. When drinking alcohol and taking MDMA, the user will feel unwell but will generally drink more than usual. The hangover will, thus, be much more intense than if the user were just drinking alcohol.

Using GHB (see page 198) after taking MDMA prolongs the effect of MDMA. This combination disinhibits the user more than if she or he were using either of the drugs on their own.

If the MDMA user also takes modern antidepressants, known as selective serotonin reuptake inhibitors (SSRIs), he or she will probably feel almost none of MDMA's effects. However, combining MDMA with an old class of antidepressants, called MAO inhibitors, is very risky. Blood pressure can rise dangerously, and there is an increased chance of serotonin syndrome.

Combining MDMA and anti-asthma or anti–hay fever remedies is not a good idea because one's blood pressure can increase to a dangerous level.

*DETECTABILITY*

MDMA is broken down by the liver. Within two to three days after use, it is no longer detectable in the blood or urine.

**KETAMINE**

Ketamine is a synthetic dissociative anesthetic that has some hallucinogenic effects. It is referred to as a "dissociative anesthetic" because it makes patients feel detached from their pain

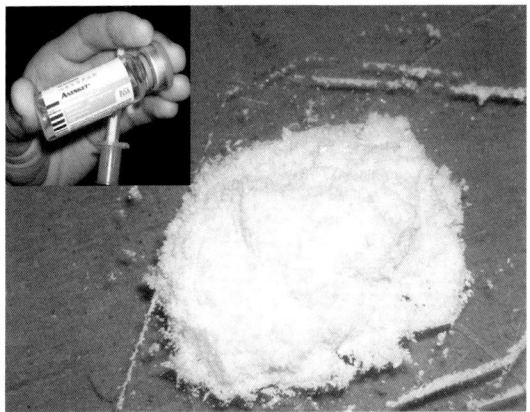

Ketamine.

and environment. It distorts perceptions of sight and sound, and makes the user feel disconnected and out of control. It is an injectable, short-acting anesthetic used in surgery, and it is also used as a means of pain management for humans and other animals. In much lower doses than are used medically, ketamine is also used as a recreational drug, primarily in the form of a crystalline powder but also in liquid form, and (rarely) in pill form. Ketamine, along with the other "club drugs," has become popular among teens and young adults at dance clubs and raves. Common street names include cat tranquilizer, cat valium, jet K, kit kat, purple, special K, special la coke, super acid, super K, and vitamin K.

*HISTORY*

Ketamine was developed in 1962 as an anesthetic for humans and other animals. It was widely marketed by the firm Parke-Davis under various brand names such as Ketalart, Ketanest, Ketaset, and Aneskin. During the Vietnam War, it was used by American surgeons in the field. Ketamine is a relatively safe anesthetic because, in contrast with other anesthetics, it hardly suppresses respiratory and heart rates. Due to adverse side effects, however—disorientation, frightening dreams, and hallucinations—that occurred during recovery from anesthesia in clinical practice, ketamine is not being used as much in surgery anymore. But these same side effects were attractive to experimenters in the therapeutic/psychiatric field.

In his 1978 book, *The Scientist*, American psychiatrist John Lilly wrote a report about his own experiments with ketamine. He came to the conclusion that ketamine opens the door for "metaprogramming," a process he describes as influencing synapses to cause behavioral and personality changes.[2] In Russia in 1985, Professor Yevgeny Krupitsky used ketamine in addiction therapy for the first time. As head of the research laboratory for addiction and psychopharmacology in Saint Petersburg, Krupitsky developed a psychedelic therapy schedule that, to his surprise, took care of abstinence from alcohol for at least a year in 66 percent of alcohol-dependent patients. Krupitsky later published the results of a study on ketamine and heroin addiction. Although ketamine caused no positive, lasting effects on alcoholics, as he had hoped at first, there was a noticeable improvement in the withdrawal process. He chalked up these results to ketamine's influence: a positive transformation of the user's self-concept and emotional, moral, and spiritual attitudes.

During the 1990s, ketamine also showed up in the New York and UK club circuits. All sorts of articles about ketamine appeared in lifestyle magazines, and during the late 1990s, ketamine popped up in alternative circuits in the Netherlands.

Today ketamine is still used in veterinary operations. In humans, it can be used in the treatment of chronic (nerve) pain, and in burn units for painful procedures. Ketamine is also still in use as an anesthetic in young children and the elderly because they are less sensitive to the side effects than other members of the population, and because of the drug's positive aspect for these two demographics: it does not suppress respiratory function as much as other anesthetics. In these cases, it is almost always co-administered with a benzodiazepine agent to suppress hallucinations. Since 2000, ketamine has also been in the spotlight because of its antidepressant effect.

## THE MODES OF ADMINISTRATION

In the drug scene, ketamine is mainly a crystalline powder consumed nasally (snorting). Ketamine is also available in liquid form, in which case it is injected intramuscularly. The liquid version, however, can also be boiled down to a crystalline powder. Ketamine is almost never available as a pill. The majority of the ketamine in recreational use was produced by the pharmaceutical industry and subsequently came into the illegal circuit.

## DOSAGE

The nasal dose varies from 15 to 150 milligrams, and users generally lie down after taking doses of 50 milligrams or more. When taken this way, ketamine's effects are felt within 5 to 15 minutes and last for approximately 45 to 60 minutes.

Ketamine can also be swallowed. The ingested dose ranges from 75 to 500 milligrams. Depending on the stomach contents, the effects are felt after 20 to 60 minutes. The experience lasts one to three hours, with after effects that can last about as long.

When the user injects ketamine intramuscularly, the dosage is usually between 50 and 125 milligrams. The user feels the drug's effects after three to five minutes, and the experience lasts for 30 to 45 minutes.

## EFFECTS

Ketamine is a dissociative trip drug, which means the user experiences a feeling of separation between his or her mind and body.

### MENTAL EFFECTS

- Dreamy, woolly daze
- Dissociative effects include
  - the feeling that one's hands no longer belong to one's body;
  - one's body feeling different, as if it is made of plastic, rubber, or wood;
  - body parts feeling much larger or smaller than they actually are;

- the feeling that one has misplaced one's arms or legs;
- the feeling that the density of one's body has decreased, as if it has dissolved;
- feeling unsure about whether one's own body parts belong to oneself, or someone else;
- the feeling that one's mind is in a totally different dimension than one's body; and
- withdrawal from the body (out-of-body experience).

- Possible confusion, a bad trip
- Possible insightful experience
- A very strong ketamine experience is called a "K-hole," which has been described variously as the feeling that one has experienced death; the feeling that one has flown at high speed through a tunnel; intense hallucinogenic effects; telepathic contacts; or the feeling of being in a world without time.

PHYSICAL EFFECTS

- Increased heart rate and blood pressure
- Increased saliva production
- Dilated airways
- Disorientation
- Difficulty with coordinating movements (drift, "robot walk")
- Possible nausea
- Possible stiff muscles

SHORT-TERM RISKS

- When using ketamine, there is a chance of nausea; if a user has taken a high dose and passes out, he or she could choke on vomit.
- The user can become disoriented and have difficulty with coordinating movements. As a result, he or she may fall and become injured.

- The user can be overwhelmed by the intensity of the experience and have a bad trip.
- Ketamine numbs, so the user feels no pain and thus can be hurt without knowing it.

*LONG-TERM RISKS*

When ketamine is used regularly, the body begins to tolerate it, and the user needs to take more ketamine every time to achieve the same effect. Ketamine can be quite addictive. After long-term use, some users become paranoid. Intense use of this drug can also lead to memory problems and brain damage. Chronic use can result in bladder and kidney problems; users talk about severe abdominal pain (K-cramp) and bladder inflammation. Urinary tract damage can result in an increased susceptibility to infections of the bladder, the urinary tract, and the kidneys, including total loss of renal function and the need for kidney dialysis.

*ADDICTION AND COMBINATIONS WITH OTHER DRUGS*

Unlike other hallucinogens, ketamine is addictive. The user can become mentally dependent on it. In addition, body tolerance for the drug's psychedelic effects lead to users taking higher and higher doses to feel the same effects.

The combination of ketamine with high doses of downers such as alcohol and GHB can lead to the suppression of respiration and then unconsciousness. The unconscious user may choke by swallowing his or her own tongue or vomit.

The combination of ketamine with stimulants such as cocaine or speed can be risky for people with heart and vascular disease because cocaine, like ketamine, stimulates the heart rate and constricts the blood vessels, so the heart receives less oxygen.

*DETECTABILITY*

Ketamine is broken down by the liver and excreted through the kidneys and urine. It is completely eliminated from the body in two to four days.

## Depressants

Depressants are also called "psycholeptics" or "downers." They slow down the activity of the central nervous system (the brain and spinal cord), thereby reducing a person's alertness. They also slow down bodily functions such as breathing and heart rate. These drugs are available in multicolored tablets and capsules, or in liquid form. Some drugs in this category are known as "major tranquilizers" or "antipsychotics," as they are supposed to reduce the symptoms of mental illness. Other depressants belong to the prescription drug group of benzodiazepines, and others still are classed as barbiturates—drugs that are used as sedatives and sleeping pills.

### BARBITURATES

Barbiturates produce a wide spectrum of central nervous system depression, from mild sedation to coma. High doses depress both nerve and muscle activity and inhibit oxygen consumption in the tissues. In low doses, barbiturates act as sedatives, so they have a tranquilizing effect; increased doses have a hypnotic or sleep-inducing effect; still larger doses work as anticonvulsants and anesthetics.

Barbiturates are usually taken as a pill or injected. They are often used as a substitute for alcohol and cause a feeling of euphoria and relaxation. On the street, they are often also used as a substitute for cocaine, amphetamines, and crystal meth. The street names of commonly used barbiturates describe the desired effect of the drug or the color of and markings on the pill. Common street names are amytal, barbs, block busters, blues, Christmas trees, downers, goof balls, nembutal, pinks, reds, red devils, reds and blues, seconal, sekkies, sleeping pills, sleepers, tuinal, and yellow jackets. Some user-created drug forums on the Internet are positive about barbiturates (in the sense that these drugs are less expensive than cocaine), with the result that users often underestimate the risks associated with taking them. Barbiturates can be extremely dangerous because the

# THE DIFFERENT DRUGS

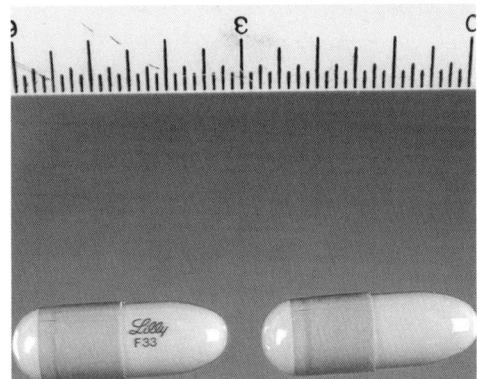

The barbiturate amobarbital.

correct dose is difficult to pin down. Even a slight overdose can cause coma or death. Barbiturates are also addictive and can cause life-threatening withdrawal symptoms.

### HISTORY

The barbiturates are all derivatives of barbituric acid, which was first prepared in 1864 by the German organic chemist Adolf von Bayer. In 1903, the first barbiturate, Barbital, was used in medical practices. In 1912, a common barbiturate, Phenobarbital, was introduced.

Barbiturates became popular in the 1960s and 1970s in treatments of anxiety, insomnia, and seizure disorders. They evolved into recreational drugs that some people used to reduce inhibitions, decrease anxiety, and treat unwanted side effects of illicit drugs. Barbiturate use has declined dramatically since the 1970s, mainly because a safer group of sedative-hypnotics called benzodiazepines are now being prescribed by the medical profession, unless a patient presents with certain specific indications (for example, sleep disturbance), in which case doctors will prescribe barbiturates. Veterinary euthanasia also employs barbiturates.

There are many different barbiturates. The primary difference among them is how long their effects last. The effects of some of the long-acting drugs may last up to two days. The effects of others may only last a few minutes.

## THE MODES OF ADMINISTRATION

Barbiturates can be injected into one's veins or muscles, but they are usually taken in pill form. Most barbiturates come in powdered form and are sold as colored capsules that are swallowed. They are also available as ampoules, suppositories, or syrup.

The effects of barbiturates can last from four to 16 hours, or longer. Symptoms of use may gradually fade over the week after use, depending on the dose. Use over a long period usually leads to tolerance, so users must take larger doses to get the same effects. When users take the drug daily for more than a month, usually beyond the therapeutic dose, the brain easily develops a need for the drug. When a user is psychologically addicted to barbiturates, finding and using the drug becomes the focus of life.

## EFFECTS

Small doses of barbiturates cause drowsiness, intoxication, and disinhibition. Higher doses can result in staggering, slurred speech, and confusion. The drug can be fatal if taken in extremely large quantities—in this case, the user may simply stop breathing.

While barbiturates are very addictive, addiction to barbiturates is uncommon today. Obvious symptoms of addiction include the following:

- Constant falling
- Bruised legs
- Nervousness
- Shaking
- Noise sensitivity
- Restlessness
- Sweating
- Hallucinations
- Insomnia

## SHORT- AND LONG-TERM RISKS

Although the medical use of barbiturates has declined since the 1970s, some surveys suggest that use by young people has been rising. Many of today's drug users may be too young to remember the deaths and dangerous effects barbiturates caused in the 1970s, so they underestimate the risks of using them. Barbiturates are also commonly used in suicide attempts.

Sudden withdrawal from high doses can result in death. Effects of withdrawal are delirium, fainting, irritability, nervousness, seizures, sickness, sleeplessness, and twitching. Overdose can be the result of an easy mistake, just a few extra tablets—a normal dose is very similar to a lethal dose.

*ADDICTION AND COMBINATIONS WITH OTHER DRUGS*

Barbiturates are highly addictive and are dangerous when mixed with alcohol. Barbiturates and alcohol both lower blood pressure and respiration, and together can cause respiratory arrest.

A common reason to use barbiturates is to counteract the symptoms of other drugs; barbiturates counteract the excitement and alertness obtained from stimulants such as cocaine and methamphetamines.

*DETECTABILITY*

The detection times in urine are as follows: four to five days (Pentobarbital); 14 to 21 days (Phenobarbital); four to five days (Secobarbital); and for chronic use, several weeks.

## BENZODIAZEPINES

Benzodiazepines belong to a group of central-nervous-system depressants called "minor tranquilizers." They come as pills in a variety of colors and shapes, depending on the brand. Chiefly, it's the fast-acting benzodiazepines that are used in the illegal drug world because of their intoxicating effects. Common street names are benzoes, downers, footballs, moggies, Normies, rohies, roofies, Sarahs, and sleepers. The most common benzodiazepines are prescribed, so many users maintain their drug supply by getting prescriptions from several doctors or forging prescriptions, as well as by buying them illicitly.

## HISTORY

The first benzodiazepine (chlordiazepoxide) was synthesized in 1954 in Austria. It was discovered by chance during research on chemical dyes, and it was found to be a very effective tranquilizer. It was marketed in 1959 under the brand name Librium. Four years later, Valium was released and became popular. Since then, many other benzodiazepines have been developed. Benzodiazepines have proved to be less dangerous than barbiturates but like barbiturates are also addictive.

Benzodiazepines are prescribed all over the world for problems such as anxiety and insomnia. They can also be prescribed for epilepsy, alcohol withdrawal, and agitation in severe psychiatric disorders. Prescribed benzodiazepines are taken orally as pills. Because there is a high risk of dependence, benzodiazepines are usually prescribed for short-term use only.

## THE MODES OF ADMINISTRATION

Benzodiazepines used illegally as recreational drugs may be ground to a powder, mixed with water, and injected; they are also swallowed as pills. Benzodiazepines take around 30 minutes to work when taken orally because they have to be digested before the drug can enter the bloodstream. Injected benzodiazepines have an almost immediate effect.

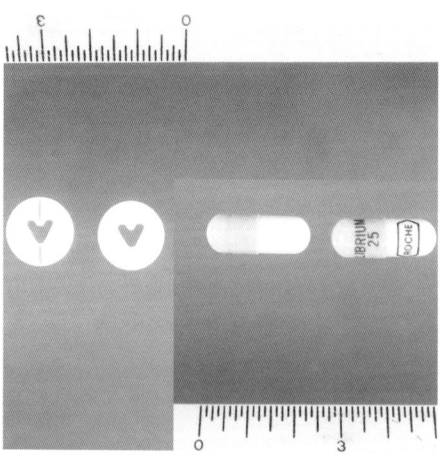

The benzodiazepine Valium in tablets and Librium in capsule shape.

## MENTAL AND PHYSICAL EFFECTS

Like other depressants, benzodiazepines affect both physical and mental performance, reducing coordination, slowing reaction times, and impairing memory. Taking this drug increases one's risk of accidents and falling, and impairment of performance in tasks such as driving. Different benzodiazepines are processed by the digestive system and eliminated from the body at different rates. For example, the effects of one of the more common, short-acting benzodiazepines, temazepam, reach a peak after two or three hours; the drug ceases to be effective after about six to eight hours. The effects of diazepam (Valium), on the other hand, peak after 30 to 90 minutes, while the drug remains in the blood for up to three days. There is also considerable variation between individuals, depending on various factors such as age and liver health.

## SHORT-TERM RISKS

The immediate effects and risks of taking benzodiazepines include the following:
- Feeling of relaxation
- Sleepiness
- Lack of energy
- Dizziness
- Euphoria
- Confusion
- Visual distortions
- Moodiness
- Short-term memory loss

## LONG-TERM RISKS

There is a long list of adverse physical and mental effects associated with long-term benzodiazepine use:
- Anxiety
- Irritability
- Paranoia

- Aggression
- Depression
- Muscle weakness
- Rashes
- Nausea
- Weight gain
- Sexual problems
- Menstrual irregularities
- Memory loss
- Confusion
- Lethargy
- Sleep problems

ADDICTION AND COMBINATIONS WITH OTHER DRUGS

Benzodiazepines are highly addictive and are therefore prescribed only for short-term use. Tolerance can develop quickly; users must increase the dosage to feel the same effects, which in turn increases the chances of dependence. After only two weeks of regular use, people can become dependent and suffer withdrawal symptoms.

Heroin users sometimes use benzodiazepines as a substitute if heroin is unavailable. Benzodiazepines can also be used both to help withdrawal from heroin and to increase its effects. Since heroin is another depressant, however, combining the two drugs greatly increases one's risk of dying from a heroin overdose; benzodiazepines are involved in about a quarter of heroin overdose deaths.

People who use amphetamines and MDMA often use benzodiazepines to help them relax or sleep when they are recovering from the effects of these stimulant drugs.

Combining the use of benzodiazepines with alcohol, which, like the benzodiazepine, is a depressant, has been shown to increase one's risk of dying from sedative overdose.

## ROHYPNOL

Rohypnol is a trade name for flunitrazepam, a central-nervous-system depressant. Like other benzodiazepines, Rohypnol produces sedative-hypnotic, anti-anxiety, and muscle-relaxant effects. Prior to 1997, it was manufactured as a white tablet (0.5–2 milligram/tablet), and when mixed in drinks, it was colorless, tasteless, and odorless. Rohypnol has been used to physically and mentally incapacitate women targeted for sexual assault. The drug is placed in the alcoholic drink of an unsuspecting victim to incapacitate her and prevent resistance to sexual assault. The drug leaves victims unaware of what has happened to them.

In 1997, the manufacturer responded to concerns about the drug's role in such sexual assaults by reformulating the drug. Rohypnol is now manufactured as an oblong, olive-green tablet with a speckled blue core that, when dissolved in light-colored drinks, will dye the liquid blue. However, generic versions of the drug may not contain the blue dye.

Adolescents may abuse Rohypnol to produce a euphoric effect often described as a "high." While high, they experience reduced inhibitions and impaired judgment. It is also used in combination with alcohol to produce an exaggerated intoxication. In addition, cocaine addicts may use benzodiazepines such as Rohypnol to relieve the side effects (for example, irritability and agitation) associated with cocaine binges.

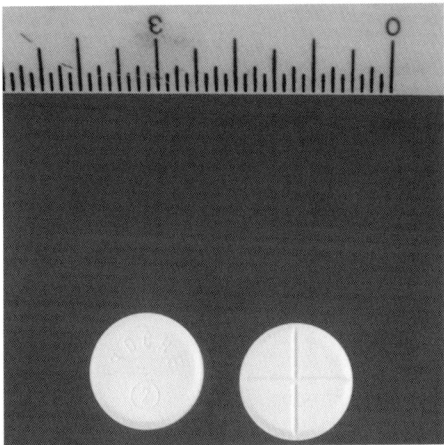

The benzodiazepine Rohypnol, pre 1997.

*DETECTABILITY*

In the urine, benzodiazepine is detectable for up to three days in therapeutic use, and in chronic users, it is detectable for four to six weeks.

## GHB

GHB is the abbreviation for gamma-hydroxybutyric, another name for the generic drug sodium oxybate. It is mainly sold as a viscous, salty liquid in small plastic bottles (5 milliliters/bottle). GHB is sometimes misleadingly called "liquid ecstasy." Other street names are blue nitro, fantasy, G, grievous bodily harm, liquid E, GBL, and 1,4-B.

GHB occurs naturally in the human body, notably in the brain. This does not mean that GHB taken as a drug is harmless; if one uses GHB, the amount of GHB in the brain becomes much higher than normal.

Gamma butyrolactone (GBL) is employed in the process of making GHB; in fact, the human body can convert GBL into GHB. As a result, sometimes GBL is sold instead of GHB, and it looks the same as GHB. But liquid GBL is at least twice as strong as liquid GHB. Differences in individuals' body weight, metabolism, stomach contents, and sensitivity to the drug can make taking GBL risky—one dose might be "right" for one person, but another may

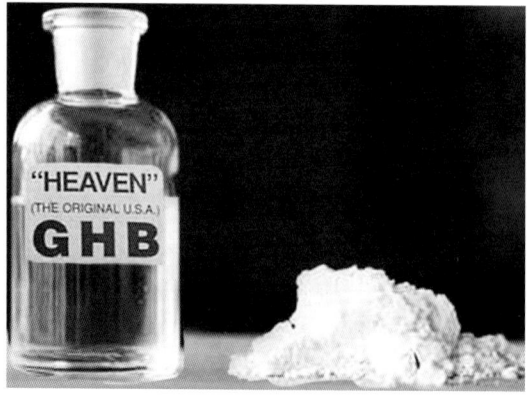

GHB.

require more or less to get the same effects, and another yet might overdose. In addition, pure GBL is a caustic substance (lactone) and is seriously harmful to the body, esophagus, mouth, and stomach.

### HISTORY

GHB is a naturally occurring substance found in the body. In 1960, it was isolated from mammalian tissues by the French researcher Henri Laborit, who was looking for a substance that has a similar effect to the neurotransmitter GABA, which depresses brain function. GABA does not cross the blood-brain barrier, but Laborit sought a substance that did. He found what he was looking for in GHB, and it was first synthesized in 1961. At first GHB was prescribed as a sedative, and later, it was used as an anesthetic. GHB has a poor analgesic effect, however, and so it is no longer generally used as an anesthetic. In addition, it is difficult to dose GHB, which is of course essential in terms of anesthesiology: the physician must be able to know exactly how long a patient will be under anesthesia when performing an operation. A final reason not to use GHB as an anesthetic is the risk of seizures.

In the 1980s, GHB was very popular among American bodybuilders because they believed the drug stimulated the release of growth hormone and promoted the building of muscle tissue. GHB stimulates the release of pituitary hormones, including growth hormone. However, with GHB use, the release of cortisol by the adrenal glands also increases, which leads to reduced muscle mass. So GHB only results in a very slight increase in muscle mass.

In the late 1980s in the Netherlands, GHB became popular and was then legally sold as an aphrodisiac powder in smart shops. In the entertainment circuit, GHB is known as an aphrodisiac, but it can also quickly render one unconscious.

Today GHB is supplied via the pharmacy under the brand name Xyrem and is used for the treatment of narcolepsy.

### THE MODES OF ADMINISTRATION

GHB usually comes as a liquid, but it is also available as a powder. A full bottle of GHB contain 5 milliliters. The liquid or powder is added to soft drinks, fruit juice, or water, and then drunk.

GBL is available only as a liquid and has to be very well diluted before it is consumed.

#### DOSAGE

GHB is extremely difficult to dose, depending on body weight, stomach contents, tolerance, and sensitivity to GHB. Also, the concentration of GHB in the liquid plays a major role. The maximum amount of the drug in the liquid is usually around 50 percent, equivalent to 2 to 3 grams of pure GHB per 5-milliliter bottle. A person can overdose by taking 2 grams (+/− 3 milliliters). Most GHB on the market is between 450 and 700 milligrams per milliliter.

#### EFFECTS

GHB is a narcotic. It is colorless, odorless, and tastes very salty. Ten to 45 minutes after taking a dose, the first effects begin. In small doses, GHB produces a relaxed, peaceful feeling and can be sexually stimulating. At higher doses, the user may feel sick or get dizzy. Sometimes the user falls asleep. The effects of this drug are sometimes described by users as similar to those of alcohol. The effects of one dose last for about 1.5 hours.

MENTAL EFFECTS
- Memory loss
- Confusion
- Recklessness
- Disinhibition
- Euphoria
- Cheerfulness, calmness

PHYSICAL EFFECTS
- Slow heartbeat
- Lowered body temperature

- Vomiting
- Talkativeness
- Agitation
- Sexual stimulation
- Tendency to vibrate
- Dizziness
- Nausea
- Headache
- Feeling weak in the muscles
- Drowsiness
- Loss of consciousness
- Convulsions

*SHORT-TERM RISKS*

There are a variety of short-term risks to taking GHB, the more serious of which are exacerbated by the difficulty in administering a safe dosage. As well, especially in combination with stimulants such as MDMA and speed, taking GHB may cause short-term movement disorders and seizures. Following are some other short-term risks associated with GHB use.

- Fainting as a result of a high dosage, or combination use with alcohol or sleeping pills and sedatives, which can cause coma or even death from respiratory arrest
- Sexual disinhibition
- Vibrating
- Nausea
- Dizziness
- Vomiting
- Impaired balance and coordination
- Confusion
- Convulsions

*LONG-TERM RISKS*
- Addiction
- Possible brain damage
- Loss of memory
- Esophagus damage after consuming too-high a pH of GHB, or undiluted GBL
- Disrupted sleep patterns

*ADDICTION AND COMBINATIONS WITH OTHER DRUGS*
Regular users easily establish tolerance to GHB; they increasingly need more to achieve the same effects. Since 2008 there has been a sharp increase in the number of GHB addiction problems in the Netherlands. Physical addiction to GHB only occurs when the drug is used daily. When a dependent user stops taking GHB, withdrawal symptoms include anxiety, insomnia, and tremors. Withdrawal from GHB is very risky—it can include hallucinations, psychosis, and seizures—and requires medical supervision.

One can also become mentally addicted to GHB. The user may not be physically dependent, but he or she may feel unable to go to a party without the drug.

It is highly inadvisable to combine GHB with alcohol, sleeping pills, and tranquilizers (like Valium) or other "downers" (like ketamine) because of the increased risk of overdose. The likelihood of the user being rendered unconscious increases strongly if he or she takes GHB in combination with alcohol. As well, when users combine GHB with drugs that impart narcotic-like effects—think antihistamines (allergy medications) and anticonvulsants (for epilepsy and restless legs)—they have an increased risk of impaired consciousness and/or respiratory depression.

Using GHB shortly after using MDMA prolongs the effects of MDMA. As well, the stimulatory effects of MDMA can make the anesthetic effects of GHB less pronounced. As long as one is under the influence of both, one will feel the effects for longer than if one had taken the same amount of GHB without MDMA. However, once the MDMA stops working, the effects of GHB suddenly stop. In addition, this combination increases the risk of seizures and movement disorders.

Some people think taking MDMA and/or amphetamines together with GHB works against loss of consciousness. They feel "brighter" than when they take GHB by itself. As a result, the user may take more GHB than she or he would when using GHB on its own. When the MDMA or amphetamines have worn off, the GHB may still be in the user's system and may still render him or her unconscious. As well, there are indications that a coma resulting from an overdose of GHB that has been taken in combination with speed or MDMA may last longer than a coma resulting from an overdose of GHB on its own.

*DETECTABILITY*

When compared with other drugs, GHB is only detectable for a short amount of time in the human body. In blood it is detectable for up to eight hours and in urine up to 12 hours. In practice, however, after about six hours, no traces of GHB can be found in the body. So if someone wants to investigate whether or not someone secretly put GHB in a drink, the victim's urine should be tested as soon as possible.

## Stimulants

Stimulants, also called "psychoanaleptics" or "uppers," increase the activity of the central nervous system, making the person more alert and aroused. This type of drug also elevates blood pressure, heart rate, and respiration, but decreases sleep and appetite. Stimulants historically were used to treat asthma and other respiratory problems, as well as obesity and neurological disorders. But as their potential for abuse and addiction became apparent, the medical profession began to prescribe them less and less.

All stimulants work by increasing dopamine levels in the brain. Dopamine is a neurotransmitter associated with pleasure, movement, and attention. When taken in high doses, stimulants can increase brain dopamine in a rapid and highly amplified manner, disrupting normal communication between brain cells, producing euphoria and, as a result, increasing the risk of addiction. Stimulants temporarily provide more energy and therefore have an energizing effect. Examples of stimulants are cocaine, khat, amphetamines, and the methamphetamines, speed and crystal.

## COCAINE

Cocaine is usually distributed as a white crystalline powder. Cocaine sold on the street is often cut or diluted with other substances, such as glucose, lactose, or baking powder. Common street names are blow, Charlie, coca, coke, crack, flake, nose candy, snow, soda cot, toot, and white dust. Cocaine is obtained from the leaves of the coca plant, but it can also be chemically synthesized. The active substance is cocaine hydrochloride, which has a stimulating and mood-enhancing effect.

In South America, the coca plant grows on small terraced plantations called *cocales*. Two main types of the plant are *Erythroxylum coca* (Bolivian coca plant) and *Erythroxylum novogranatense* (Colombian coca plant). This flowering shrub mainly grows at altitudes of 500 to 2,000 feet (152–610 m) in the Andes of South America. The cocaine-manufacturing process takes place in remote jungle labs where the raw product undergoes a series of chemical transformations.

The coca plant from which cocaine is derived.

Cocaine.

## CRACK

A pure form of freebase cocaine is made by adding sodium bicarbonate or ammonia to cocaine hydrochloride and water, and then cooking that concoction. This product is called a variety of names: base, bori, cooked coke, clean coke, crack, freebase, pure coke, rock, or white. The most-used street name for this drug, "crack," got its name from the crackling sound produced by the coke base during heating.

Within eight seconds of smoking crack, usually by means of a "base pipe," the effects can be felt in the form of a "flash," which lasts about 20 seconds. The length of the "experience" one feels when taking cocaine thus depends on the method of use: snorting, up to about 30 minutes; injecting, one to two minutes; and smoking crack, a few minutes.

Cocaine hydrochloride cannot be smoked effectively because it is destroyed at high temperatures; however, if the hydrochloride is removed through a chemical process, the drug is converted into "freebase," which can be smoked. Crack is a particularly pure form of freebase cocaine. It often comes in the form of small lumps known as "rocks."

Crack.

## HISTORY

For more than five thousand years, coca was the holy plant of the Incas. The Incas in the Andes chewed coca leaves to increase their heart rate and accelerate their breathing to counter the effects of living in thin mountain air. The original inhabitants of Peru only chewed coca leaves during religious ceremonies. This taboo was broken when Spanish soldiers invaded Peru in 1532. The Indigenous people, who were forced to work in the Spanish silver mines, were given coca leaves—when they were under the influence of the coca, the people were easier to control and exploit.

The plant has been cultivated in South America for so long that the original, wild plant no longer exists. The shrubby bush can reach heights between 35 and 71 inches (90 and 180 cm) and is found in the Andes. The plant also grows in Brazil and on the islands of Java and Sumatra. The leaves of the coca plant are delicate, and the flower is a soft-yellow color. The plant grows year round and can be harvested every three months.

In Incan culture, the chewing of coca leaves was at first reserved for the nobility and priests, but later everyone was allowed to participate in the practice, particularly because coca keeps hunger and tiredness at bay. This practice continues among the Indigenous peoples of the Andes, especially among the tin-mine workers of Bolivia. Most of the time, people mix the leaves with lime before chewing them. A coca leaf is between 0.25 and 1.31 percent cocaine. Europeans first came in contact with the use of the coca plant in the 16th century. The chewing of coca didn't become popular in Europe, however, because the leaves would lose their effect during their long journey across the ocean.

In the 19th century, European chemists became interested in the effects of coca leaves. In 1859, the German chemist Albert Niemann isolated cocaine for the first time from *Erythroxylum*. He extracted the primary alkaloid and named the ingredient "cocaine." He wrote of the alkaloid's "colorless, transparent prisms" and said, "Its solutions have an alkaline reaction, a bitter taste, promote the flow of saliva and leave a peculiar numbness, followed by a sense of cold when applied to the tongue."[3]

In 1884, modern-day local anesthesia began with a discovery by a young ophthalmologist from Vienna named Carl Koller, who used a cocaine solution as a local anesthetic on the cornea. Koller's colleague, Sigmund Freud, was already aware of the pain-killing properties of cocaine. The news of this discovery spread throughout the world in less than a month. Near the end of the 19th century, Italian neurologist Paolo Mantegazza especially praised the drug for its stimulating effect on cognition,[4] which prompted the production and sale of a variety of tonics claiming health benefits. The original Coca Cola was one of these tonics, and from 1886 until 1901, cocaine was an ingredient in Coca Cola because of its stimulating effects.

In 1892, physician Carl Ludwig Schleich discovered that an injection of cocaine solution worked as a local anesthetic. Medical cocaine was used for a long time in eye and dental surgeries, as a local anesthetic, but today, these same fields use synthetic anesthetics for the same purpose.

The Dutch Cocaine Factory was founded in 1900, making the Netherlands a leader in the production of cocaine. In particular, the Dutch colony of Java became a leading exporter of coca leaves. By 1912, shipments to Amsterdam, where the leaves were processed into cocaine, reached 2,204,622 pounds (1,000,000 kg), overtaking the Peruvian export market. Java was a greater exporter of coca than Peru until the end of the 1920s (except during World War I).

In 1928, the Netherlands adopted The Opium Act, which prohibits the non-medical use of cocaine. After the act came into effect, sales from the Dutch factory decreased sharply. In the late 1970s and early 1980s, cocaine again became popular as a recreational drug in the Netherlands and in North America.

### THE MODES OF ADMINISTRATION

Cocaine as a white, crystalline powder can be snorted or injected into the veins after being dissolved in water. Cocaine is also abused in combination with an opiate such as heroin in a practice known as "speed balling." Although injecting into veins or muscles, snorting, and smoking are the most common ways of using cocaine, all mucous membranes readily absorb the drug. Cocaine base (crack), which looks like small, irregularly shaped chunks (or "rocks") of a whitish solid, is smoked, either alone or with marijuana or tobacco.

### SNORTING

Cocaine powder is placed in a "line" and sniffed via a tube up into the nose. There, the cocaine is absorbed by the nasal mucosa. From the mucous membrane, the coke enters the bloodstream and reaches the brain in about three minutes. When consumed in this, most popular, manner, the effects of the drug last from 15 to 30 minutes.

### INJECTING

When powdered coke is dissolved in water and then injected into the bloodstream, it reaches the brain after about 14 seconds. The effects of the drug taken this way last from one to three minutes.

## SMOKING

When powdered cocaine is smoked in a cigarette, also called a "puff," most of the cocaine burns and so does not impart its effects on the user. At 387°F (197°C), also the temperature at which cocaine evaporates, cocaine powder shatters and/or burns. Before it evaporates, it is thus rendered ineffective. Only a small portion of smoked, powdered cocaine will come through the lungs into the bloodstream, giving the user a brief and intense high.

Those who smoke cocaine usually use crack. To make crack, cocaine is mixed with water and sodium bicarbonate, or ammonia, and then cooked. Crack has a melting point of 208°F (98°C) and begins to evaporate at that temperature. It does not shatter and so can be smoked. When smoked as crack, the level of cocaine in the blood rises quickly, but it also goes down again very quickly.

## *DOSAGE*

A safe dose of cocaine does not exist, and risks increase as users take the drug more often and more each time. Most cocaine available to users is cut with other substances, which are often harmful.

Almost every drug sold on the black market has been cut with another substance. Adulterants, such as boric acid, flour, laundry detergent, or laxatives, are typically used to stretch the dealer's cocaine supply. Other fillers include local anesthetics (lidocaine, procaine, and tetracaine), which work to mimic some of the effects of cocaine (at a cheaper cost than cocaine itself). The practice of using fillers increases the bulk of the product, which in turn increases profit for the dealer.

Adulterants can cause several problems for users, including issues related to toxicity caused by the adulterant, overdose due to variable levels of purity, and toxicity issues caused by the combination of adulterants and drugs the person is taking. Following are some examples of fillers put in cocaine:

- Acetaminophen (Paracetamol, APAP), a common analgesic and fever reducer, can cause liver damage at higher doses, particularly when combined with alcohol.

- Atropine is an anti-muscarinic with various clinical applications. Severe adverse effects are possible, including amnesia, ataxia, difficulty swallowing, disorientation, disturbed speech, psychosis, restlessness, tachycardia, urinary retention, visual disturbances, and coma at high doses.
- Caffeine is a common stimulant.
- Cornstarch is used as a low-end adulterant. It is dangerous if injected.
- Diltiazem is a calcium channel blocker used to combat cardiovascular disease. It can cause adverse cardiovascular reactions, diarrhea, fainting, nausea, and vomiting.
- Hydroxyzine is a sedative, anxiolytic, and antihistamine that can cause dizziness.
- Lactose is a milk sugar and is one of the most common substances used over the last century to cut cocaine.
- Levamisole, an anthelmintic (dewormer) and immunomodulatory, is often used to cut cocaine. It can cause diarrhea, dizziness, and nausea, and is increasingly found in cocaine supplies. It is associated with cases of reversible immune system dysfunction.
- Lidocaine, procaine, and other local anesthetics are used to mimic the numbing effect of cocaine. They can cause convulsions, dizziness, nausea, tremors, and vomiting.
- Mannitol (mannite) is a sugar alcohol and a diuretic that adds a sweet taste to cocaine.
- Methylephedrine is a stimulant.
- Phenacetin is an analgesic and fever reducer, withdrawn by the US FDA in 1983 because of possible carcinogenicity and kidney toxicity.
- Quinine, an odorless, bitter chemical used to cut cocaine and heroin, is dangerous when injected.
- Talc (magnesium trisilicate) is a soft mineral, pharmacologically inert and dangerous to inject.

## EFFECTS

The intensity of cocaine's euphoric effects depends on how quickly the drug reaches the brain, which depends on the dose and method of use. Some long-term users of inhaled cocaine have contracted a unique respiratory syndrome ("crack lung"), and chronic snorting of cocaine has led to the erosion of the upper nasal cavity.

MENTAL EFFECTS
- Clear mind
- Excitement and happiness
- Fears and inhibitions disappear
- Talkativeness
- Confidence; one feels one performs better
- All personal problems seem to evaporate
- Feel more creative than usual
- Sometimes aggressive behavior

PHYSICAL EFFECTS
- Temporary increase in muscle strength and endurance
- Energy
- Suppressed appetite
- Increased heart rate and blood pressure
- Shortness of breath
- Sexual stimulation
- Increased alertness
- Slight increase in body temperature
- Sensory nerve conduction is blocked, so users feel no or less pain
- Dry (nasal) mucosa
- Laxative effect
- Bladder irritant and diuretic

### SHORT-TERM AND LONG-TERM RISKS

Under the influence of cocaine, the user will not sleep because cocaine suppresses fatigue. Days after taking coke, the user may still be exhausted and feel dejected. The longer cocaine is used, the longer these feelings persist. Cocaine users are highly energetic and at the same time have no interest in eating, which may reduce resistance to illness, and the user can lose weight. Cocaine has a strong influence on the heart and blood vessels. With each dose, blood vessels constrict, blood pressure rises, and heart rate accelerates. This places a heavy burden on the heart and can cause heart arrhythmia, heart attack, hypertension, and stroke. When injecting and smoking, the risks are the same, even greater to some extent.

Cocaine is often cut with agents that cause their own and/or additional risks when combined with coke. For instance, levamisole as an agent to cut cocaine is used in veterinary medicine as dewormer. Regularly sniffing coke that is cut with levamisole can lead to a dangerously low level of white blood cells, which might reduce resistance to disease. Phenacetine, an outdated painkiller that causes kidney damage, is also used to cut cocaine. Caffeine is also regularly used to cut coke.

### SHORT-TERM RISKS

- Exhaustion and fatigue.
- Cocaine can enter the sinus frontalis and sinus maxillaris cavities and cause constipation and headache.
- Snorting cocaine may produce inflammation in the nasal mucosa. When inflamed, the mucosa produces extra mucus and the user gets a runny and painful nose.
- When sharing a pipe, users run the risk of contracting hepatitis C (a liver disease).
- Mainly because of careless and unhygienic injecting, infection and inflammation can occur. When sharing syringes and base pipes, users run the risk of spreading or contracting infectious diseases. Resistance to infectious diseases decreases when using cocaine.

- Those who take high doses may have trouble having an erection or reaching orgasm.
- Overdose causing restlessness, anxiety, and suspicion.
- Overdose leading to heart and respiratory problems resulting in death. When injecting, death can come speedily, after only a few minutes. Even when smoking, a fatal overdose can happen quickly. Whether a dose is toxic or lethal depends on the individual. Some people stay alive after taking a few grams, whereas people who are allergic to cocaine may fail after taking only a small dose.

LONG-TERM RISKS

Cocaine leads to narrowing of blood vessels, increased heart rate, and high blood pressure. Because the blood vessels constrict, the heart receives less blood and oxygen. But due to the increase in heart rate, the heart requires more oxygen. As a result, the heart becomes overburdened. Cocaine use can lead to diseases of the cardiovascular system such as arteriosclerosis, heart arrhythmias, heart attacks, and strokes. The risk of contracting these increases when blood vessels are older and already affected by atherosclerosis.

Regular use of cocaine alters the user's interactions with others. The user becomes cool, arrogant, and selfish, and also is often irritable, annoyed, and restless. Many cocaine users lose contact with reality, and feel suspicious and threatened. This can lead to aggressive and paranoid behavior.

Other long-term risks associated with cocaine use follow:
- Loss of sense of smell.
- Frequent use can lead to a hole in the septum.
- Frequent use can lead people to believe that there are bugs under their skin. They become itchy and sometimes scratch until they draw blood.
- Regular use of cocaine can cause psychosis.
- Damage to the lungs (crack use).
- Prolonged use can reduce one's interest in sex and lower the quality of sperm.

*ADDICTION AND COMBINATIONS WITH OTHER DRUGS*

The greatest risk to using cocaine is addiction. People are not immediately addicted by using cocaine once in a while. In fact, many individuals use cocaine recreationally. But the body does build tolerance to the drug, which means users need more and more to achieve the same effects.

Cocaine can also lead to psychological dependence. The effect of cocaine is short and the contrast between the positive feeling and the feeling afterward is sharp. When users feel exhausted and worn down, their craving for cocaine increases. The addiction to cocaine is persistent and annoying, and it hurts users financially, mentally, and socially.

Combining different drugs with cocaine is especially risky and unpredictable.

By combining alcohol and cocaine, the agent coca-ethylene is created. This psychoactive substance is more harmful to the liver than alcohol alone, loading an extra burden on the heart and blood vessels. It is also more addictive than only alcohol or only cocaine. Coca-ethylene's half-life lasts four times longer than cocaine, and, therefore, it takes longer to break down, allowing more opportunity for toxic effects to arise. People may also come to associate alcohol with cocaine use—so when they drink, they want to take coke, and vice versa. If users snort cocaine while drinking, they feel less drunk than they really are, which can lead to drinking more than they would have done without the coke, as well as drunk driving. Hangovers from this combination of drugs are horrific.

Combining coke and MDMA increases the risk of dehydration and overheating and can lead to changes in the brain: impaired memory, moodiness, and problems with concentration. This combination exerts pressure on the heart and increases the risk of physical exhaustion. Cocaine may also flatten the MDMA intoxication.

Combining cocaine and cannabis increases one's risk of acquiring psychological problems such as anxiety and restlessness.

## FIND ON THE FARM

After a long journey over rough terrain, we approach an outlying farm building. When we look around outside the building, we feel as if we are in a museum. Several old agricultural vehicles, a collection of tractors of various models, fire equipment, and mowers—all are lined up together. A friendly cat sits, alert, on a pile of firewood. The ground-level space inside the barn is also brimming with old equipment. We wonder if the cache could be inside.

"Maybe," the dog handler says. "But we will start the search outside, because dealers often prefer to hide drugs outside of buildings—the caches seem to be safer that way."

His drug-detector dog Ann begins her search with enthusiasm. With short words and hand signals, the handler directs her to the parked vehicles. She searches along the collection and easily climbs over containers and engines. Soon, she finds an old fire-hose cart. Getting more and more excited, she digs with her snout into the coiled hose. Dust and cobwebs cling to her fur as she tries to pull up the hose. The handler finds a route to his dog and helps her pull up the hose, under which have been hidden a cache of well-filled plastic bags. The handler throws Ann's toy out into the clear space of the yard, beyond the vehicles. Ann expertly finds a path to her toy and plays with it vigorously.

## KHAT

Khat (*Catha edulis*) is a flowering evergreen shrub native to East Africa and the Arabian Peninsula, where its leaves are chewed as part of an established cultural tradition and used for its stimulant-like effects to decrease fatigue and hunger. Khat comes as leaves, twigs, and shoots. Common street names are Abyssinian tea, African salad, catha, chat, kat, mira, oat, or quat. Khat has two active ingredients: cathine and cathinone.

Khat is grown and regularly used in Kenya, Somalia, and Yemen, where it is legal. Khat is exported from Kenya all over the world, mostly to expatriate Kenyans, Somalis, and Yemenis. Shipping has to be quick—khat can only be used when fresh.

Khat.

### HISTORY

The use of khat is traditional in Djibouti, Ethiopia, Kenya, Somalia, and Yemen, where chewing khat is linked to a deep-rooted sociocultural tradition. Here, chewing khat with a group is somewhat similar to drinking coffee with friends and family in the Western world. Khat sessions may last for hours, especially in Yemen, where a large portion of the population chews khat daily. In recent decades, khat use has increased dramatically in its countries of origin.

### THE MODE OF ADMINISTRATION

Khat is chewed. The fresher the leaves, the better.

### DOSAGE

Several leaves per person.

### EFFECTS

The active ingredient in khat is the alkaloid cathinone, found particularly in young, fresh leaves. The chemical structure of this compound is similar to amphetamine. Chewing khat provides one with an amphetamine-like effect. The drug stimulates and is uplifting. Users are active, and fatigue and hunger disappear. The drug also makes users talkative. The effects are felt after 60 minutes and last for several hours.

MENTAL EFFECTS
- Increased energy and alertness
- Mild euphoria and excitement
- Increased desire to talk

PHYSICAL EFFECTS
- Suppressed hunger and fatigue
- Slightly increased blood pressure and heart rate
- Dry mouth
- Increased sexual desire but decreased sexual potency
- Brown stains on the teeth
- Insomnia
- Gastrointestinal disorders

*SHORT-TERM RISKS*
The biggest short-term risks for khat users are depression and mood swings. The user feels dejected when the khat has worn off. He or she can also be easily irritated. With prolonged use, mood swings can increase.

*LONG-TERM RISKS*
Long-term users of khat increase their risks of having psychotic reactions and hallucinations. Especially if overused, there is a risk of delusions, hearing voices, and feeling paranoid. Taking a high dose also increases the risk of psychotic reactions. But because khat is chewed and only slowly absorbed into the body, users cannot quickly ingest a high dose.

*ADDICTION AND COMBINATIONS WITH OTHER DRUGS*
Physically, khat is not especially addictive.
Because khat makes users feel awake and alert, they may drink more alcohol than normal without feeling very drunk. This combination may lead to aggressive, rash, or reckless behavior.

*DETECTABILITY*
In urine, khat is detectable for one day after use.

## (METH)AMPHETAMINES

Amphetamines, also called speed, are stimulants that speed up the body's systems. Many are legally prescribed in tablet form and used to treat attention-deficit hyperactivity disorder (ADHD), narcolepsy, and obesity. Common prescription amphetamines include methylphenidate (Ritalin), amphetamine and dextroamphetamine (Adderall), and dextroamphetamine (Dexedrine).

Amphetamines are also used as performance and cognitive enhancers, and recreationally as aphrodisiacs and euphoriants. Common street names are bennies, black beauties, crank, speed, and uppers.

Speed is usually sold in powder form, but it also comes in pills. Many people who use speed think "wet" speed (a moist powder or paste) is better than dry speed, but wet speed contains all kinds of residues from the production process. It's often said that this wet speed comes directly from the source and is of higher quality. Tests, however, show that this speed is damp because it still contains the volatile solvents (including toxic methanol) that were used in the production process. These solvents are harmful to human health and therefore pose additional risks to those carried by dry speed.

Amphetamines are generally taken orally or injected. However, the development of "ice," the slang term for crystallized

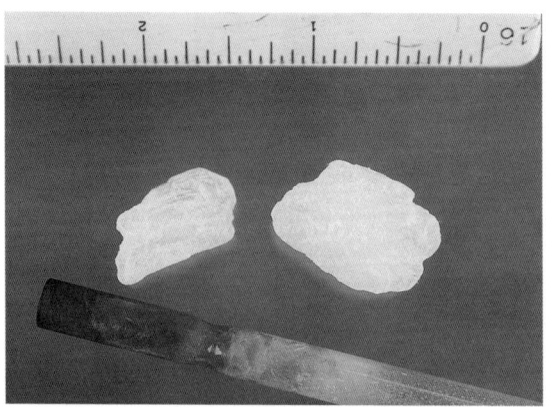

Ice, smokable methamphetamine, and a pipe.

methamphetamine hydrochloride, in 1919, means that speed can also be smoked. Just as crack is smokable cocaine, ice is smokable methamphetamine.

## HISTORY

Amphetamine was first synthesized in 1885 as a chemical alternative to the stimulant ephedrine. But it only started being used as a medicine in 1927. First, it was used as a blood-pressure-increasing agent. In the 1930s, it was sold under the name Benzedrine as a remedy for asthma because it widens the airways and as an over-the-counter inhaler to treat nasal congestion. During World War II (and also during the 2003 war in Iraq), amphetamine was used by soldiers to combat fatigue. Amphetamine has also been used as a medicine to treat attention deficit disorder, depression, a type of epilepsy, narcolepsy, obesity, and Parkinson's disease. After World War II, amphetamine entered the world market and, over the years since then, the use of clandestinely produced amphetamines has increased.

There are various types of amphetamines or substances similar to amphetamine, including the following:

- Ephedrine, which is found in the ephedra plant. Amphetamine is a counterfeit ephedrine made in the laboratory.
- L-amphetamine, which is levorotatory (anti-clockwise rotating) amphetamine, and dex or d-amphetamine, or dextrorotatory amphetamine. Amphetamines can be dextrorotatory or levorotatory. Dextrorotatory amphetamine fits better to the receptors in the brain than levorotatory, and is therefore stronger. You can compare dextrorotatory or levorotatory amphetamine with a right and a left glove, both of which you would like to put on your right hand. One just fits better. Illegal amphetamine is mostly a combination of dextrorotatory or levorotatory amphetamine.
- 4-fluoro-amphetamine, a designer drug with effects that more closely resemble those of MDMA.

- 4-methylamphetamine (4-MA), which is also sold as speed. Compared to amphetamine, 4-MA facilitates the release of more serotonin, which can lead to overheating. It looks and smells the same as dex-amphetamine.
- Methamphetamine (meth) is a different form of amphetamine. An important difference between the two is that methamphetamine is more readily soluble in fat than dex-amphetamine and is broken down slower. Methamphetamine, therefore, penetrates the brain with greater ease and works longer. It is two times stronger than dex-amphetamine.

Drug-trafficking organizations from Latin America are the primary manufacturers and distributors of methamphetamine to cities throughout the United States. Domestic, clandestine laboratory operators also produce and distribute meth, but usually on a smaller scale. The methods used to produce the drug depend on the availability of precursor chemicals. Usual street names include batu, bikers' coffee, chalk, chicken feed, crystal, glass, go-fast, hiropon, ice, meth, poor man's cocaine, shabu, trash, vidrio, and yaba.

Crystal, ice, and shabu are methamphetamine in crystal form. Crystal meth resembles glass fragments or shiny blue-white "rocks" of various sizes. In Thailand, yaba refers to dextrorotatory and levorotatory methamphetamine in pill form.

As well as being stronger than other types of amphetamine, methamphetamine is smokable. Therefore, its effects are much more severe. Users smoke the drug by putting it into a glass pipe and heating it with a lighter. After breathing it in several times, the user feels the first effects. Methamphetamine is also injected, particularly in the United States. It can come as dextrorotatory or levorotatory, and usually it is a mixture of both methamphetamines.

## THE MODES OF ADMINISTRATION

### NASAL

After the user snorts amphetamine powder, the drug is absorbed by the nasal mucosa, through which it enters the bloodstream. Effects are felt within minutes.

### ORAL

Amphetamine can be administered orally in pill form or by dissolving a bit of powder in a drink. Some users also place a bit of the powder into a piece of cigarette paper, fold it up, and swallow it. This method is called a "speed bomblet." When speed is taken orally, it takes 15 to 30 minutes for the user to feel it. Amphetamines "work" for a longer period if one swallows them than if one snorts them—snorting provides a quick, intense experience.

### INJECTION

When speed is injected into a vein, the effects are felt almost immediately.

### DOSAGE

Amphetamine is available on the illicit market in very different strengths. In the Netherlands, for example, the drug market mostly deals amphetamine powder cut with high concentrations of caffeine. It is difficult to ascertain the amount of amphetamine per gram of powder, but a usual dose is 5 to 40 milligrams of the powder. Of course, what one user takes compared to another user depends on the actual amount of amphetamine in the powder available, and also on the manner in which the drug is administered, since the body absorbs the drug in different ways depending on administration.

### EFFECTS

When swallowed, amphetamine takes 15 to 20 minutes to work. When snorted, it works after several minutes, and when injected, the user feels the effects almost immediately. The effects of amphetamine on average last between five and eight hours, or longer. Many users still experience after effects up to 12 hours after taking the drug. During those hours, it is impossible or very difficult to eat and sleep.

Amphetamine is a stimulant that increases blood pressure, body temperature, heart rate and respiration. The user gets large pupils and a dry mouth because less saliva is produced. The amphetamine user has to urinate frequently, sweats more, and eventually has a stiff jaw because of the tendency to tense the muscles when under the influence of the drug. Bronchi (the airways) expand, making breathing easier. The user feels cheerful and full of energy, and hunger and tiredness disappear like snow in the sun. The user talks a lot and quickly, is alert, and has a lot of energy. He or she could, for example, dance the whole night through. The user has more stamina and muscle strength. Some gain confidence; others feel aggressive, anxious, irritable, paranoid, or restless. A typical behavior performed by users under the influence of amphetamine is repetitive motion, such as moving objects around, only to replace them. After the amphetamine wears off, fatigue sets in and users begin to feel ill. It is difficult to fall asleep after amphetamine use, and amphetamine depletes the energy reserves in the body. For days after using the drug, users may be tired, and some people feel depressed. The amphetamine hangover is worse if one does not eat enough before, during, and after use.

MENTAL EFFECTS
- Cheerfulness
- Increased alertness
- Suppressed fatigue
- Restlessness
- Increased energy and stamina
- Confidence, even overconfidence
- Talkativeness
- Perception of an increased ability to think quickly
- Sometimes irritability and aggressiveness
- Sometimes decreased libido

PHYSICAL EFFECTS
- Increased heart rate and blood pressure
- Increased body temperature
- Large pupils

- Dry mouth
- Loss of appetite
- Dilated airways
- Tight muscles
- Stiff jaw, twitching of the face, and gnashing of teeth
- Restless movements
- Palpitations
- Sometimes dizziness, headache, nausea, and sweatiness
- Post-experience: insomnia

*SHORT-TERM RISKS*

Overdose is a short-term risk to amphetamine use—also a long-term risk, depending on the consequences of the overdose. The user may feel sick or vomit, have a high fever, and overheat. Furthermore, he or she could develop liver and kidney dysfunction and may have seizures. An overdose may result in coma and even, in rare cases, death.

Overheating (hyperthermia) may also result. One's body temperature rises after taking amphetamine. This tendency to have a higher body temperature when taking the drug is exacerbated if the user takes the drug in a hot, crowded environment (such as in a club or at a party, or in the sun at a festival). If the user then also dances for a long period and does not drink much water, he or she can become overheated. If the user's body temperature rises to 104 to 106°F (40–41°C), his or her life is at risk. (See description of overheating on page 181, in the section related to MDMA.)

An acute state of arousal is another short-term risk associated with this drug. One can tell if a user is in this state when he or she behaves restlessly and aggressively. He or she may strike out wildly and not calm down. The aggression is not focused but random. Often it is impossible to make contact with the user. A person in this state will go on fighting, even when he or she is overpowered by police or security. It is a dangerous situation in which the user will continue to fight, and his or her heart rate and blood pressure will continue to rise. When in this state, the user's life is in danger and action should be taken by medical professionals.

Other short-term risks include the following:
- Increased risk of heart (cardiovascular) problems
- Epileptic seizures
- Psychological problems and hangover
- Vivid hallucinations (bugs under the skin)
- In case of contaminated syringes, HIV and/or hepatitis infection
- Liver damage

*LONG-TERM RISKS*

If someone uses amphetamine too much and too often, his or her chances of developing psychosis may increase. Amphetamine psychosis can cause anxiety, delusions, and hallucinations, and can include sensations such as tingling and itching, as well as the feeling that small animals are under the skin. This kind of psychosis often begins with the feeling of being watched; users may have delusions of persecution. Users developing psychosis may also see flashes in their peripheral vision. However, if users stops using amphetamine, the psychosis will also stop. Heavy and prolonged amphetamine use also often causes depression or anxiety.

Other long-term risks to amphetamine use follow:
- Addiction
- Increased risk of cardiac arrhythmias, myocardial infarction, and stroke
- Fatigue and exhaustion
- Susceptibility to infections; for women, this usually means bladder infections
- Reduced resistance to health risks
- Reduced level of physical fitness
- Weight loss

- Inflamed nasal mucosa
- Reduced ability to smell and taste
- Chronic colds and nosebleeds
- Damaged teeth
- Blemishes on the skin (acne)

### ADDICTION AND COMBINATIONS WITH OTHER DRUGS

Users of amphetamine can become mentally dependent on the drug, the manifestation of which can vary from no longer liking to attend parties party without speed, or the need for speed to feel good or a little energetic. Someone who uses for a long time eventually needs 20 times more than he or she did at the start. There may be mental withdrawal symptoms. During the days following taking the drug, users often feel depressed, fatigued, lethargic, and restless. After a day or two, the user feels rested and his or her appetite increases. Physical withdrawal symptoms are relatively mild.

Combining the use of amphetamine and MDMA or cocaine adds extra pressure on the heart and blood vessels. The hangover is often worse if one takes this combination than it would be after taking any single one of these drugs. Amphetamine works against the amorous effects of MDMA. With this combination, users increase their risk of brain damage (it could be that amphetamine increases the brain damage caused by MDMA). This combination also increases the chances of overheating; and the combined use of MDMA and amphetamine increases the risk of serotonin syndrome (see page 182).

Because amphetamine increases alertness, keeps sleep at bay, and makes users feel physically stronger than normal, they are able to drink more alcohol without feeling very drunk. However, the hangover the next day is awful. The combination of amphetamine and alcohol may also lead users to engage in (extremely) aggressive behavior. The risk of rash or reckless behavior also increases with this combination.

Combining GHB with amphetamine is similar to combining alcohol with the drug: a downer with an upper. The body receives conflicting signals. GHB can alleviate the stimulant effect of amphetamines. If the amphetamine begins to wear off and there is sufficient GHB in the body, the user may be rendered unconscious by the GHB.

Combining amphetamine with antidepressants may result in a dangerous rise in blood pressure. Use of the old-class antidepressants (monoamine oxidase inhibitors [MAOIs]) with amphetamine is risky; the user's blood pressure may rise dangerously, and the risk of developing serotonin syndrome also increases (see page 182).

Some users smoke cannabis after using amphetamine with the aim of calming down or getting some sleep. However, smoking dope with amphetamine may make the user feel anxious and restless.

### DETECTABILITY

How long (meth)amphetamine is detectable in the blood or urine depends on several factors, including the dose taken, personal metabolism (the rate at which waste products are broken down, especially by the liver), and stomach contents at the time of use. Generally speaking, amphetamine will no longer be detectable in a user's urine two to three days after use. If the user takes amphetamines excessively, it may take four to five days for the body to flush the drug.

## Narcotics

Narcotics are also known as opioids. The term "narcotic" originally referred to a variety of substances that dulled the senses and relieved pain. Though some people still refer to all drugs as narcotics, today, medical use of the term "narcotic" is always in reference to opium, opium derivatives, and their semi-synthetic substitutes. Opium has been used since ancient times as an analgesic and a source of other drugs.

The natural source of opium is the poppy, an herbaceous plant often grown for its colorful flowers. One species of poppy that grows in Asia and South America, *Papaver somniferum*, is the source for all natural opioids. Some opioids, such as morphine and codeine, occur naturally in opium, the gummy substance collected from the seedpod of the opium poppy.

Semi-synthetic opioids are synthesized by changing the chemical structure of naturally occurring opium products, such as morphine and codeine, and include heroin, oxycodone, hydrocodone, and hydromorphone.

Synthetic opioids, such as methadone, meperidine, and fentanyl, are made from chemicals without using a naturally occurring opioid as a starting material.

Several opioids are prescribed by doctors to relieve pain and come in a variety of forms, including tablets, capsules, syrups, solutions, and suppositories. When used carefully and with a health care provider's guidance, these drugs can effectively reduce pain.

Continued use of opioids, prescribed or otherwise, can result in physical dependence and addiction. The body adapts to the presence of the drug, and withdrawal symptoms occur if use is reduced or stopped. These symptoms include cold flashes with goose bumps, diarrhea, insomnia, muscle and bone pain, restlessness, and vomiting. Tolerance can also occur, meaning that long-term users must increase their doses to achieve the same high they achieved when they first used the drug. If dependent users cannot get the opioid they are addicted to, they may turn to the black market for them, and in the absence of the prescription drugs they are used to, resort to taking cheaper and riskier substitutes such as heroin.

#### OPIUM

Opium is obtained by first making an incision in an unripe poppy seedpod, which will then leak a milky substance. This substance is then dried to create a dark-brown powder, called raw opium, which can be smoked. Morphine, a heavy narcotic and analgesic

## RAW OPIUM

For centuries, the opium poppy has been cultivated in Asia, and it is an important part of the economy. The whole plant is used after opium is harvested: oil is pressed from the poppy seeds, and the remaining plant is used as fodder for cattle. The plant grows best in mountainous areas, at an altitude of about 3,280 feet (1000 m). The plant needs a lot of attention and must be weeded regularly, so individual farmers do not cultivate large poppy fields.

About half a million people in Thailand's mountainous areas, which produce 150 tons of opiate per year, work in the opium fields. About two weeks after the plants have flowered and the flower leaves have fallen off, the farmer and his family begin the harvest. Bit by bit, the green pods are slashed—not too deeply and not too shallowly—with a special knife. The white milk drips out of the pods and coagulates when exposed to the air. Slowly the milk becomes a brown, sticky mass. About 24 hours after leaking out, the sticky stuff is scraped from the pods and collected. One poppy produces about 1 gram of raw opium—a plantation that is 328 square feet (100 m$^2$) produces about 22 pounds (10 kg) of raw opium.

A more modern method of harvesting, used for pharmaceutical-grade opium, is to extract the alkaloids from the mature, dried plant.

used for pain control, can be made from the raw opium. Codeine, also a painkiller, can be made from morphine. Compared to morphine, codeine is a weak painkiller, but it is a powerful cough suppressant. Morphine can also be processed chemically to create heroin, which looks like a grainy (white, gray, or brown) powder. One street name for heroin is "brown," referring to the brown powder.

Street names for opium include Auntie, black pill, chandu, Chinese molasses, Chinese tobacco, dopium, dream gun, God's medicine, gondola, goric, great tobacco, hop/hops, O, O.P., ope, and zero.

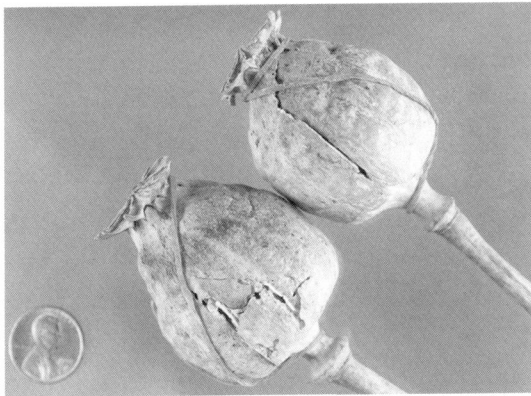

The opium poppy's seedpod.

## HISTORY

The history of opium is deep. Ancient Egyptians used it, as did many other peoples of the same period in the Middle East. By the seventh century, opium came to China via Arab traders. At first, the Chinese used it to cure diarrhea, but it soon was used as a pain reliever. Opium was introduced to Europe around 1525 as a medicinal drink called "laudanum," a mixture of alcohol and opium. It was popular and used by both adults and children as sleep aid and pain reliever. Eventually, opium came to be seen as a panacea for almost all diseases and complaints.

Early Chinese opium users were supplied by merchants coming from India. But the Portuguese took over this trade in the 16th century. After the first Portuguese ship arrived in Canton in 1514, the popularity of smoking opium increased. In 1567, the Chinese emperor gave the Portuguese permission to start a settlement in Macao, which became an opium-trading center. There was much profit to importing opium to China, where it was not only smoked recreationally but also used as a remedy for malaria. Many Chinese users became addicted, and it became such a problem that the Yongzheng Emperor, who ruled from 1722 to 1735, decided to ban the drug. Importing the drug and cultivating the plant became illegal—the opium trade should have collapsed. However, the emperor was powerless in the face of foreign opium merchants, who were protected by their governments. Besides, the new laws regarding cultivation, importation, and use were nearly impossible to enforce.

Alongside the Portuguese, Dutch merchants also continued to import opium to China, and soon the English began to take over the opium trade in the area. In 1839, the Chinese emperor decided that protests and laws against the trade written on paper were not effective. He sent an emissary to Canton, who confiscated more than 20,000 boxes of opium and then burned them in public. This incident kicked off the first Opium War (1839–1842), and a few months later a British fleet hit back hard, destroying, in just 45 minutes, a large part of the Chinese navy in the Battle of Chuenpi.

The British demanded a legalization of the opium trade, compensation for the destroyed drugs, sovereignty over some islands along the Chinese coast, and freedom to enter all Chinese harbors. The war ended in 1842 with the Agreement of Hanking—the English got what they wanted, and Hong Kong became a Crown colony.

Subsequently, other Western countries, including the United States, gained the same privileges as the English in China. But 12 years later, in 1856, another war broke out, this one between the French and English, each trying to protect their spheres of interest in the trade. This second war ended with the bringing down of Beijing and another agreement favorable to the Western traders, who were insensitive to the opium problem in China. This agreement lasted until about 1908, when an international commission came together in Shanghai whose discussions led to the International Opiate Conference in The Hague, Netherlands, in 1912. Up until that point, opium in the United States and in England was an over-the-counter drug.

Today, experts think that between 70 and 80 percent of the world's raw opium comes from the Golden Triangle, an isolated border region in Thailand, Burma, and Laos. Almost all of this opium is produced for the illegal drug trade. An area called the Golden Sickle (Iran, Afghanistan, and Pakistan) also produces a lot of illegal opium. The most important producer of the legal opium used for prescription drugs is India.

### THE MODES OF ADMINISTRATION

Opium can be a liquid, solid, or powder, but most illegal opium is available commercially as a fine brownish powder. It can be smoked, intravenously injected, or taken in pill form.

### EFFECTS

Opioids impart a general sense of well-being, reducing tension, anxiety, and aggression. These effects are helpful in a therapeutic setting but contribute to users' risk of dependence.

### MENTAL EFFECTS

Opioid use comes with a variety of unwanted effects, including drowsiness, inability to concentrate, and apathy. Use can lead to psychological dependence. Long after the physical need for the drug has passed, the user may continue to think and talk about using opioids and feel overwhelmed when coping with daily activities. Even if a user is able to stop taking the drug, relapse is common if changes have not been made to the physical environment or to the behavioral motivators that prompted the abuse in the first place.

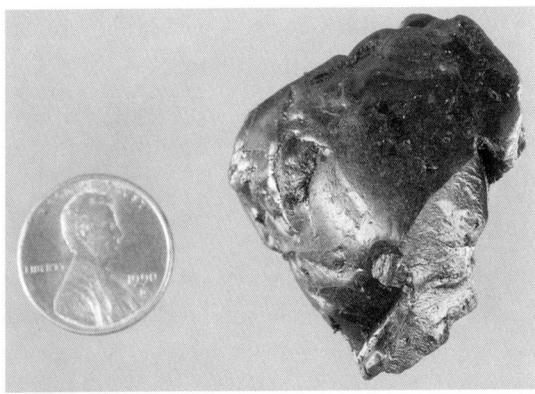

Solid opium.

## PHYSICAL EFFECTS

Opioids are prescribed by doctors to treat pain, suppress coughs, cure diarrhea, and put people to sleep. Effects depend heavily on the dose, how the drug is taken, and previous exposure. Negative effects include the following:

- Slowed physical activity
- Constriction of the pupils
- Flushing of the face and neck
- Constipation
- Nausea
- Vomiting
- Slowed breathing

With an increased dose, both pain relief and harmful effects also increase. However, except in cases of extreme intoxication, there is no loss of motor coordination or slurred speech. Some opioid preparations are so potent that a single dose can be lethal to an inexperienced user.

## SHORT-TERM RISKS

Opium can provide pain relief and impart euphoria, followed by a sense of well-being and calm drowsiness or sedation. Short-term risks can be that breathing slows, potentially to the point of unconsciousness and death with large doses. Other effects can include confusion, constipation, and nausea. Use of opium with other substances that depress the central nervous system, such as alcohol, antihistamines, barbiturates, benzodiazepines, or general anesthetics, increases the risk of life-threatening respiratory depression.

## LONG-TERM RISKS

Long-term use of opium can lead to drug tolerance: the user needs more and more of the drug to get similar euphoric effects. Opium use can also lead to physical dependence and addiction. Withdrawal symptoms can occur if long-term use is reduced or stopped.

Many of the long-term risks of opium use arise from smoking the drug. Smoking opium can be more damaging than smoking tobacco or marijuana. Those who smoke opium do so by combining it with marijuana or tobacco, which damages the lungs. Smoking opium can also lead to heart disease and other consequences that result from a lack of oxygen in the regulatory system. Eating and smoking opium can lead to liver and kidney damage. Long-term use of the drug may cause renal failure. In addition, if the drug is injected, or if derivatives of the drug are injected, there can be severe damage to veins, and illness can result from using contaminated needles. Long-term risks can also include abdominal distention and bloating; brain damage due to hypoxia, resulting from respiratory depression; constipation; liver damage (especially prevalent in abuse of drugs that combine opiates with acetaminophen); nausea; and vomiting.

### ADDICTION AND COMBINATIONS WITH OTHER DRUGS

Physical dependence is a consequence of chronic opioid use, and withdrawal takes place when drug use is discontinued. Early withdrawal symptoms often include watery eyes, runny nose, yawning, and sweating. As the withdrawal continues, symptoms can include the following:

- Restlessness
- Irritability
- Loss of appetite
- Nausea
- Tremors
- Drug craving
- Severe depression
- Vomiting
- Increased heart rate and blood pressure
- Chills alternating with flushing and excessive sweating

## FENTANYL

Fentanyl is a type of morfinomimeticum, a substance whose effects are like those of morphine. However, fentanyl is also about a hundred times stronger than morphine. Dr. Paul Janssen of Belgium developed the drug in 1959, and it was distributed by his company, Janssen Pharmaceutica. In a medical context, it is used as a potent painkiller during surgery. The painkilling effects are short-lived and can be counteracted by administering naloxone, a substance that blocks or reverses the effects of opioid medications.

In addition to its use in operations, fentanyl topical patches are prescribed for chronic pain—a 100-milligram patch contains about 16.8 milligrams of the drug, which slowly releases into the skin at a rate of about 0.1 milligrams per hour. Fentanyl can also be injected; when employing this format, in comparison to patches, users receive less of the drug (0.05 milligrams per milliliter). Fentanyl comes in the form of fentanyl citrate, too, a lozenge on a stick like a lollipop. The lozenge dissolves slowly in the mouth and is absorbed by the oral mucosa. The drug is also available as a nasal spray and a dissolving (buccal) tablet.

Fentanyl's most common side effects (which affect more than 10 percent of users) include abnormal physical weakness, confusion, constipation, diarrhea, dry mouth, nausea, somnolence, and sweating. Between 3 and 10 percent of fentanyl users also experience abdominal pain, anorexia and weight loss, anxiety, apnea, depression, dizziness, fatigue, flu-like symptoms, hallucinations, headache, hypoventilation, indigestion, labored breathing, nervousness, and urinary retention. Fentanyl use has also been associated with brain-damage-associated aphasia, which is an inability to understand and formulate language.

A number of synthesized fentanyl analogs are available to users, all of which have slightly different effects. For example, alfentanil (Rapifen) is an ultra-short-lived (5–10 minutes) opioid analgesic. Carfentanil (Wildnil) is a highly potent analog that is used by veterinarians to anesthetize large animals; it is about 10,000 times as strong as morphine, so 10 milligrams is sufficient for an adult elephant. Sufentanil (Sufenta) is highly potent, too, about 10–15 times stronger than fentanyl.

Fentanyl is also used as a recreational drug, which has led to hundreds of overdose deaths per year in the 2000s. In fact, death from fentanyl overdose was declared a public health crisis in Canada in September 2015, and it continues to be a major killer in that country. In 2016, deaths from fentanyl overdoses in British Columbia, Canada, averaged two persons per day. That same year, news media identified that the mass production of fentanyl pills in North America is partly due to illegal trade in fentanyl powder from China. The powder is received and then pressed into pills that sometimes look identical to the prescription painkiller Oxycontin. The contraband fentanyl powder is also added to Xanax pills. In 2016, police took down a lab near Calgary, Alberta, Canada, that was allegedly shipping 100,000 fentanyl pills a month to that city, where 90 people overdosed on the drug in 2015. The British Columbia Coroners Service showed the deadly opioid was linked to nearly half of more than 250 overdose deaths tallied for the first four months of 2016.

Opium is also used in combination with other drugs. For example, "black" is a combination of marijuana, opium, and methamphetamine; "Buddha" is potent marijuana spiked with opium. Combining opium with alcohol or other drugs is a dangerous practice. Opium should never be mixed with other substances that similarly depress the central nervous system, such as alcohol, anesthetics, antihistamines, barbiturates, and benzodiazepines. Mixing these substances can cause breathing to stop and can lead to coma or death. The combination of multiple sedative drugs has an effect on the central nervous system that is greater than the sum of each drug's individual effect.

*DETECTABILITY*

In urine, opium is detectable for two to three days after use; and in saliva, opium is detectable from one hour to three days after use (depending on the quality and amount of the opium, the frequency of use, and the individual characteristics of the user, such as metabolism and weight).

**MORPHINE**

Morphine is a non-synthetic narcotic with high potential for abuse and is the principal constituent of opium. It is one of the most effective drugs known for the relief of severe pain, acting directly on the central nervous system to decrease the feeling of

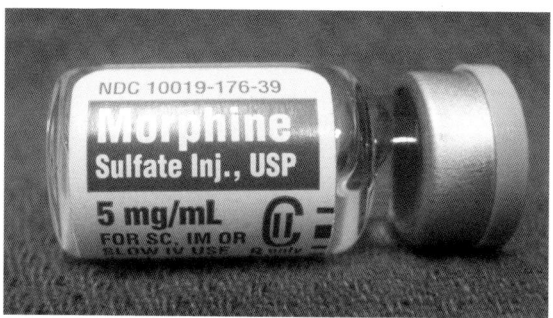

Morphine.

both acute pain and chronic pain. Common street names include dreamer, first line, hows, M.S., morf, and morpho.

### HISTORY

German pharmacist Friedrich Wilhelm Adam Sertürner from Paderborn was the first to isolate morphine from raw opium between 1803 and 1805. He called the isolated alkaloid "morphium" after the Greek god of dreams, Morpheus, the son of Hypnos, the Greek god of sleep. Morphine was not only the first alkaloid to be extracted from opium but also the first alkaloid to be isolated from any plant. The firm Merck in Darmstadt began marketing the drug in 1827, and in 1846, German research chemists began to produce morphium tablets, which were sold under the name "Morphine." Morphine was more widely used after the invention of the hypodermic syringe in 1854.

Raw opium contains both morphine and codeine. Usually raw opium's monetary value depends on its percentage of morphine. This amount varies depending on the origin of the opium (opium from Turkey, for example, has a high percentage of morphine, while opium from India has a high percentage of codeine). Medicinal, legal, opium is standardized to include 10 percent morphine.

Merchants collect illegal opium from farmers, and then it is whisked off to different illegal labs in the country of origin, or in neighboring countries, where lab workers isolate the morphine.

These labs often consist of only a few tents containing chemicals, barrels, and pots and pans. The raw opium is cooked in old oil barrels. After that, chemicals are added to the cooked substance to isolate the morphine.

## THE MODES OF ADMINISTRATION

Pharmaceutical forms of morphine include oral solutions, immediate- and sustained-release tablets and capsules, injectable preparations, and suppositories. Those dependent on morphine prefer injection because the drug enters the bloodstream more quickly than it does when ingested.

Morphine is a very strong painkiller, so users must be careful with doses. Tablets, capsules, drinks, and suppositories work within one to two hours. Injections and infusions work faster. The maximum oral dose is 10 to 20 milligrams at a time, every four hours. The dose for subcutaneous or intramuscular injection is usually 10 milligrams at a time; the intravenous dose is 2.5 to 5 milligrams in 4 to 5 milliliters of the liquid over the course of four to five minutes. The effect lasts four to seven hours. Slow-release tablets and capsules work for about 12 hours.

## MENTAL AND PHYSICAL EFFECTS

Morphine's effects include euphoria and relief from physical pain. Chronic use of morphine results in tolerance and physical and psychological dependence. Morphine also decreases feelings of hunger and inhibits the cough reflex.

### MENTAL EFFECTS

- Euphoria
- Repression of emotional pain
- Possible hallucinations

### PHYSICAL EFFECTS

- Pain control
- Possible constipation
- Loss of appetite and nausea

### SHORT-TERM RISKS

- Risk of infection. Unhygienic and shared needles increase this risk. Diseases and disorders that can be transmitted include blood poisoning, hepatitis, HIV, and vein inflammation.
- Overdose. When one takes too much morphine, breathing, blood pressure, and heart rate decrease, which can lead to death. The final stages of an overdose include unconsciousness and coma.

### LONG-TERM RISKS

- Malnutrition, because morphine can reduce the user's appetite. This can lead to serious complications and can even be lethal.
- Chronic constipation.
- In women, there is the chance that the menstrual cycle will stop or be disrupted.
- Prolonged use of morphine can cause both physical and psychological dependence.

### ADDICTION AND COMBINATIONS WITH OTHER DRUGS

Morphine is mentally addictive because of the significant difference between how the patient feels with and without morphine. Physical dependence also occurs because the body becomes habituated to a regular dose of morphine and adjusts itself accordingly.

Since morphine and alcohol (and other drugs) suppress respiration and heart rate, it is dangerous to combine them. This combination suppresses breathing and heart rate to such a degree that the user may be rendered unconscious, slip into a coma, and possibly die.

The combination of morphine and cocaine (and other stimulants) is also very dangerous. Because morphine suppresses respiration and heart rate, while cocaine increases them, there is a high risk of cardiac arrhythmia (irregular heart rate) and death.

### DETECTABILITY

In urine, morphine is detectable for two to three days after use; in saliva, it is detectable from one hour to three days after use.

## SPEEDY'S NOSE

Some days, we only have everyday tasks to complete with our detector dogs. But other days, like today, we must get to work and help uncover a drug-smuggling ring. Today, the suspects have made our job especially difficult. When they realized they were busted, they tried to escape in a rain of gunfire. This escape attempt failed, thanks to border patrol officers and a guard dog. But now, it's time for our dog Speedy to take on the case and search for the undoubtedly well-hidden drugs in the smugglers' car. First he searches the outside of the car, clockwise, sticking his nose into every crevice. Poised at one of the fenders, he waits, sniffs, crawls between the wheel and the body of the car and, with mounting excitement, begins to scratch. Officers find bags of drugs in the place Speedy indicated. In the meantime, Speedy continues his investigation, giving the now-cooled engine a once over. After an extensive search, he finds a big packet of drugs cleverly hidden in the air filter, a place where it can hardly be missed by Speedy's efficient nose. Failures due to Speedy's nose are almost never reported. No matter how expertly the contraband may be packed and hidden, the smell always gives it away.

## HEROIN

Heroin is manufactured from morphine, which is obtained from the opium poppy. Its effects are similar to those of morphine. Both are central-nervous-system depressants and very effective painkillers. Heroin is highly addictive; after only two to 10 days of use, users can be addicted, and kicking that habit is next to impossible. It is a very effective painkiller, in a clear form is about four to six times stronger than morphine, and is often better tolerated than morphine, but because it is so addictive, it is rarely prescribed for medical purposes. It comes in several forms, including "black tar" from Mexico and white heroin from Colombia. Common street names include big H, black tar, boy, brown, Chiva, H, Harry, hell dust, horse, junk, negra, shit, skag, smack, and thunder.

Black-tar heroin.

## HISTORY

Heroin was first synthesized in 1874 by C.R. Alder Wright, an English chemistry and physics researcher at St. Mary's Hospital Medical School in London. He synthesized diacetylmorphine (heroin) by adding two acetyl groups to a morphine molecule. Heinrich Dreser, a chemist at Bayer Laboratories in Germany, continued to test heroin, and Bayer marketed it as an analgesic and "sedative for coughs" in 1888. When its addictive potential was recognized, Bayer ceased its production in 1913.

In the 1960s and 1970s, a scheme headed by Corsican criminals, called the French Connection, involved Turkish morphine being smuggled to Italy and the south of France, where it was synthesized into heroin in labs before it was moved along to Canada and then into the United States. The operation was responsible for bringing in most of the heroin used in the United States at the time. The scheme fell apart when the United States, through the United Nations, exerted pressure on the Turkish government to institute controls on poppy cultivation and exports, and when the French police and Drug Enforcement Administration (DEA) worked to curtail the activities of heroin producers in Europe.

Still, six provinces in Turkey continue to cultivate poppies for the pharmaceutical industry. Unfortunately, legal opium does enter the illegal market, despite stricter laws.

# THE DIFFERENT DRUGS

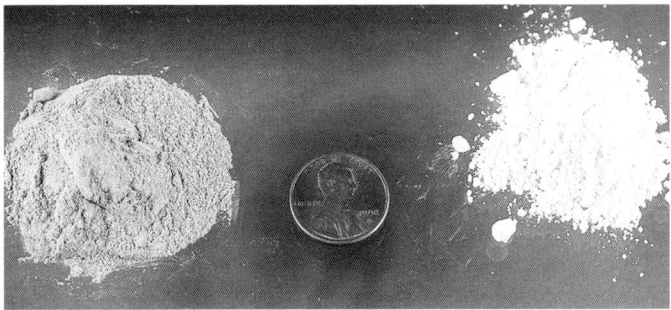

Asian heroin.

Since about 1975, heroin smugglers in Southeast Asia have been targeting the European market, smuggling heroin from Bangkok, Hong Kong, and Singapore. This Asian heroin is of another quality and form than the white heroin produced in Europe. European (Turkish) heroin does not dissolve well in water. It is especially suitable for smoking. Asian (Chinese) heroin is prepared in a different way and dissolves easily in water so it can be injected.

### MANUFACTURE

Heroin is made in illegal laboratories, often by chemists who need the money or are pressed to do so. The risks are huge, both in terms of being arrested and incarcerated (even accruing the death penalty in some countries) and in terms of becoming an addict oneself as one works to create heroin from opium. To produce heroin, some equipment and knowledge is necessary, but really, the production is rather simple. Blocks of raw morphine are ground into powder, which is then dried. The chemist makes sure the powder is totally dry before proceeding because moisture will affect the next phase: the acetyl process. During this process, the chemist adds acetic anhydride to the raw morphine powder to create the desired product, diacetylmorphine. A drug-detector dog recognizes heroin by the smell of the acetic acid.

### THE MODES OF ADMINISTRATION

Heroin is typically sold as a white or brownish powder, or as the black sticky substance known on the streets as "black-tar heroin."

Although purer heroin is becoming more common, most street heroin is cut with other drugs or with substances such as corn starch, powdered milk, quinine, or sugar. Heroin can be smoked, snorted, or injected. The purest heroin is usually snorted or smoked.

Some users "chase the dragon" to take heroin. This is a slang phrase of Cantonese origin from Hong Kong, referring to inhaling the vapor from heated opium, morphine, and heroin. The drug is placed and heated on a piece of aluminum foil. The moving smoke is chased after with a tube held by the user and through which the user inhales the smoke.

When injected, powdered heroin is first laid on a spoon and mixed with water and lemon juice or ascorbic acid. The mixture is then heated and the dissolved heroin is pulled up into a syringe and injected directly into a vein.

*DOSAGE*

The dose a user needs to achieve the desired effect varies widely and highly depends on the user and the degree to which the user is habituated to the drug. When someone with no tolerance to the drug injects it, a normal dose is between 5 and 10 milligrams. Users with high tolerance need a dose of 20 to even 60 milligrams to achieve the desired results. The effects begin to be felt after about 10 to 20 seconds and last for about four hours. A typical dose for the drug when nasally administered is between 15 and 25 milligrams.

*EFFECTS*

Morphine and heroin have approximately the same effects, although heroin is stronger. The effects of heroin depend on the dose, purity, and method of administration. The experience and physical condition of the user also play roles in the effects felt. The first few times one uses heroin are almost always unpleasant. The user can suffer dizziness, headaches, nausea, vomiting, and/or itching all over the body, but especially on the face. After several times, the body tolerates these effects and they disappear, allowing the narcotic and analgesic effects to predominate. The user is left with warm, happy feelings of contentment and security. Feelings of cold, fear, hunger, pain, and sadness seem to evaporate. The user enters a drowsy, dreamlike state. When under the influence of heroin, many users are passive and quiet and are easily irritated by "whining in their heads" when someone tries to speak to them. Their heart rate and breathing slow down and their body temperature goes down slightly. Their pupils reduce to the size of pinpricks. The motility of the intestines decreases, as well. Many users have trouble with bowel movements (constipation) and their needs for sex decrease.

**MENTAL EFFECTS**

- Feelings of bliss, warmth, and safety
- Complete relaxation
- Feelings of emotional indifference or superficiality
- Disappearance of all unpleasant feelings such as pain and sorrow

**PHYSICAL EFFECTS**

- Pain relief
- Cough suppressant
- Slow heartbeat and breathing
- Lower body temperature
- Drowsiness, sleepiness, possible unconsciousness
- Pupils like pinpricks
- Decreased intestinal motility (constipation)
- Inhibition of sexual function (reduced libido, impotence in men)
- In women, cessation of menstruation
- Poor appetite
- Vague upper abdominal discomfort

### SHORT-TERM RISKS

The user may simply stop breathing as a result of taking heroin. Users undergoing an overdose look pale and are limp, breathe shallowly (if they are breathing at all), sometimes foam at the mouth, and may vomit or have seizures. Common causes of overdose include the following:

- The user is a novice, unused to the drug's strength.
- The user has taken a break from using the drug, but then started again using the same dose as the last time he or she used.
- The user has consumed contaminated heroin.
- The user has taken heroin that is stronger than anticipated.
- The user took the drug when feeling exhausted or physically unwell.

Another short-term risk to heroin use is contracting HIV and/or hepatitis through contaminated needles, syringes, or syringe attributes.

### LONG-TERM RISKS

Heroin itself is not especially harmful to the body, but the way of life that accompanies heroin use *is* harmful. Many heroin users live on the streets, eat poorly, are socially isolated, and may use contaminated needles. Besides being victims of overdoses from heroin and AIDS contracted by using contaminated needles, users may also die as the result of accidents, cancer, cardiovascular disease, cirrhosis of the liver, respiratory disease, suicide, or violence.

Because heroin suppresses pain, some users may ignore complaints and leave them so they worsen unnecessarily or until they are too late to address.

When a woman uses heroin, menstruation is often irregular or ceases. But she can become pregnant. Pregnancies are often only detected at an advanced stage, and babies born to heroin-dependent women are at first physically dependent on heroin, too, and will go through withdrawal. A baby in withdrawal cries a lot, is nervous, and is often awake. Babies born to mothers who used heroin during their pregnancies may also have developmental disorders.

In the long term, users may experience anxiety, depression, personality disorders, and psychotic episodes.

### ADDICTION AND COMBINATIONS WITH OTHER DRUGS

Heroin is highly addictive. The body quickly gets used to heroin, and so to feel the desired effect of euphoria every time, users must continually use more and have an increasing need to use. Withdrawal symptoms occur quickly—after only two or three weeks of use—and cause users to feel sick, clammy, and cold, with abdominal cramps, chills, diarrhea, runny nose, and muscle pain in the arms and legs. These symptoms disappear when heroin is taken again. But each time the user stops taking the drug, the withdrawal symptoms become more intense. The dependent user puts everything aside and does anything (even steal) for a dose. Psychological dependence is almost a given.

Heroin is often used in combination with other agents, for example, with alcohol or cocaine. The combination of heroin with other depressants is dangerous. The respiration-inhibitory activity of opioids, for example, is enhanced by the use of alcohol. Combining heroin with monoamine oxidase inhibitors (MAOIs, used to treat depression or Parkinson's disease) may lead to high blood pressure.

### DETECTABILITY

Heroin is usually detectable in blood for up to about eight hours after use. As well, there are tests that scan for the breakdown products of heroin, which are detectable in urine for three to five days after use. Heroin is detectable in saliva for one to four days, and in hair for up to 90 days after use.

## Party Drugs

Party drugs are used regularly at dance or house parties. Of course, party drugs can also be used on other occasions. These are usually stimulants that give users a joyful, ecstatic outlook, but the user's perception is often distorted. For instance, music seems more "intense" than usual, and users often become totally absorbed in "the rhythm of the bass." Many party drugs give users a burst of temporary energy and prevent the feeling of fatigue. Users can "party" longer than usual, drink more alcohol without passing out, and hold their own on the dance floor for longer than normal. The extra energy is a short-term effect; in the longer term, the drug plunges the user into exhaustion and depression. Party drugs can be addictive, causing psychological and physical dependency. Typical party drugs include, but are not limited to, alcohol, amphetamines, cocaine, ecstasy, GHB, and poppers.

**POPPERS**

"Poppers" is the term given to alkyl nitrites that are inhaled for recreational purposes, especially in preparation for sex. American magazines such as *Time*, *Queerty*, and the *Wall Street Journal* report that popper use among homosexual men began as a way to enhance sexual pleasure, but "quickly spread to avant-garde heterosexuals" as a result of aggressive marketing.[5]

Poppers come as a yellowish liquid sold in small bottles. Formerly it came in the form of small capsules that, if broken open, made a popping noise—hence the name. The liquid is flammable,

Poppers.

evaporates quickly, irritates the skin, and smells very strongly of dirty socks. Poppers usually contain amyl nitrite but also butyl nitrite or isoamyl nitrite.

### HISTORY
In 1844, the French chemist Antoine Jérôme Balard synthesized amyl nitrite, which was first used in 1859 to combat heart pain. It wasn't until the 1960s, however, that the medical establishment began prescribing the substance in pill form. Poppers thus became available to recreational users, and the drug became popular among homosexual men and in the dance party circuit.

### THE MODES OF ADMINISTRATION
The liquid is dripped onto a handkerchief and then its vapor is inhaled. Some users dip a cigarette into the bottle and inhale the drug's vapor through the unlit cigarette. Poppers irritate the skin, so users take care not to allow the liquid to come into contact with skin or mucous membranes.

### DOSAGE
One sniff is enough for most people to feel this drug's impact, or sometimes even to lose consciousness.

### EFFECTS
Inhaling amyl nitrate for 10 seconds results in a one- to two-hour daze that enhances sexual experiences and strengthens erections. The drug causes the smooth muscles and blood-vessel walls to relax. The blood vessels dilate, which lowers blood pressure and may increase one's risk of feeling dizzy or fainting. The lowered blood pressure may also have a negative effect on erections. The heart has to work harder under these conditions, and a throbbing headache might ensue. Users experience a mild, brief, blissful feeling that is often described as a brief sensation of almost unconsciousness, somewhat similar to the effect of nitrous oxide. Users suddenly feel very relaxed, weak, and dizzy, and a warm feeling rises to the head.

MENTAL EFFECTS
- Feeling almost unconsciousness, blissful, and relaxed
- Sexual excitement

PHYSICAL EFFECTS
- Widened blood vessels
- Decreased blood pressure
- Fast heartbeat, palpitations
- Warm feelings go to the user's head
- Weakness and dizziness that can lead to fainting
- Throbbing headache
- Slackened smooth muscles
- Weakened and short-lived erection, or strengthened and long-lasting erection
- Nausea
- Sometimes: blue lips or fingernails
- Rarely: loss of consciousness

SHORT-TERM RISKS
- Throbbing headache
- Dizziness
- Loss of consciousness/fainting
- Palpitations
- Hemolytic anemia due to hemolysis, the abnormal breakdown of red blood cells
- When the skin comes into direct contact with poppers, skin rashes may arise. If the popper-infused liquid is swallowed or comes into contact with nasal mucosa, severe irritation and poisoning may result.

LONG-TERM RISKS

With sporadic and limited use, the risks to using poppers are few and minor. With prolonged and frequent use, there are risks to one's physical health. Because poppers increase intraocular pressure, visual disturbances may occur. Brain damage, as a result of damaged blood vessels, may result. Long-term users may also develop methemoglobinemia, a blood disorder in which a higher than normal amount of methemoglobin is produced in red blood cells and a decreased amount of oxygen is available to tissues.

*ADDICTION AND COMBINATION WITH OTHER DRUGS*

Psychological dependence can occur with regular use of poppers. Because use is often combined with sex, some users say that sex is not enjoyable without poppers. With regular use, tolerance develops.

Some users combine poppers with Viagra. But poppers contain nitrates, substances that have the same effect on blood pressure as Viagra. Combined use of Viagra and poppers can cause extremely low blood pressure, stroke, heart attack, and/or even death.

Combining GHB and poppers is particularly dangerous to levels of oxygen in the blood. Taking poppers increases heart rate and decreases blood pressure. Poppers also hinder the transport of oxygen through the bloodstream. GHB can delay breathing.

The combination of MDMA or speed and poppers can cause heart palpitations.

*DETECTABILITY*

Poppers are broken down very quickly in the body and are virtually impossible to detect in blood or urine. There are no known drug tests that can reveal the use of poppers.

## Smart Drugs and Eco Drugs

**SMART DRUGS**

A smart drug is one that is prescribed for dementia, epilepsy, and forgetfulness. Sometimes smart drugs are used by healthy people for other purposes, for instance if they want to improve memory, concentration, and intelligence. Examples of smart drugs include amphetamine pharmaceuticals and methylphenidate (a substituted phenethylamine), both of which improve cognitive control;

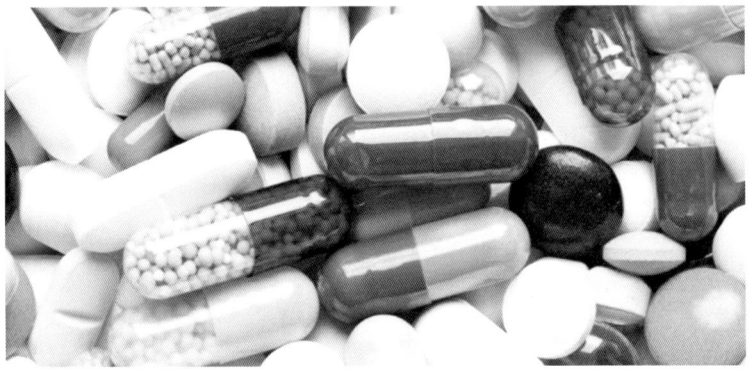
Smart drugs.

eugeroics (armodafinil and modafinil), which are wakefulness-promoting agents; and xanthines (most notably, caffeine), which increase alertness and performance.

### ECO DRUGS

Eco drugs have a consciousness-influencing effect and are all directly derived from natural sources. Some examples include stimulating (energizing) eco drugs such as guarana (*Paulinnia cupana*) and kola nut (*Cola nitida*)—which both contain caffeine—and ginseng (*Panax ginseng*).

Ginseng affects blood pressure, the immune system, and metabolism. Eastern medicine has deemed it necessary to many prescriptions, and it is regarded as both a preventive and curative agent. Ginseng is believed to eliminate mental and physical fatigue, cure pulmonary complaints, dissolve tumors, and reduce problems related to aging. Eastern medicine practitioners also prescribe it to combat diabetes, protect people from radiation and the side effects of chemotherapy, combat colds and chest problems, and to stimulate appetite and sleep. Ginseng is also often used in energizer drinks and concoctions.

Other eco drugs act as narcotics or sedatives. Kava kava (*Piper methysticum*), for example, has multiple effects. It acts as a relaxant, local anesthetic, and analgesic. Valerian (*Valeriana officinalis*) has

Ginseng root.

Kava kava.

soothing effects on the central nervous system and is sometimes used to counteract insomnia. St. John's wort (*Hypericum perforatum*), too, has a calming effect.

Still other eco drugs act like hallucinogens or aphrodisiacs. Consider salvia (*Salvia divinorum*), which is usually smoked to provide a strong, brief, hallucinatory trip. Yohimbe (*Yohimbe pausinyatalia*) contains yohimbine, which has been shown in several studies to enhance sexually stimulation and potency.

### SHORT- AND LONG-TERM RISKS

Some eco drugs can poison users, like the nightshades (*Solanaceae*) henbane (*Hyoscyamus niger*), mandrake (*Mandragora officinarum*), and datura, also called devil's trumpets (*Datura stramonium*).

*Salvia divinorum* extract.

Guarana.

Yohimbe.

Guarana (*Paulinnia cupana*) can cause allergic reactions. Some eco drugs contain substances whose functions are unknown or disputed.

High doses of smart drugs can be dangerous for people with cardiovascular problems. Also, high doses of these stimulants can result in users having difficulty absorbing certain vitamins (such as A and D), and they can suppress fatigue for so long that it is hazardous. Prescription drugs are, after all, intended for use by people who have certain conditions.

The use of hallucinogens, including eco-drug hallucinogens, can be risky because users might have a bad trip or perform dangerous activities when on them.

### ADDICTION

The risk of physical dependence on most eco drugs and smart drugs is small, and there is no evidence that these drugs are stepping stones to riskier drugs. However, the possibility of psychological dependence exists, depending on the user.

## New Psychoactive Substances (NPS)

New psychoactive substances are chemicals about whose effects, short- and long-term, we still know little. We also know little about their addictive qualities and safe (or unsafe) dosages. Included in this category are the following:

- Methylone (Xplosion)
- Mephedrone (4-MMC, meow meow)
- Methoxetamine (MTX, MXE)
- 2,5-dimethoxy-4-iodophenethylamine (2-CB, 2-CT-7, 2-CI, 2-CE)
- 4-fluoroamphetamine (4-FA, 4-FMP, PAL-303, "Flux")
- 1-benzofuran-6-ylpropan-2-amine or 6-(2-aminopropyl) benzofuran (6-APB, Benzo Fury)
- DOx is a chemical class of substituted amphetamine derivatives, such as 2,5-dimethoxy-4-methylamphetamine

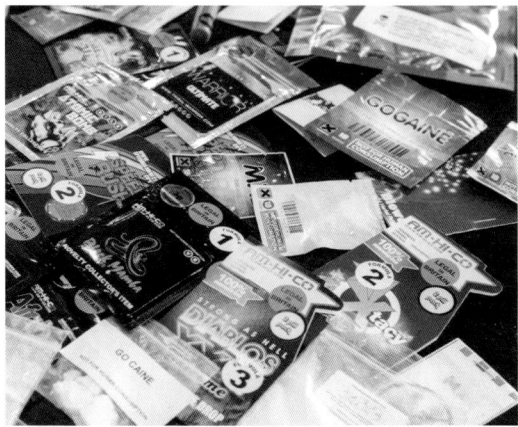
New psychoactive substances.

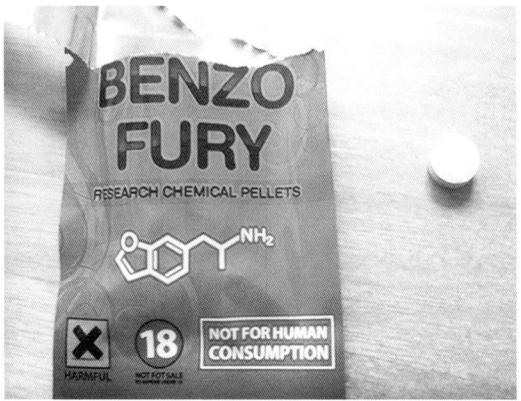
Benzo Fury, a new psychoactive substance.

(DOM), 2,5-dimethoxy-4-chloroamphetamine (DOC), or 2,5-dimethoxy-4-bromoamphetamine (DOB)
- Butylone (bk-MBDB)
- Benzylpiperazine (BZP)

## HISTORY

As soon as a drug is forbidden, people try to find a way to either take it or produce something similar, something that is not covered by legislation. In the 1920s, in response to the Opium Act, for example, alternatives such as morphine and heroin were developed. In the 1960s, alternatives for PCP and LSD were created.

Alexander "Sasha" Shulgin, an American pharmacologist and chemist from Berkeley, California, developed a new method to synthesize MDMA, the active ingredient in ecstasy, and strongly supported the use of MDMA in a therapeutic setting. He synthesized hundreds of substances, including mescaline, and tested these drugs with his wife and a group of friends. He described his experiments in the books *PiHKAL* (Phenethylamines I Have Known and Loved, published in 1991), *TiHKAL* (Tryptamines I Have Known and Loved, published in 1997), and *The Shulgin Index* (2011).

In the 1990s, the term "research chemicals" became a euphemism for chemicals sold for industrial or academic research rather than human consumption. This term originated, however, with online sellers who wanted to appear to be selling psychoactive chemical substances (often analogs of prohibited substances) for legitimate purposes. The sellers felt that this marketing strategy would ensure they would not be prosecuted. In the United States, however, it is illegal to sell substances that resemble a prohibited substance, but only if the prosecutor can demonstrate that the substances are intended for human consumption. Later, other

Bath salts.

euphemisms came into being to "protect" sellers of NPSs, including air freshener, bath salts, knife grinder, and plant food.

In 2004, the American Drug Enforcement Agency (DEA) set up operation WebTryp to investigate websites under suspicion of distributing unscheduled, unregulated, illegal tryptamines and phenethylamines. WebTryp came on the heels of a rapid growth in online NPS sales, as well as increasing drug-related hospitalizations and deaths. The operation led to the arrest of 10 online store owners and hefty punishments, including life sentences, since it was proved that the culprits knew the products sold were used for human consumption.

The users were not prosecuted; however, customer databases on the websites investigated by the DEA were shared internationally. The British police arrested 22 residents who had purchased drugs through the seized websites.

This operation resulted in a silencing of online talk about NPSs. Users worry that if the drugs and their sources are discussed openly, another DEA operation will soon be under way. A negative consequence of this silence is that there is now little information available to users about the sellers and chemicals. This makes users vulnerable to scams and unreliable and unsafe sellers.

# Conclusion

Chemical odorants mimicking the smells of drugs have been used in detector-dog training since the first drug-detector dog was trained in the early 1960s. Caryophyllene epoxide, for example, was used to help dogs learn to identify cannabis; acetic acid was used for training dogs to recognize heroin; and both methyl benzoate and benzoic acid were used in training dogs to detect cocaine. Benzaldehyde was used to train dogs to detect methamphetamine.

However, these chemical substances are also present in other products around the home. Acetic acid, for example, is found in detergents and in food as a flavoring, preservative, and acidity regulator. And caryophyllene epoxide is a constituent in the essential oils in many plants, including oregano and lavender. So, after some problems associated with dogs identifying the "wrong" items, training centers began to use the drugs themselves in training exercises. With this change came attention to other details: more attention was paid, for example, to the quantities and the various cuts, mixtures, and combinations of drugs. Dogs' sense of smell can, after all, discriminate between complex mixtures of odors. Their ability to accurately discriminate among odors makes them invaluable in odor detection.

One cannot effectively mask an odor with a stronger odor when it comes to canine detection. Dogs can detect minute quantities of odorants, even beneath heavier odors, and because they are capable of discriminating between individual molecular combinations, attempts to fool detector dogs by packaging contraband with other strong-smelling items are usually unsuccessful.

As well, as dogs move, they pick up scant traces of odor. By moving their heads back and forth, all the while constantly sampling the air, dogs compare the strength of scent received in each of their mobile nostrils and find the direction of increasing concentration. By following the molecular concentration gradient to its strongest point or source, dogs achieve a stereoscopic pinpointing of odor. This characteristic movement of the head also alerts the dog handler to the possibility of a find.

Dogs are ideally suited for drug-detection searches in buildings, out of doors, on people, in large containers such as shipping crates, in large amounts of luggage, in mail, and in and around all sorts of vehicles. A dog can usually search a large vehicle in about five minutes and a small vehicle in as little as two minutes. These times compare favorably with the screening times needed for other methods of detection, such as physical searches conducted by security guards or searches using X-ray–based portals. The drug-detector dog's ability to rapidly and successfully screen a large area and to follow a scent gradient until he locates the object from which the scent is emanating greatly exceeds that of technology-based sniffer systems. So let's go on with professionally training and employing highly effective K9 drug–detection teams!

# Appendix A

# Canada's Controlled Drugs and Substances Act: Drug Schedules I–IV and VIII

## Schedule I

1. Opium poppy (*Papaver somniferum*), its preparations, derivatives, alkaloids, and salts, including opium, codeine (methylmorphine), morphine, and thebaine (paramorphine), and the salts, derivatives, and salts of derivatives of the substances set out in the four sub-items mentioned above, including the following:

    acetorphine (acetyletorphine)
    acetyldihydrocodeine
    benzylmorphine
    codoxime
    desomorphine (dihydrodeoxymorphine)
    diacetylmorphine (heroin)
    dihydrocodeine
    dihydromorphine
    ethylmorphine
    etorphine
    hydrocodone (dihydrocodeinone)
    hydromorphinol
    hydromorphone (dihydromorphinone)
    methyldesorphine
    methyldihydromorphine
    metopon (dihydromethylmorphinone)

morphine-N-oxide (morphine oxide)
myrophine (benzylmorphine myristate)
nalorphine (N-allylnormorphine)
nicocodine (6-nicotinylcodeine)
nicomorphine (dinicotinylmorphine)
norcodeine (N-desmethylcodeine)
normorphine (N-desmethylmorphine)
oxycodone (dihydrohydroxycodeinone)
oxymorphone (dihydrohydroxymorphinone)
pholcodine
thebacon (acetyldihydrocodeinone)

but not including the following:

apomorphine            naltrexone
cyprenorphine          narcotine
nalmefene              papaverine
naloxone               poppy seed

2. Coca (*Erythroxylon*), its preparations, derivatives, alkaloids, and salts, including coca leaves, cocaine (benzoylmethylecgonine), and ecgonine.
3. Phenylpiperidines, their intermediates, salts, derivatives, and analogs and salts of intermediates, derivatives, and analogs, including the following:

allylprodine           hydroxypethidine
alphameprodine         ketobemidone
alphaprodine           methylphenylisonipecotonitrile
anileridine            morpheridine
betameprodine          norpethidine
betaprodine            pethidine
benzethidine           phenoperidine
diphenoxylate          piminodine
difenoxin              properidine
etoxeridine            trimeperidine
furethidine            pethidine intermediate C

4. Phenazepines, their salts, derivatives, and salts of derivatives, including proheptazine.

5. Amidones, their intermediates, salts, derivatives, and salts of intermediates and derivatives, including the following:

    dimethylaminodiphenylbutanonitrile
    dipipanone
    isomethadone
    methadone
    normethadone
    norpipanone
    phenadoxone

6. Methadols, their salts, derivatives, and salts of derivatives, including the following:

    acetylmethadol
    alphacetylmethadol
    alphamethadol
    betacetylmethadol
    betamethadol
    dimepheptanol
    noracymethadol

7. Phenalkoxams, their salts, derivatives, and salts of derivatives, including dimenoxadol, dioxaphetyl butyrate, and dextropropoxyphene.
8. Thiambutenes, their salts, derivatives, and salts of derivatives, including diethylthiambutene, dimethylthiambutene, and ethylmethylthiambutene.
9. Moramides, their intermediates, salts, derivatives, and salts of intermediates and derivatives, including dextromoramide, diphenylmorpholinoisovaleric acid, levomoramide, and racemoramide.
10. Morphinans, their salts, derivatives, and salts of derivatives, including the following:

    buprenorphine
    drotebanol
    levomethorphan
    levorphanol
    levophenacylmorphan
    norlevorphanol
    phenomorphan
    racemethorphan
    racemorphan

11. Benzazocines, their salts, derivatives, and salts of derivatives, including phenazocine, metazocine, and pentazocine.
12. Ampromides, their salts, derivatives, and salts of derivatives, including diampromide, phenampromide, and propiram.
13. Benzimidazoles, their salts, derivatives, and salts of derivatives,

including clonitazene, etonitazene, and bezitramide.
14. Phencyclidine, its salts, derivatives, and analogs, and salts of derivatives and analogs, including ketamine.
15. Piritramide, its salts, derivatives, and salts of derivatives.
16. Fentanyls, their salts, derivatives, and analogs, and salts of derivatives and analogs, including the following:

> acetyl-α-methylfentanyl
> alfentanil
> carfentanil
> p-fluorofentanyl
> fentanyl
> β-hydroxyfentanyl
> β-hydroxy-3-methylfentanyl
> α-methylfentanyl
> α-methylthiofentanyl
> 3-methylfentanyl
> 3-methylthiofentanyl
> remifentanil
> sufentanil
> thiofentanyl

17. Tilidine, its salts, derivatives, and salts of derivatives.
   17.1 Methylenedioxypyrovalerone (MDPV), its salts, derivatives, isomers, and analogs, and salts of its derivatives, isomers, and analogs.
18. Methamphetamine, its salts, derivatives, isomers, and analogs, and salts of derivatives, isomers, and analogs.
19. Amphetamines, their salts, derivatives, isomers, and analogs, and salts of derivatives, isomers, and analogs, including the following:

> amphetamine
> N-ethylamphetamine
> 4-methyl-2,5-dimethoxyamphetamine (STP)
> 3,4-methylenedioxyamphetamine (MDA)
> 2,5-dimethoxyamphetamine
> 4-methoxyamphetamine
> 2,4,5-trimethoxyamphetamine
> N-methyl-3,4-methylenedioxyamphetamine
> 4-ethoxy-2,5-dimethoxyamphetamine
> 5-methoxy-3,4-methylenedioxyamphetamine
> N,N-dimethyl-3,4-methylenedioxyamphetamine
> N-ethyl-3,4-methylenedioxyamphetamine
> 4-ethyl-2,5-dimethoxyamphetamine (DOET)
> 4-bromo-2,5-dimethoxyamphetamine
> 4-chloro-2,5-dimethoxyamphetamine

4-ethoxyamphetamine
benzphetamine
N-propyl-3,4-methylenedioxyamphetamine
N-(2-hydroxyethyl)-α-methylbenzeneethanamine
N-hydroxy-3,4-methylenedioxyamphetamine
3,4,5-trimethoxyamphetamine
20. Flunitrazepam and any of its salts or derivatives.
21. 4-hydroxybutanoic acid (GHB) and any of its salts.

## Schedule II

1. Cannabis, its preparations and derivatives, including the following:

   | | |
   |---|---|
   | cannabis resin | cannabinol |
   | cannabis (marijuana) | tetrahydrocannabinol |
   | cannabidiol | |

   but not including non-viable cannabis seed (with the exception of its derivatives) and mature cannabis stalks that do not include leaves, flowers, seeds, or branches (and fiber derived from such stalks).

2. Synthetic cannabinoid receptor type 1 agonists, their salts, derivatives, isomers, and salts of derivatives and isomers, including those that fall within the following core chemical structure classes:

   - Any substance that has a 2-(cyclohexyl)phenol structure with substitution at the 1-position of the benzene ring by a hydroxy, ether, or ester group and further substituted at the 5-position of the benzene ring, whether or not further substituted on the benzene ring to any extent, and substituted at the 3-position of the cyclohexyl ring by an alkyl, carbonyl, hydroxyl, ether, or ester, and whether or not further substituted on the cyclohexyl ring to any extent, including the following:

   | | |
   |---|---|
   | nabilone | CP 47,497 |
   | parahexyl | CP 55,940 |
   | DMHP | |

- Any substance that has a 3-(1-naphthoyl)indole structure with substitution at the nitrogen atom of the indole ring, whether or not further substituted on the indole ring to any extent and whether or not substituted on the naphthyl ring to any extent, including the following:

  | | |
  |---|---|
  | JWH-018 | JWH-210 |
  | JWH-073 | JWH-267 |
  | JWH-122 | AM-1220 |
  | JWH-019 | AM-2201 |
  | JWH-022 | MAM-2201 |
  | JWH-080 | EAM-2201 |
  | JWH-081 | WIN 55,212–2 |
  | JWH-200 | |

- Any substance that has a 3-(1-naphthoyl)pyrrole structure with substitution at the nitrogen atom of the pyrrole ring, whether or not further substituted on the pyrrole ring to any extent and whether or not substituted on the naphthyl ring to any extent, including JWH-307.
- Any substance that has a 3-phenylacetylindole structure with substitution at the nitrogen atom of the indole ring, whether or not further substituted on the indole ring to any extent and whether or not substituted on the phenyl ring to any extent, including JWH-250, JWH-251, and JWH-302.
- Any substance that has a 3-benzoylindole structure with substitution at the nitrogen atom of the indole ring, whether or not further substituted on the indole ring to any extent and whether or not substituted on the phenyl ring to any extent, including AM-2233.
- Any substance that has a 3-methanone(cyclopropyl) indole structure with substitution at the nitrogen atom of the indole ring, whether or not further substituted on the indole ring to any extent and whether or not substituted on the cyclopropyl ring to any extent, including UR-144, 5F-UR-144, and A-796,260.
- Any substance that has a quinolin-8-yl 1H-indole-3-carboxylate structure with substitution at the nitrogen

atom of the indole ring, whether or not further substituted on the indole ring to any extent and whether or not substituted on the quinolin-8-yl ring to any extent, including PB-22 and 5F-PB-22.
- Any substance that has a 3-carboxamideindazole structure with substitution at the nitrogen atom of the indazole ring, whether or not further substituted on the indazole ring to any extent and whether or not substituted at the carboxamide group to any extent, including AKB48, 5F-AKB48, AB-FUBINACA, and AB-PINACA.
- Any substance that has a 3-carboxamideindole structure with substitution at the nitrogen atom of the indole ring, whether or not further substituted on the indole ring to any extent and whether or not substituted at the carboxamide group to any extent, including STS-135 and APICA.

## Schedule III
1. Methylphenidat and any salt thereof.
2. Methaqualone and any salt thereof.
3. Mecloqualone and any salt thereof.
4. Lysergic acid diethylamide (LSD) and any salt thereof.
5. N,N-diethyltryptamine (DET) and any salt thereof.
6. N,N-dimethyltryptamine (DMT) and any salt thereof.
7. N-methyl-3-piperidyl benzilate (LBJ) and any salt thereof.
8. Harmaline and any salt thereof.
9. Harmalol and any salt thereof.
10. Psilocin and any salt thereof.
11. Psilocybin and any salt thereof.
12. N-(1-phenylcyclohexyl)ethylamine (PCE) and any salt thereof.
13. 1-[1-(2-thienyl)cyclohexyl]piperidine (TCP) and any salt thereof.
14. 1-phenyl-N-propylcyclohexanamine and any salt thereof.
15. Rolicyclidine and any salt thereof.
16. Mescaline and any salt thereof, but not peyote (Lophophora).
17. 4-Methylaminorex and any salt thereof.
18. Cathinone and any salt thereof.

19. Fenetylline and any salt thereof.
20. 2-methylamino-1-phenyl-1-propanone and any salt thereof.
21. 1-[1-(phenylmethyl)cyclohexyl]piperidine and any salt thereof.
22. 1-[1-(4-methylphenyl)cyclohexyl]piperidine and any salt thereof.
23. 4-bromo-2,5-dimethoxybenzeneethanamine and any salt, isomer, or salt of an isomer thereof.
24. Aminorex and any salt thereof.
25. Etryptamine and any salt thereof.
26. Lefetamine and any salt thereof.
27. Mesocarb and any salt thereof.
28. Zipeprol and any salt thereof.
29. Amineptine and any salt thereof.
30. Benzylpiperazine (BZP) and its salts, isomers, and salts of isomers.
31. Trifluoromethylphenylpiperazine (TFMPP) and its salts, isomers, and salts of isomers.

## Schedule IV

1. Barbiturates, their salts and derivatives, including

allobarbital
alphenal
amobarbital
aprobarbital
barbital
barbituric acid
butabarbital
butalbital
butallylonal
butethal
cyclobarbital
cyclopal
heptabarbital
hexethal

hexobarbital
mephobarbital
methabarbital
methylphenobarbital
propallylonal pentobarbital
phenobarbital
probarbital
phenylmethylbarbituric acid
pecobarbital
pigmodal
talbutal
vinbarbital
vinylbital

2. Thiobarbiturates, their salts and derivatives, including thialbarbital, thiamylal, thiobarbituric acid, and thiopental.
3. Chlorphentermine and any salt thereof.
4. Diethylpropion and any salt thereof.
5. Phendimetrazine and any salt thereof.
6. Phenmetrazine and any salt thereof.
7. Pipradol and any salt thereof.
8. Phentermine and any salt thereof.
9. Butorphanol and any salt thereof.
10. Nalbuphine and any salt thereof.
11. Glutethimide.
12. Clotiazepam and any salt thereof.
13. Ethchlorvyno.
14. Ethinamate.
15. Mazindol.
16. Meprobamate.
17. Methyprylon.
18. Benzodiazepines, their salts and derivatives, including the following:

| | |
|---|---|
| alprazolam | ketazolam |
| bromazepam | loprazolam |
| brotizolam | lorazepam |
| camazepam | lormetazepam |
| chlordiazepoxide | medazepam |
| clobazam | midazolam |
| clonazepam | nimetazepam |
| clorazepate | nitrazepam |
| cloxazolam | nordazepam |
| delorazepam | oxazepam |
| diazepam | oxazolam |
| estazolam | pinazepam |
| ethyl loflazepate | prazepam |
| fludiazepam | quazepam |
| flurazepam | temazepam |
| halazepam | tetrazepam |
| haloxazolam | triazolam |

but not including the following:
clozapine (and any salt thereof)
flunitrazepam (and any salts or derivatives thereof)
olanzapine (and its salts)
19. Catha edulis Forsk, its preparations, derivatives, alkaloids, and salts, including cathine.
20. Fencamfamin and any salt thereof.
21. Fenproporex and any salt thereof.
22. Mefenorex and any salt thereof.
23. Anabolic steroids and their derivatives, including the following:

androisoxazole
androstanolone
androstenediol
bolandiol
bolasterone
bolazine
boldenone
bolenol
calusterone
clostebol
drostanolone
enestebol
epitiostanol
ethylestrenol
4-hydroxyl-19-
    nortestosterone
fluoxymesterone
formebolone
furazabol
mebolazine
mesabolone
mesterolone

metandienone
metenolone
methandriol
methyltestosterone
metribolone
mibolerone
nandrolone
norboletone
norclostebol
norethandrolone
oxabolone
oxandrolone
oxymesterone
oxymetholone
prasterone
quinbolone
stanozolol
stenbolone
testosterone
tibolone
tiomesterone
trenbolone

24. Zeranol
25. Zolpidem and any salt thereof
25. 1 Pemoline and any salt thereof.
26. Pyrovalerone and any salt thereof.

## Schedule VIII

The Controlled Drugs and Substances Act details that for amounts not exceeding those set in Schedule VIII, a maximum fine of $1000 and/or maximum six months' imprisonment is the only punishment.

| Substance | Amount |
| --- | --- |
| Cannabis resin | 1 g |
| Cannabis (marijuana) | 30 g |

# Appendix B

## Canada's Controlled Drugs and Substances Act: Punishments

### Possession of Substance
1. Except as authorized under the regulations, no person shall possess a substance included in Schedule I, II, or III.

### Obtaining Substance
2. No person shall seek or obtain
   a. a substance included in Schedule I, II, III, or IV, or
   b. an authorization to obtain a substance included in Schedule I, II, III, or IV from a practitioner, unless the person discloses to the practitioner particulars relating to the acquisition by the person of every substance in those schedules, and of every authorization to obtain such substances, from any other practitioner within the preceding 30 days.

### Punishment
3. Every person who contravenes subsection (1) where the subject matter of the offense is a substance included in Schedule I
   a. is guilty of an indictable offense and liable to imprisonment for a term not exceeding seven years; or
   b. is guilty of an offense punishable on summary conviction and liable

> i. for a first offense, to a fine not exceeding one thousand dollars or to imprisonment for a term not exceeding six months, or to both, and
> ii. for a subsequent offense, to a fine not exceeding two thousand dollars or to imprisonment for a term not exceeding one year, or to both.

## Punishment

> 4. Subject to subsection (5), every person who contravenes subsection (1) where the subject matter of the offense is a substance included in Schedule II
>    a. is guilty of an indictable offense and liable to imprisonment for a term not exceeding five years less a day; or
>    b. is guilty of an offense punishable on summary conviction and liable
>       ii. for a first offense, to a fine not exceeding one thousand dollars or to imprisonment for a term not exceeding six months, or to both, and
>       ii. for a subsequent offense, to a fine not exceeding two thousand dollars or to imprisonment for a term not exceeding one year, or to both.

## Punishment

> 5. Every person who contravenes subsection (1) where the subject matter of the offense is a substance included in Schedule II in an amount that does not exceed the amount set out for that substance in Schedule VIII is guilty of an offense punishable on summary conviction and liable to a fine not exceeding one thousand dollars or to imprisonment for a term not exceeding six months, or to both.

## Punishment

> 6. Every person who contravenes subsection (1) where the subject matter of the offense is a substance included in Schedule III

a. is guilty of an indictable offense and liable to imprisonment for a term not exceeding three years; or
b. is guilty of an offense punishable on summary conviction and liable
   i. for a first offense, to a fine not exceeding one thousand dollars or to imprisonment for a term not exceeding six months, or to both, and
   ii. for a subsequent offense, to a fine not exceeding two thousand dollars or to imprisonment for a term not exceeding one year, or to both.

## Punishment

7. Every person who contravenes subsection (2)
   a. is guilty of an indictable offense and liable
      i. to imprisonment for a term not exceeding seven years, where the subject matter of the offense is a substance included in Schedule I,
      ii. to imprisonment for a term not exceeding five years less a day, where the subject matter of the offense is a substance included in Schedule II,
      iii. to imprisonment for a term not exceeding three years, where the subject matter of the offense is a substance included in Schedule III, or
      iv. to imprisonment for a term not exceeding 18 months, where the subject matter of the offense is a substance included in Schedule IV; or
   b. is guilty of an offense punishable on summary conviction and liable
      i. for a first offense, to a fine not exceeding one thousand dollars or to imprisonment for a term not exceeding six months, or to both, and
      ii. for a subsequent offense, to a fine not exceeding two thousand dollars or to imprisonment for a term not exceeding one year, or to both.

## Determination of Amount

8. For the purposes of subsection (5) and Schedule VIII, the amount of the substance means the entire amount of any

mixture or substance, or the whole of any plant, that contains a detectable amount of the substance.

## Trafficking in Substance

No person shall traffic in a substance included in Schedule I, II, III, or IV or in any substance represented or held out by that person to be such a substance.

## Possession for Purpose of Trafficking

No person shall, for the purpose of trafficking, possess a substance included in Schedule I, II, III, or IV.

## Importing and Exporting

Except as authorized under the regulations, no person shall import into Canada or export from Canada a substance included in Schedule I, II, III, or IV.

## Possession for the Purpose of Exporting

Except as authorized under the regulations, no person shall possess a substance included in Schedule I, II, III, or IV for the purpose of exporting it from Canada.

## Production of Substance

Except as authorized under the regulations, no person shall produce a substance included in Schedule I, II, III, or IV.

# Appendix C

## United States Controlled Substances Act: Drug Schedules I–V

### Schedule I
Schedule I drugs, substances, or chemicals are defined as drugs with no currently accepted medical use and a high potential for abuse. Schedule I drugs are the most dangerous drugs in all the drug schedules and can be potentially severe in terms of psychological or physical dependence. There is a lack of accepted safety for use of the drug or other substance under medical supervision. Examples of Schedule I drugs, with trade names and street names included in parentheses, include the following:

> 3,4-methylenedioxymethamphetamine (MDMA, ecstasy, XtC)
> diacetylmorphine, diamorphine (heroin)
> JWH (synthetic marijuana)
> lysergic acid diethylamide (LSD)
> marijuana (cannabis)
> methaqualone (Quaalude, Parest, Somnafac, Opitimil, Mandrax)
> peyote (cactus, which contains mescaline)

### Schedule II
Schedule II drugs, substances, or chemicals are defined as drugs with a high potential for abuse, but less abuse potential than Schedule I drugs, with use potentially leading to severe psychological or physical dependence. Drugs or other substances in this schedule have a currently accepted medical use in treatment in the United States or a currently accepted medical use with severe

restrictions. These drugs are also considered dangerous. Examples of Schedule II drugs include the following:

amphetamine (Dexedrine, Adderall, Obetrol)
coca leaves
fentanyl (Duragesic, Oralet, Actiq, Sublimaze, Innovar)
hydrocodone (Dihydrocodeinone)
hydromorphone (Dilaudid)
meperidine (Demerol, Mepergan, Pethidine)
methadone (Dolophine, Methadose, Amidone)
methamphetamine (Desoxyn, d-desoxyephedrine, ICE, crank, speed)
methyl benzoylecgonine (cocaine, crack)
methylphenidate (Ritalin, Concerta, Methylin)
morphine (MS Contin, Roxanol, Oramorph, RMS, MSIR)
morphine methyl ester, (codeine, methyl morphine)
opium
oxycodone (Oxycontin, Percocet, Endocet, Roxicodone, Roxicet)
phencyclidine (PCP)

## Schedule III

Schedule III drugs, substances, or chemicals are defined as drugs that have moderate or low potential for physical dependence or high psychological dependence. Schedule III drugs' abuse potential is less than that of Schedule I and II drugs but more than that for those listed in Schedule IV. The drugs or other substances in this schedule have a currently accepted medical use in treatment in the United States. Examples of Schedule III drugs include the following:

anabolic steroids (body-building drugs)
barbituric acid derivative (barbiturates not specifically listed)
codeine and isoquinoline alkaloid 90 mg/du (codeine with papaverine or noscapine)
codeine combination product 90 mg/du (codeine with Empirin, Fiorinal, Tylenol, Asperin [acetylsalicylic acid—ASA], or paracetamol [acetaminophen—APAP])

ketamine (Ketaset, Ketalar, special K, K)
lysergic acid (LSD precursor)
testosterone (Android-T, Androlan, Depotest, Delatestryl)

## Schedule IV

Schedule IV drugs, substances, or chemicals may lead to limited physical or psychological dependence relative to the drugs or other substances in Schedule III. The drugs or other substances on this list have a currently accepted medical use in treatment in the United States. Examples of Schedule IV drugs include the following:

alprazolam (Xanax)
clonazepam (Klonopin, Clonopin)
dextropropoxyphene dosage forms (Darvon, Propoxyphene, Darvocet, Propacet)
diazepam (Valium, Diastat)
flunitrazepam (Rohypnol, Narcozep, Darkene, Roipnol)
lorazepam (Ativan)
pentazocine (Talwin, Talacen)
tramadol (Contramal, Doctramado, Dolzam, Tradonal, Tramal, Ultram, Zytram)
zolpidem (Ambien, Ivadal, Stilnoct, Stilnox)

## Schedule V

Schedule V drugs, substances, or chemicals are defined as drugs with lower potential for abuse than those included in Schedule IV and consist of preparations containing limited quantities of certain narcotics. Schedule V drugs are generally used for antidiarrheal, antitussive, and analgesic purposes. Examples of Schedule V drugs include the following:

codeine preparations, 200 milligrams/100 milliliters (Cosanyl, Robitussin, Cheracol, Cerose)
difenoxin preparations (Motofen)
diphenoxylate preparations (Lomotil, Logen)
lacosamide (Vimpat)
opium preparations, 100 milligrams/100 milliliters (Parepectolin, Kapectolin, Kaolin Pectin)
pregabalin (Lyrica)

# Appendix D

# United States Federal Trafficking Penalties for Drugs Included in Schedules I–V

Federal Trafficking Penalties for Schedules I, II, III, IV, and V (Except Marijuana)

| Schedule | Substance/quantity | Penalties |
|---|---|---|
| II | Cocaine / 500–4999 grams mixture | **First offense**: Not less than five years and not more than 40 years. If death or serious bodily injury, not less than 20 years or more than life. Fine of not more than $5 million if an individual, $25 million if not an individual. **Second offense**: Not less than 10 years and not more than life. If death or serious bodily injury, life imprisonment. Fine of not more than $8 million if an individual, $50 million if not an individual. |
| II | Cocaine base / 28–279 grams mixture | |
| IV | Fentanyl / 40–399 grams mixture | |
| I | Fentanyl analog / 10–99 grams mixture | |
| I | Heroin / 100–999 grams mixture | |
| I | LSD / 1–9 grams mixture | |
| II | Methamphetamine / 5–49 g pure OR 50–499 g mixture | |
| II | PCP / 10–99 g pure OR 100–999 g mixture | |

*(Continued)*

(Continued from previous page)

| Schedule | Substance/quantity | Penalties |
|---|---|---|
| II | Cocaine / 5 kilograms or more mixture | **First offense**: Not less than 10 years and not more than life. If death or serious bodily injury, not less than 20 years or more than life. Fine of not more than $10 million if an individual, $50 million if not an individual.<br><br>**Second offense**: Not less than 20 years and not more than life. If death or serious bodily injury, life imprisonment. Fine of not more than $20 million if an individual, $75 million if not an individual.<br><br>**Two or more prior offenses**: Life imprisonment. Fine of not more than $20 million if an individual, $75 million if not an individual. |
| II | Cocaine base / 280 grams or more mixture | |
| IV | Fentanyl / 400 grams or more mixture | |
| I | Fentanyl analog / 100 grams or more mixture | |
| I | Heroin / 1 kilogram or more mixture | |
| I | LSD / 10 grams or more mixture | |
| II | Methamphetamine / 50 grams or more pure OR 500 grams or more mixture | |
| II | PCP / 100 grams or more pure OR 1 kilogram or more mixture | |

| Substance/quantity | Penalty |
|---|---|
| Any amount of other Schedule I and II substances<br><br>Any drug product containing gamma hydroxybutyric acid<br><br>Flunitrazepam (Schedule IV) – 1 gram | **First offense**: Not more than 20 years. If death or serious bodily injury, not less than 20 years or more than life. Fine of $1 million if an individual, $5 million if not an individual.<br><br>**Second offense**: Not more than 30 years. If death or serious bodily injury, life imprisonment. Fine of $2 million if an individual, $10 million if not an individual. |
| Any amount of other Schedule III drugs | **First offense:** Not more than 10 years. If death or serious bodily injury, not more than 15 years. Fine not more than $500,000 if an individual, $2.5 million if not an individual.<br><br>**Second offense**: Not more than 20 years. If death or serious bodily injury, not more than 30 years. Fine not more than $1 million if an individual, $5 million if not an individual. |

# United States Federal Trafficking Penalties

| Substance/quantity | Penalty |
|---|---|
| Any amount of all other Schedule IV drugs (other than 1 gram or more of Flunitrazepam) | **First offense**: Not more than five years. Fine not more than $250,000 if an individual, $1 million if not an individual.<br><br>**Second offense**: Not more than 10 years. Fine not more than $500,000 if an individual, $2 million if not an individual. |
| Any amount of all Schedule V drugs | **First offense**: Not more than one year. Fine not more than $100,000 if an individual, $250,000 if not an individual.<br><br>**Second offense**: Not more than four years. Fine not more than $200,000 if an individual, $500,000 if not an individual. |

Federal Trafficking Penalties for Marijuana, Hashish, and Hashish Oil, Schedule I Substances

| Substance/quantity | Penalty |
|---|---|
| Marijuana / 1000 kilograms or more marijuana mixture OR 1000 or more marijuana plants | **First offense**: Not less than 10 years or more than life. If death or serious bodily injury, not less than 20 years or more than life. Fine not more than $10 million if an individual, $50 million if not an individual.<br><br>**Second offense**: Not less than 20 years or more than life. If death or serious bodily injury, life imprisonment. Fine not more than $20 million if an individual, $75 million if not an individual. |
| Marijuana / 100–999 kilograms marijuana mixture OR 100–999 marijuana plants | **First offense**: Not less than five years or more than 40 years. If death or serious bodily injury, not less than 20 years or more than life. Fine not more than $5 million if an individual, $25 million if not an individual.<br><br>**Second offense**: Not less than 20 years or more than life. If death or serious bodily injury, life imprisonment. Fine not more than $8 million if an individual, $50 million if other than an individual. |

(*Continued*)

(Continued from previous page)

| Substance/quantity | Penalty |
|---|---|
| Marijuana / 50–99 kilograms marijuana mixture, 50–99 plants<br><br>Hashish / more than 10 kilograms<br><br>Hashish oil / more than 1 kilogram | **First offense:** Not more than 20 years. If death or serious bodily injury, not less than 20 years or more than life. Fine of $1 million if an individual, $5 million if not an individual.<br><br>**Second offense:** Not more than 30 years. If death or serious bodily injury, life imprisonment. Fine of $2 million if an individual, $10 million if not an individual. |
| Marijuana / less than 50 kilograms marijuana (but does not include 50 or more marijuana plants, regardless of weight), one to 49 marijuana plants<br><br>Hashish / 10 kilograms or lessHashish oil / 1 kilogram or less | **First offense:** Not more than five years. Fine not more than $250,000 if an individual, $1 million if not an individual.<br><br>**Second offense:** Not more than 10 years. Fine of $500,000 if an individual, $2 million if not an individual. |

# Notes

## Selecting the Drug-Detector Dog and Handler

1. See K. Soproni, A. Miklősi, J. Topál, and V. Csányi, "Comprehension of Human Communicative Signs in Pet Dogs (*Canis familiaris*)," *Journal of Comparative Psychology*, 115, no. 2 (June 2001): 122–126. See also, K. Soproni, A. Miklősi, J. Topál, and V. Csányi, "Dogs' (*Canis familaris*) Responsiveness to Human Pointing Gestures," *Journal of Comparative Psychology*, 116, no. 1 (2002): 27–34.

## Reading Your Dog

1. See L.P. Waggoner, J.M. Johnston, M. Williams, J. Jackson, and M.H. Jones, "Canine Olfactory Sensitivity to Cocaine Hydrochloride and Methyl Benzoate," *Proc. SPIE* 2937, Chemistry- and Biology-Based Technologies for Contraband Detection, 216 (February 17, 1997).

## Influence of Air Currents in Search Work

1. "Marvels of Mini-Weather," *The Sciences*, 5, no. 2 (July 1965): 1–4.

## The Different Drugs

1. See Albert Hofmann, *LSD: mein Sorgenkind, Die Entdeckung einer "Wunderdroge"* (Stuttgart: Verlag G. Cotta'sche Buchhandlung, 1979). See also, Albert Hofmann, *LSD: My Problem Child* (New York: McGraw-Hill Book Company, 1980).

2. C.J. Lilly, *The Scientist: A Novel Autobiography* (Philadelphia: Lippincott, 1978).

3. Albert Niemann, "*Über eine neue organische Base in den Cocablättern*" ("On a New Organic Base in the Coca Leaves"), *Archiv der Pharmazie* 153, no. 2 (1860): 129–256.

4 P. Mantegazza, "*Sulle virtù igieniche e medicinali della coca e sugli alimenti nervosi in generale*" ("On the Hygienic and Medicinal Properties of Coca and on Nervous Nourishment in General"), *Annali Universali di Medicina* 167 (1859): 1–76.

5 See *Time*, "Nation: Rushing to a New High," Monday, July 17, 1978. See also Graham Gremore, "'Sudden Sniffing Death' Is Now a Thing Thanks to the New Gay Poppers," *Queerty*, January 28, 2015. And also, J. Sansweet, "Poppers, Legally Sniffable, Becoming a Big Business," *The Wall Street Journal*, October 10, 1977.

# *Bibliography*

Allison, A.C. "The Morphology of the Olfactory System in the Vertebrates." *Biological Reviews of the Cambridge Philosophical Society* 28, no. 2 (May 1953): 195–244. http://dx.doi.org/10.1111/j.1469-185X.1953.tb01376.x.

Boyse, E.A. "HLA and the Chemical Senses." *Human Immunology* 15, no. 4 (April 1986): 391–5. http://dx.doi.org/10.1016/0198-8859(86)90016-9.

Craven, B.A., E.G. Paterson, and G.S. Settles. "The Fluid Dynamics of Canine Olfaction: Unique Nasal Airflow Patterns as an Explanation of Macrosmia." *Journal of the Royal Society, Interface* 7, no. 47 (June 6, 2010): 933–43. http://dx.doi.org/10.1098/rsif.2009.0490.

Gerritsen, R., and R. Haak. *K9 Scent Training: A Manual for Training Your Identification, Tracking and Detection Dog*. Calgary: Brush Education Inc, 2015.

———. *K9 Search and Rescue: A Manual for Training the Natural Way*. Calgary: Brush Education Inc, 2013.

Gibbons, B. "The Intimate Sense of Smell." *National Geographic* (1986).

Haak, R. *Het Africhten tot Verdedigingshond*. Best: Zuid Boekprodukties, 1984.

———. *Het Speuren van Honden in Theorie en Praktijk*. Best: Zuid Boekprodukties, 1986.

Hofmann, Albert. *LSD: mein Sorgenkind, Die Entdeckung einer 'Wunderdroge.'* Stuttgart: Verlag G. Cotta'sche Buchhandlung, 1979.

———. *LSD: My Problem Child*. New York: McGraw-Hill Book Company, 1980.

Hondebrink, H., and C. Boomaars. *Opleiding Speurhondengeleider Narcotica*. Oosterhout: Dog Training Center Oosterhout, 2015.

Horowitz, A. *Inside of a Dog: What Dogs See, Smell, and Know*. New York: Scribner, 2009.

Lancet, D. "Vertebrate Olfactory Reception." *Annual Review of Neuroscience* 9, no. 1 (March 1986): 329–55. http://dx.doi.org/10.1146/annurev.ne.09.030186.001553.

Lilly, C.J. *The Scientist: A Novel Autobiography*. Philadelphia: Lippincott, 1978.

Mantegazza, P. "*Sulle virtù igieniche e medicinali della coca e sugli alimenti nervosi in generale* (On the Hygienic and Medicinal Properties of Coca and on Nervous Nourishment in General)." *Annali Universali di Medicina* 167 (1859): 1–76.

"Marvels of Mini-Weather." *Sciences* 5, no. 2 (July 1965): 1–4. http://dx.doi.org/10.1002/j.2326-1951.1965.tb00178.x.

Menzel, R., and R. Menzel. *Die Verwertung der Riechfähigkeit des Hundes im Dienste der Menschheit*. Berlin: Kameradschafts Verlagsgesellschaft, 1930.

Moncrieff, R.W. "The Sense of Smell." *Manufacturing Chemist and Aerosol News* 17, no. 10 (October 1946): 453.

———. "Olfactory Adaptation and Odor-Intensity." *American Journal of Psychology* 70, no. 1 (March 1957): 1–20. http://dx.doi.org/10.2307/1419225.

Neuhaus, W. "Die Bedeutung des Schnüffelns für das Riechen des Hundes." *Zeitung für Säugetierkunde* 46 (1981): 301–10.

Niemann, Albert. "*Über eine neue organische Base in den Cocablättern* (On a New Organic Base in the Coca Leaves)." *Archiv der Pharmazie* 153, no. 2 (1860): 129–155. http://dx.doi.org/10.1002/ardp.18601530202.

Pfungst, O. *Das Pferd des Herrn von Osten (Der Kluge Hans). Ein Beitrag zur experimentellen Tier—und Menschen—Psychologie*. Leipzig: Verlag von Johan Ambrosius Barth, 1907.

Schoon, A. *The Performance of Dogs in Identifying Humans by Scent*. PhD. Diss., Leiden. 1997.

Schoon, A., and R. Haak. *K9 Suspect Discrimination: Training and Practicing Scent Identification Line-Ups*. Calgary: Detselig Enterprises Ltd, 2002.

Soproni, K., A. Miklósi, J. Topál, et al. "Comprehension of Human Communicative Signs in Pet Dogs (*Canis familiaris*)." *Journal of Comparative Psychology* 115, no. 2 (June 2001): 122–6. http://dx.doi.org/10.1037/0735-7036.115.2.122.

Soproni, K., A. Miklósi, J. Topál, et al. "Dogs' (*Canis familaris*) Responsiveness to Human Pointing Gestures." *Journal of Comparative Psychology* 116, no. 1 (2002): 27–34. http://dx.doi.org/10.1037/0735-7036.116.1.27.

Stoddart, D.M. *The Ecology of Vertebrate Olfaction*. London: Chapman and Hall, 1980. http://dx.doi.org/10.1007/978-94-009-5869-2.

———. *The Scented Ape*. Cambridge: Cambridge University Press, 1990.

Waggoner, L.P., J.M. Johnston, M. Williams, J. Jackson, M.H. Jones, T. Boussom, and J.A. Petrousky. "Canine Olfactory Sensitivity to Cocaine Hydrochloride and Methyl Benzoate." *Proc. SPIE* 2937, Chemistry- and Biology-Based Technologies for Contraband Detection, 216 (February 17, 1997). DOI: 10.1117/12.266775.

# About the Authors

Ruud Haak (1947–2023) was the author of more than 30 dog books in Dutch and German, and served as the editor-in-chief of the biggest Dutch dog magazine, *Onze Hond* (*Our Dog*), from 1979 to the end of his career. He was born in 1947 in Amsterdam, the Netherlands. At the age of 13, he was training police dogs at his uncle's security dog training center, and when he was 15, he worked after school with his patrol dog (which he trained himself) at the Amsterdam harbor. He later started training his dogs in Schutzhund and IPO, and he successfully bred and showed German Shepherds and Saint Bernards.

Ruud worked as a social therapist in a government clinic for criminal psychopaths. From his studies in psychology, he became interested in dog behavior and training methods for nose work, especially the tracking dog and the search-and-rescue dog. He trained drug- and explosive-detector dogs for the Dutch police and the Royal Dutch Airforce and was a visiting lecturer at Dutch, German, and Austrian police-dog schools.

In the 1970s, Ruud and his wife, Dr. Resi Gerritsen, a psychologist and jurist, attended many courses and symposia with their German Shepherds for Schutzhund, tracking dog, and search-and-rescue dog training in Switzerland, Germany, and Austria. In 1979, they started the Dutch Rescue Dog Organization in the

# ABOUT THE AUTHORS

Ruud Haak with his German shepherd Yes van Sulieseraad and Malinois Google van het Eldenseveld.

Resi Gerritsen with her Malinois Halusetha's All Power and Malinois Google van het Eldenseveld.

Netherlands. With that unit, they attended many operations responding to earthquakes, gas explosions, and lost persons in wooded or wilderness areas. In 1990, Ruud and Resi moved to Austria, where they were asked by the Austrian Red Cross to select and train operational rescue and avalanche dogs. They lived for three years at a height of 6,000 feet (1800 m) in the Alps and worked with their dogs in search missions after avalanches.

With their Austrian colleagues, Ruud and Resi developed a new method for training search-and-rescue dogs. This way of training showed the best results after a major earthquake in Armenia (1988), an earthquake in Japan (1995), two major earthquakes in Turkey (1999), and big earthquakes in Algeria and Iran (2003). Ruud and Resi also demonstrated the success of their unique training methods for tracking dogs as well as search-and-rescue dogs at the Austrian, Czech, Hungarian, and World Championships, where both were several times the leading champions. Later, they served as training directors and international judges for the International Rescue Dog Organisation (IRO) and the Fédération Cynologique Internationale (FCI).

Resi and Ruud held many symposia and master classes all over the world on their unique training methods, which are featured in their books:

- *K9 Drug Detection: A Manual for Training and Operations*
- *K9 Explosive and Mine Detection: A Manual for Training and Operations*
- *K9 Investigation Errors: A Manual for Avoiding Mistakes*
- *K9 Personal Protection: A Manual for Training Reliable Protection Dogs*
- *K9 Professional Tracking: A Complete Manual for Theory and Training in Clean-Scent Tracking*
- *K9 Scent Training: A Manual for Training Your Identification, Tracking, and Detection Dog*

- *K9 Schutzhund Training: A Manual for IGP Training through Positive Reinforcement*
- *K9 Search and Rescue: A Manual for Training the Natural Way*
- *The Labrador Retriever: From Hunting Dog to One of the World's Most Versatile Working Dogs*
- *The German Shepherd Dog: A Historical View of the Breed's Development, Prime, and Deterioration*
- *The Malinois: The History and Development of the Breed in Schutzhund, Detection, and Police Work*

With Simon Prins they wrote *K9 Behavior Basics: A Manual for Proven Success in Operational Service Dog Training* and *K9 Line-up Training: A Manual for Suspect Identification and Detection Work*. All of these books are published by Dog Training Press.

Ruud is survived by Resi, who now lives in the Netherlands. You can contact Resi by e-mail at resigerritsen@gmail.com.

# Index

**A**
abuse, definition, 142
Abyssinian tea (khat), 215
accidental drug uptake, first aid for dog, 45–54
acetic acid, 257
acid (LSD), 171
acquired behavior, 56
active response of dog, 31–36
Adam (ecstasy/MDMA), 175
adaptation to odor, 69
adaptive intelligence of dog, 2
addiction to drugs, 142. *See also* specific drugs
administration modes for drugs. *See* specific drugs
African salad (khat), 215
airflow and air currents. *See also* wind
   in buildings, 88–96
   outdoors, 76–77
   and search work, 71, 73–74, 77, 78–79, *89*, *90*, *94*, *95*, *96*
air pressure, and search work, 91–93, *92*
air-scenting dogs, 66
airplanes, search action on, 122–123
alert response, in training, 20
amobarbital, *191*
amphetamines. *See* methamphetamines (meth)/amphetamines
amytal (barbiturates), 190
animal barns, search action in, 112
Anti-Drug Abuse Act (1988, USA), 138–139
apomorphine, 47, 48
Aunt Mary (marijuana), 151
Auntie (opium), 228

**B**
1,4-B (GHB), 198
Balard, Antoine Jérôme, 247
bald heads (magic mushrooms), 163
*banga* (cannabis), 151

barbiturates, *191*
   addiction and mix with other drugs, 192, 193
   administration modes, 192
   description, 190–191
   detectability, 193
   effects and risks, 192–193
   history, 191
   street names, 190
barbs (barbiturates), 190
barking, as response, 32
barns, search action in, 112
base (crack), 205
bath salts, *255*
batu (methamphetamines), 220
Bayer, Adolf von, 191
BC bud (marijuana), 151
beans (ecstasy/MDMA), 175
Beaufort scale, 78–79
behavior of dog, 6, 56–58
bennies (methamphetamines), 218
benzaldehyde, 257
Benzo Fury, *254*
benzodiazepines, *194*
   addiction and mix with other drugs, 196
   administration modes, 194
   description, 191, 193
   detectability, 198
   effects and risks, 195–196
   history, 194
   street names, 193
benzoes (benzodiazepines), 193
benzoic acid, 257
*bhang* (cannabis), 151
big H (heroin), 239
bikers' coffee (methamphetamines), 220
biting, as response, 32
black beauties (methamphetamines), 218
black glass (hashish), 155
black magic (synthetic cannabinoids), 156

black pill (opium), 228
black-tar heroin, *240*, 241
black tar (heroin), as street name, 239
blaze (synthetic cannabinoids), 156
blind search, 27–28
block busters (barbiturates), 190
blotter acid (LSD), 171
blow (cocaine), 204
blue nitro (GHB), 198
blues (barbiturates), 190
blunts (marijuana), 151
body language of dog, 61–62
boldness of dog, 7–8
*boom* and boom (cannabis), 151
bori (crack), 205
boy (heroin), 239
breed and variety of dog, 9–10
bring drive of dog, 8, 20, 21
brown (heron), 239
brown (opium), 228
budder (hashish), 155
buildings. See also indoor locations
  dangers in, 96–98
  indoors search work, 88–96
  outdoors search work, 84–88
butane hash oil, 155, *155*
butane honey oil (BHO) (hashish), 155
buttons (peyote), 168

C

cactus (peyote), 168
Canada
  drug schedules, 134–135, 259–269
  hazmat, 99
  laws and enforcement, 134–135
  punishments for drugs, 135, 270–273
cannabinoids, 150, 158
  synthetic cannabinoids, 156, *157*
cannabis (marijuana and hashish)
  addiction and mix with other drugs, 160–161, 226
  administration modes, 150, 151, 157–158
  description, 149–150, 151–155
  detectability, 161
  dosages, 158
  effects on dogs, 49–50
  effects on humans, 158–159
  history, 150
  ingestion, 49, 157–158
  in Netherlands, 131–132
  as psychoactive drug, 148–149
  resin, 149–150
  risks, 156, 160
  and THC, 147, 151, 153, 154–156, 159
  varieties, 151–152, 153–154
cannabis oil (hashish), 154
*Cannabis sativa L.*, 149, 151
caryophyllene epoxide, 257
cat tranquilizer (ketamine), 185

cat valium (ketamine), 185
catha (khat), 215
CBD (cannabidiol), 158
chalk (methamphetamines), 220
chandu (opium), 228
Charlie (cocaine), 204
chat (khat), 215
Chemical Abuse Prevention Act (Netherlands), 130
chemical odorants, 257
chewing, as intake method, 145
chicken feed (methamphetamines), 220
chimney effect, 92–95, *94*
Chinese molasses (opium), 228
Chinese tobacco (opium), 228
Chiva (heroin), 239
Christmas trees (barbiturates), 190
chronic (marijuana), 151
cities, temperature in, 82
clarity (ecstasy/MDMA), 175
*Claviceps purpurea*, 171
clean coke (crack), 205
"Clever Hans" problems, 11
climate, and odor of drug, 71
coat of dog, cleaning of, 52–54
coca (cocaine), 204
cocaine, *204–205*
  addiction and mix with other drugs, 183–184, 214–215, 238
  administration modes and dosages, 208–210
  adulterants/fillers in, 209–210, 212
  description, 204–205
  effects and risks, 211–213
  effects on dogs, 50
  field test, *52*
  history, 206–208
  odor thresholds for dog, 66–67
  street names, 204
codeine, 228
coke (cocaine), 204
collar, as equipment, 18
combination of drugs. *See specific drugs*
Controlled Drugs and Substances Act (Canada)
  drugs included, 134–135, 259–269
  overview, 134–135
  punishments, 135, 270–273
controlled search, 26–27
Controlled Substances Act (USA)
  overview, 135–136
  penalties, 138–139, 277–280
  schedules, 136–138, 274–276
cooked coke (crack), 205
*Copelandia cyanescens*, 163
crack (cocaine), 204, 205, *206*, 208, 209
crank (methamphetamines), 220
crazy clown (synthetic cannabinoids), 156
crystal/crystal meth (methamphetamines), 220

# INDEX

**D**
dabs (hashish), 155
*dagga* (cannabis), 151
dangers for dog
  from gases, 96
  hazmat, 98–99
  houses and buildings, 96–98
  in search action, 101–102
dehydration, first aid for, 54
demon (synthetic cannabinoids), 156
dependency to drugs. *See* addiction to drugs
depressants (downers or psycholeptics). *See also* specific drugs
  description, 148, 190
  types and uses, 190–203
detectability of drugs. *See* specific drugs
detection of drug. *See* drug-detector dog
diazepam, field test, *52*
disco biscuit (ecstasy/MDMA), 175
dog handler. *See* handler of dog
dogs for drug detection. *See* drug-detector dog
dope (marijuana), 151
dopium (opium), 228
dosages of drugs. *See* specific drugs
dots (LSD), 171
downers. *See* depressants
downers (barbiturates), 190
downers (benzodiazepines), 193
dream gun (opium), 228
dream (synthetic cannabinoids), 156
dreamer (morphine), 236
Dreser, Heinrich, 247
drinking of drugs. *See* ingestion
drive of dog, 5–6
drug abuse, definition, 142
drug complexes, 68–69
drug-detector dog
  chemical odorants, 257
  cues from handler, 11–12
  description as search dog, 66–67
  detection skills, 257–258
  environmental influences, 76–88
  examples of search work, 162, 177, 215, 239
  mental characteristics, 2–5
  and odor print, 63, 67–72
  physical characteristics, 1–2
  selection and qualities, 5–10
  thresholds for drug odors, 66–67
  training (*See* training of dog)
  at young age, 4–5
drug (ecstasy/MDMA), 175
Drug Enforcement Administration (DEA), 136, 256
drug schedules. *See* schedules of drugs
drug tourism, in Europe, 131–132
drug uptake by accident, first aid for dog, 45–54
drugs
  addiction, 142
  definition, 125–126
  dreamlike state from, 127
  effects and factors, 141–142
  history, 126–127
  intake methods, 143–147
  in modern society, 127–128
  odor (*See* odor of drug)
  types of, 148–149
Dutch shepherd breed, qualities, 9–10

**E**
E (ecstasy/MDMA), 175
ear wax (hashish), 155
ears of dog, positions and meanings, 60
eating drugs. *See* ingestion
eco drugs, 250–253, *251, 252*
ecstasy (MDMA), *176*
  addiction and mix with other drugs, 183–184, 196, 201, 202–203, 214, 225–226, 249
  administration modes and dosages, 178–179
  description, 163, 175
  detectability, 184
  effects and risks, 179–183
  history, 175–177
  search work example, 177
  street names, 175
effects of drugs. *See also* specific drugs
  on dogs, 49–51
  generally, 141–142
equipment and tools, in training, 18–20, *19, 25–26, 30*
ergot and ergotamine, 171
errl (hashish), 155
evaporation, for cannabis, 157
eve (ecstasy/MDMA), 175
excretion of drugs, 147
eyes of dog, 58–59

**F**
fantasy (GHB), 198
fatigue of dog, 6–7, 24
FDA (USA), 138
fentanyl, 234–235
ferries, search action on, 123–124
fire (synthetic cannabinoids), 156
firm dogs, 7
first aid for dog
  effects of drugs, 49–51
  field tests, 52
  injections and muscles of dog, *49*
  other health issues, 52–54
  steps in, 45–46
  vomiting or not vomiting, 46–48
first drug (scent) training, 29–31
first line (morphine), 236
flake (cocaine), 204
flashbacks, 174
focus of dog, 7–8
footballs (benzodiazepines), 193
free search, 105

freebase (crack), 205
Fruhstorfer, Wolfgang, 176

**G**
G (GHB), 198
gangster (marijuana), 151
ganja (marijuana), 151
gases, dangers and labelling, 96, 99
GBL (gamma butyrolactone), 197–198
genie (synthetic cannabinoids), 156
German shepherd, qualities, 9–10
GHB (gamma-hydroxybutyric), *198*
   addiction and mix with other drugs, 202–203, 226, 249
   administration modes and dosages, 199–200
   description, 198–199
   detectability, 203
   effects and risks, 200–201
   excretion, 147
   history, 199
   street names, 198
ginseng and root, 250, *251*
glass (methamphetamines), 220
go (ecstasy/MDMA), 175
go-fast (methamphetamines), 220
God's medicine (opium), 228
golden retrievers, qualities, 10
gondola (opium), 228
goof balls (barbiturates), 190
goric (opium), 228
grass (marijuana), 151
great tobacco (opium), 228
grievous bodily harm (GHB), 198
guarana, 250, *252*, 253

**H**
H (heroin), 239
hallucinogens (psychedelic drugs or psychodysleptics). *See also* specific drugs
   description, 148, 161–163
   types and uses, 163–189
handler of dog
   actions of, 15
   and cues, 11–12
   drug knowledge, 125–128
   qualities and character, 10–13
   selection, 13–15
   voice, 7, 14–15
hard drugs
   effects on dogs, 51
   field test, *52*
Harry (heroin), 239
hash (marijuana), 151
hash oil (hashish), 154
hashish, *154*, *155*. *See also* cannabis
   description and use, 149, 150, 152–154, 157
   search example, 162
hashish bonbon, 157
hashish oil, 154, 157
"Hawaiian" (magic mushrooms), 163

Haze (marijuana), 151
hazmat (hazardous materials), dangers of, 98–99
head and ears of dog, 59–60
hell dust (heroin), 239
hemp resin, 149–150
herb (marijuana), 151
herbal incense (synthetic cannabinoids), 156
herbs, as drugs, 127
heroin, *240*, *241*
   addiction and mix with other drugs, 196, 245
   administration modes and dosages, 241–242
   description, 239
   detectability, 245
   effects and risks, 242–245
   history, 240–241
   manufacture, 241
   street names, 239
hidden drugs training, 24–26
hiropon (methamphetamines), 220
Hofmann, Albert, 164, 171–172
Hollandse herder breed, qualities, 9–10
honey oil (hashish), 154
hop/hops (opium), 228
horse (heroin), 239
houses and properties, search action, 110–111
hows (morphine), 236
*hsien ma tze* (cannabis), 151
hug drug (ecstasy/MDMA), 175
humans, search action on, 112–114
humidity, and odor of drug, 71, 74
hydro (marijuana), 151
hydrogen peroxide, 47

**I**
ice (methamphetamines), *218*, 218–219, 220
imprinting phase, 8
independence of dog, and training, 21
Indo (marijuana), 151
indoor locations. *See also* buildings
   search action, 108–114
   types and examples, 100–101
   wind in, 109–110
ingestion
   cannabis, 49, 157–158
   as intake method, 145
   LSD, 147, 171
   magic mushrooms, 165
   methamphetamines, 50
inhalation, as intake method, 143
injection of drugs, as intake method, 144
injections, and muscles of dog, *49*
innate behavior, 56
instinct of dog, 6
instinctive intelligence of dog, 2
intake methods for drugs, 143–147
intelligence of dog, 2
intranasal intake, as method, 144–145

**J**
Janssen, Paul, 234
jet K (ketamine), 185
joint (marijuana), 151
junk (heroin), 239

**K**
K9 drug detectors. *See* drug-detector dog
K2 (marijuana), 151
K2 (synthetic cannabinoids), 156
kat (khat), 215
kava kava, 250, *251*
ketamine, *185*
   addiction and mix with other drugs, 189
   administration modes and dosages, 187
   description, 184–185
   detectability, 189
   effects and risks, 187–189
   field test, 52
   history, 185–186
   street names, 185
khat, 215–217, *216*
*kiff* and kif (cannabis), 151
kit kat (ketamine), 185
kola nut, 250
Koller, Carl, 207
Krupitsky, Yevgeny, 186

**L**
Laborit, Henri, 199
Labrador breed, qualities, 10
land areas, and wind, 79–80
landscape, and search work, 79–81
leash, 18–19, 106
liberty caps (magic mushrooms), 163
Lily, John, 186
lineups, in search action, 121
lips of dog, 61
liquid ecstasy/liquid E (GHB), 198
liquid hash (hashish), 154
List I and List II drugs, 128
long leash, 18–19, 106
lover's speed (ecstasy/MDMA), 175
LSD (lysergic acid diethylamide), *170*
   addiction and mix with other drugs, 174–175
   administration modes and dosages, 172–173
   description, 163, 170–171
   detectability, 175
   effects and risks, 173–174
   history, 163, 171–172
   ingestion, 147, 171
   street names, 171
luggage and parcels, search action, 120–121, 162

**M**
*maconha* (cannabis), 151
magic mushrooms, *164*
   addiction and mix with other drugs, 167–168
   administration modes and dosages, 165
   description, 163

   detectability, 168
   effects and risks, 165–167
   history, 164–165
   ingestion, 165
   street names, 163
Malinois breed, qualities, 9–10
marijuana, *151, 152*. *See also* cannabis
   description and use, 149, 150, 151–152
   street names, 151
Mary Jane (marijuana), 151
MDMA (ecstasy). *See* ecstasy (MDMA)
medical drugs, 136, 138
mellow yellow (LSD), 171
mesc (peyote), 168
mescaline, 162, 168
meth (methamphetamines), as street name, 220
meth pipe, *103*
methamphetamines (meth)/amphetamines, *218*
   addiction and mix with other drugs, 196, 225–226, 249
   administration modes and dosages, 220–221
   description and types, 218–220
   detectability, 226
   effects and risks, 221–225
   effects on dogs, 50–51
   history, 219–220
   ingestion, 50
   street names, 218, 220
methyl benzoate, 257
3,4-methylenedioxymethamphetamine. *See* ecstasy (MDMA)
Mexican magic mushrooms, 163
mira (khat), 215
Misuse of Drugs Act (1971, UK), 132–133
mix of drugs. *See* specific drugs
mobile homes, search action of, 120
moggies (benzodiazepines), 193
*momea* (cannabis), 151
morf (morphine), 236
morphine, *236*
   addiction and mix with other drugs, 238
   administration modes, 237
   description, 227–228, 235–236
   detectability, 238
   effects and risks, 237–238
   history, 236–237
   street names, 236
morpho (morphine), 236
mota (marijuana), 151
mountains, and wind, 80–81
mouth and lips of dog, 61
Mr. Nice Guy (synthetic cannabinoids), 156
M.S. (morphine), 236
musculature/muscles of dog, *49*

**N**
naloxone, 234
narcotics (opioids). *See also* specific drugs
   definition, 125–126
   description, 226–227, 232

nasal cavity and nose of dog, 64
Nederweed (marijuana), 151, 152
negra (heroin), 239
nembutal (barbiturates), 190
Netherlands, drugs and enforcement, 129–132
new psychoactive substances (NPS). *See* NPS
Niemann, Albert, 207
ninja (synthetic cannabinoids), 156
noise shyness of dog, 8
Normies (benzodiazepines), 193
Northern Lights (marijuana), 152
nose and nasal cavity of dog, 64
nose candy (cocaine), 204
NPS (new psychoactive substances), *254*
   description, 253–254
   history, 254–256

## O

O (opium), 228
oat (khat), 215
Oberlin, Max, 175
odor of drug
   adaptation to, 69
   chemical odorants, 257
   complexes in, 68–69
   covering of, 72
   detection skills of dog, 257–258
   first drug training, 29–31
   indoors, 88–96
   influence on search work, 68–72
   number of odors in training, 30–31
   outdoors, 76–88
   and reward, 20–21
   "soaking time," 70
   sorting test, 24–25
   sterile tools, 25–26, *30*
   and sun, 82–83, *88*, *89*
   thresholds for dog, 66–67
   weather influences, 71–76
   and wind (*See* air flow and air currents; wind)
"odor print"
   description, 63, 67–68
   influence on search work, 68–72
odors (generally)
   in dog's world, 63–65
   weather influences, 73–75
olfactory area, bulb and cells, 64–66
O.P. (opium), 228
ope (opium), 228
open-air locations. *See* outdoor locations
operational search, 28, 29
opioids. *See* narcotics
opium, *231*
   addiction and mix with other drugs, 233, 235
   administration modes, 231
   description, 226–228, 236–237
   detectability, 235
   effects and risks, 231–233
   history and trade, 229–231
   poppy, *229*

raw opium, 227–228, 236–237
street names, 228
Opium Act (Netherlands), 129–130, 208
oral intake, as intake method, 145. *See also* ingestion
oral-mucosal administration, as intake method, 146–147
"orientational" scratching, 32
outdoor locations
   and buildings, 84–88
   examples, 100, 107
   search work in, 76–88, 106–108
overheating (hyperthermia), 181, 223

## P

paradise (synthetic cannabinoids), 156
paraphernalia, *97*, *103*
parcels, search action, 120–121, 162
party drugs
   addiction and mix with other drugs, 249
   administration modes and dosages, 247
   description, 245–246
   detectability, 249
   effects and risks, 247–249
   history, 247
passive response of dog, 36–42, *115*, *140*
paws of dog, cleaning of, *53*
peacep (ecstasy/MDMA), 175
perseverance of dog, 6–7, 24
peyote, *168*
   addiction and mix with other drugs, 169–170
   administration modes, 169
   description, 162, 168
   detectability, 170
   effects, 169
   history, 168
   street names, 168
peyoto (peyote), 168
pharmaceuticals, 127–128
phencyclidine (PCP), 163
philosopher's stone (magic mushrooms), 163
pinks (barbiturates), 190
pipes, *103*, *218*
pointy bald heads (magic mushrooms), 163
poisoning by drugs, first aid for dog, 45–54
poor man's cocaine (methamphetamines), 220
poppers, *246*, 246–249
pot (marijuana), 151
potpourri (synthetic cannabinoids), 156
Power Plant (marijuana), 152
practical intelligence of dog, 2
pre-training of dog, 4
prescription drugs, 136, 138
pressure (air), and search work, 91–93, *92*
prisons, search action in, 112
properties, search action on, 110–111
*Psilocybe cubensis*, 163, *164*
*Psilocybe semilanceta*, 163
*Psilocybe tampanensis*, 163

psilocybin/psilocin, 163, 165, 168
psychedelic drugs. *See* hallucinogens
psychoactive drugs, description, 148–149
psychoanaleptics. *See* stimulants
psychodysleptics. *See* hallucinogens
psycholeptics. *See* depressants
pure coke (crack), 205
purple (ketamine), 185

**Q**
quat (khat), 215
quick scan, 105

**R**
rain, and search work, 71, 83
raw opium, 227–228, 236–237
reading of dog
  body language, 61–62
  classification of behavior, 56–57
  and dog's world, 63–64
  expression of behavior, 57–58
  eyes, 58–59
  head and ears, 59–60
  mouth and lips, 61
  nasal cavity and nose, 64
  overview, 55
  tail, 60
  training of dog, 22
rectal insertion, as intake method, 145–146
red devils (barbiturates), 190
reds and blues (barbiturates), 190
reds (barbiturates), 190
redx dawn (synthetic cannabinoids), 156
reefer (marijuana), 151
relative humidity, 74
response of dog (in training)
  active response, 31–36
  box for, 37–39, *38–39, 41*
  lineup of boxes, 38–39, *42*
  passive response, 36–42, *115, 140*
  physical response, 42–44
  training steps, 34–35, 40–41
retrieve ability of dog, 8, 20, 21
reward in training, 19–21
risks of drugs. *See* specific drugs
rock (crack), 205
rohies (benzodiazepines), 193
rohypnol (flunitrazepam), 197, *197*
  field test, *52*
roofies (benzodiazepines), 193
RVs, search action in, 120

**S**
salvia (*Salvia divinorum*), 162, 251, *252*
Sarahs (benzodiazepines), 193
scent-detection dogs. *See* drug-detector dog
scent of drug. *See* odor of drug
schedules of drugs
  background, 128–129
  Canada, 134–135, 259–269

  in Single Convention, 129
  USA, 136–138, 274–276
*Sclerotia tampanensis,* 164
scratching, as response, 31–32, *34, 36*
sea, and wind, 79–80
search action
  airplanes, 122–123
  checks before, 104–105
  of humans, 112–114
  indoors, 108–114
  luggage and parcels, 120–121, 162
  methods for searching, 105–106
  outdoors, 106–108
  procedures, 102–103, 106
  ships and ferries, 123–124
  vehicles, 115–120, *117,* 239
  working conditions, 101–102
search dogs, 66
seconal (barbiturates), 190
secretion of drugs, 147
sekkies (barbiturates), 190
sence (synthetic cannabinoids), 156
sensitivity of dog, 7
serenity (synthetic cannabinoids), 156
serotonin syndrome, 182–183
Sertürner, Friedrich Wilhelm Adam, 236
710 (hashish), 155
shabu (methamphetamines), 220
shatter (hashish), 155
ships and ferries, search action on, 123–124
shit (heroin), 239
short leash, 18, 106
Shulgin, Alexander "Sasha," 176, 255
Single Convention on Narcotic Drugs (1961), 129
sinsemilla (marijuana), 151
skag (heroin), 239
skunk (marijuana), 151, 152
skunk (synthetic cannabinoids), 156
sleepers (barbiturates), 190
sleepers (benzodiazepines), 193
sleeping pills (barbiturates), 190
smack (heroin), 239
smart drugs and eco drugs, *250, 251, 252*
  addiction, 253
  description, 249–251
  effects and risks, 251, 253
smell (generally)
  in dog's world, 63–65
  weather influences, 73–75
smell (of drug). *See* odor of drug
smoke (marijuana), 151
smoke (synthetic cannabinoids), 156
smuggling, search action, 115–116
snorting/sniffing, as intake method, 144–145
snow (cocaine), 204
"soaking time," 70
social behavior of dog, 8

soda cot (cocaine), 204
sodium oxybate. *See* GHB
sorting test, 24–25
space cake, 157, 158
spaniels, qualities, 10
special K (ketamine), 185
special la coke (ketamine), 185
speed (methamphetamines), 218. *See also* methamphetamines (meth)/amphetamines
St. John's wort, 251
stimulants (uppers or psychoanaleptics). *See also* specific drugs
  description, 148, 203–204
  types and uses, 204–249
STP (ecstasy/MDMA), 175
sun, in search work, 82–83, *88*, *89*
super acid (ketamine), 185
super K (ketamine), 185
swallowing, as intake method. *See* ingestion
synthetic cannabinoids, 156, *157*
systematic search, 105–106

T
tail of dog, 60
temperature, and search work, 71–72, 73, 74–75, *75*, 79–80, 82–84, 93
Thai stick marijuana, 152, *152*
THC (tetra-hydro-cannabinol)
  in cannabis, 151, 153
  effects, 159
  excretion, 147
  extractions, 154–156, *155*
thunder (heroin), 239
tools in training, 18–20, *19*, 25–26, 30
toot (cocaine), 204
tracking dogs, 66
trailers, search action in, 120
trailing dogs, 66
trained behavior, 56–57
training case, *30*, 30–31
training of dog
  agility and obstacles, 22–23
  categories of work, 26–28
  and compulsion, 16–17
  concentration and distractions, 22–24
  at early age, 4
  equipment and tools, 18–20, *19*, 25–26, 30
  first drug training, 29–31
  hidden drugs, 24–26
  location and environment, 22
  principles and rules, 17–18, 20–22
  reading of dog, 22
  response of dog (*See* response of dog)
  reward in, 19–21
trash (methamphetamines), 220
tubers trip (magic mushrooms), 163
tuinal (barbiturates), 190

U
UN Single Convention on Narcotic Drugs (1961), 129

United Kingdom (UK), drugs and enforcement, 132–133
United States of America (USA)
  cannabis, 150
  drug schedules, 136–138, 274–276
  hazmat, 99
  laws and enforcement, 135–139
  medical drugs, 136, 138
  NPS, 255–256
  penalties for drugs, 138–139, 277–280
uppers. *See* stimulants
uppers (methamphetamines), 218
urban areas, temperature in, 82

V
vaginal insertion, as intake method, 145
valerian, 250–251
Valium (diazepam), 194, *194*, 195
valleys, and wind, 80–81
vaporizing, for cannabis, 157
variety and breed of dog, 9–10
vehicles, search action in, 115–120, *117*, 239
vidrio (methamphetamines), 220
vitamin K (ketamine), 185
vomiting or not, as first aid, 46–48

W
water intoxication (hyponatremia), 182
Watson, R. Gordon, 164
wax (hashish), 155
WebTryp, 256
weed (marijuana), 151
white (crack), 205
white dust (cocaine), 204
White Widow (marijuana), 152
wind. *See also* airflow and air currents
  assessment of, 76
  direction and speed, 76, 78–79
  indoor locations, 109–110
  and search work, 76–81, *80*, *81*, 83–88, *84*, *85*, *87*, *92*
  upwinds and downwinds, 86, 88–90
window pane (LSD), 171
Wright, C.R. Alder, 240

X
X-Dutch shepherd breed, qualities, 9–10
X (ecstasy/MDMA), 175
X-Malinois breed, qualities, 9–10
XTC (ecstasy/MDMA), 175

Y
yaba (methamphetamines), 220
yellow jackets (barbiturates), 190
yerba (marijuana), 151
yohimbe, 251, *252*
Yucatan (synthetic cannabinoids), 156

Z
zero (opium), 228
zohai (synthetic cannabinoids), 156